THEOLOGY · PHILOSOPHY · RELIGION

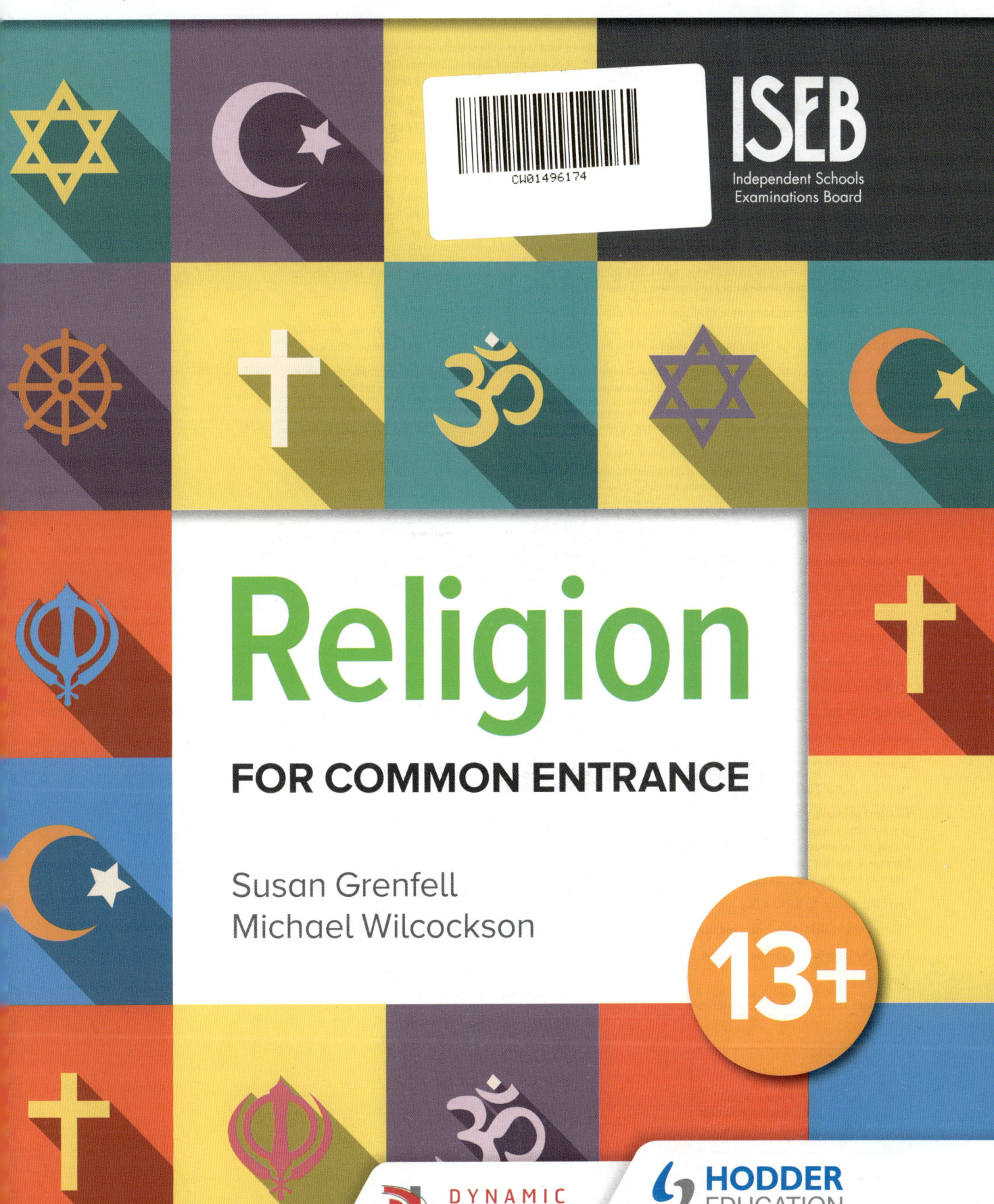

ISEB
Independent Schools
Examinations Board

Religion
FOR COMMON ENTRANCE

Susan Grenfell
Michael Wilcockson

13+

DL
DYNAMIC
LEARNING

HODDER
EDUCATION
AN HACHETTE UK COMPANY

Susan Grenfell

Susan Grenfell started teaching in secondary schools and moved to working in Prep schools in the 1990s. She has a Bachelor of Education degree from Oxford and a Diploma in Special Needs from Kingston. She was SENCo at Caldicott School until 2004 where she also taught RS at scholarship level. She has given lectures in study skills to leavers at Prep schools. Between 2005 and 2015, she was head of RS at St Hugh's School, Faringdon and for several years was secretary for the ISRSA. She has been writing RS textbooks for Common Entrance since 2004 and has spoken on the subject at teachers' conferences. She is a member of the local SACRE in Oxford and governor of a Church of England Primary School in Oxford.

Michael Wilcockson

Michael Wilcockson studied Theology at Balliol College, Oxford and is currently Head of Philosophy at Eton College as well as being Chief Setter for ISEB Theology, Philosophy and Religion and Chief Setter for A Level Religious Studies at a large examination board. He is author of many textbooks for Common Entrance, GCSE and A Level. He was Visiting Scholar at Pembroke College, Cambridge in 2010 and is a Fellow of the Chartered Institute of Educational Assessors.

Every effort has been made to trace all copyright holders, but if any have been inadvertently overlooked, the Publishers will be pleased to make the necessary arrangements at the first opportunity.

Although every effort has been made to ensure that website addresses are correct at time of going to press, Hodder Education cannot be held responsible for the content of any website mentioned in this book. It is sometimes possible to find a relocated web page by typing in the address of the home page for a website in the URL window of your browser.

Hachette UK's policy is to use papers that are natural, renewable and recyclable products and made from wood grown in well-managed forests and other controlled sources. The logging and manufacturing processes are expected to conform to the environmental regulations of the country of origin.

The logging and manufacturing processes are expected to conform to the environmental regulations of the country of origin.

Orders: please contact Bookpoint Ltd, 130 Park Drive, Milton Park, Abingdon, Oxon OX14 4SE. Telephone: (44) 01235 827827. Fax: (44) 01235 400401. Email education@bookpoint.co.uk. Lines are open from 9 a.m. to 5 p.m., Monday to Saturday, with a 24-hour message answering service.

You can also order through our website: www.hoddereducation.co.uk

ISBN: 9781510422322

© Susan Grenfell and Michael Wilcockson 2018

First published in 2018 by

Hodder Education,

An Hachette UK Company

Carmelite House

50 Victoria Embankment

London EC4Y 0DZ

www.hoddereducation.co.uk

Impression number   10 9 8 7 6 5 4 3 2

Year   2022 2021 2020 2019

Cover illustration by Barking Dog

Illustrations by Oxford Designers and Illustrators and Integra Software Services

Typeset by Integra Software Services Pvt. Ltd., Pondicherry, India

Printed in India

A catalogue record for this title is available from the British Library.

Contents

What is religion?

▲ What is religion?

In the beginning

Since the first humans walked the Earth, they have believed in powerful beings they called 'the gods'. The gods provided the necessary conditions for existence: rain and sunshine for good harvests, wildlife for hunting, fruit-bearing trees, seas and rivers for fishing. Human beings needed to keep these gods on their side and, over time, a relationship of sorts developed between people and their gods. People believed that if they behaved in certain ways and offered the gods things of value, the gods would be kind to them and be on their side. This relationship is what we have come to recognise as 'religion'.

Not everyone believed the same things about the gods and different parts of the world practised religion differently. In India, which has one of the oldest civilisations, belief in many gods (polytheistic religion) dominated their culture. Their religion is called Hinduism after the Indus Valley where the first Hindus lived. Two other major world faiths grew from this religion. The first was Buddhism, which was founded in about 500BCE, and the second was Sikhism, which started many centuries later, in the 1400CE.

In the Middle East, one tribe moved away from the idea that there were many gods and believed instead that there was only one God. Therefore, Judaism emerged as a monotheistic religion amid polytheistic tribes. Four thousand years later, Christianity made its appearance, firstly as a part of Judaism and then as a major world faith in its own right. Several centuries after that, Islam began. It had its roots in Judaism and Christianity and became a prominent religion in parts of the world.

Discuss

- Does it matter what we believe?
- Can all religions be true?
- Although religions are different, deep down do they all do the same thing?

Activity

Find out when each of the six religions began. Create a timeline showing how long each one has existed. Mark in major historical events or rulers as they occur along the line. You could add key Philosophical thinkers who you may have met in Book 1 (Theology and Philosophy) to see how ideas and beliefs developed at particular times.

Religion in the world

Many people think that being religious means following a set of rules and performing rituals. While it often includes elements of such things, religion is more than that. It does not always involve belief in the supernatural or life after death, heaven or hell, although it will have something to say about those things. It does not necessarily explain creation either, but many stories about how things began are similar. In religion, a set of beliefs about what is sacred and holy can be found and these beliefs influence how a person behaves within a community of like-minded people. So, you could say that religion offers a way of life.

Usually, what people believe shows in how they live and, because religion is important, cultures grow up around them. Special men or women become spiritual leaders and play a key role in how ordinary people interact with God and their community.

Rituals and ceremonies within religion have much in common. Many involve things like lighting candles, praying, singing hymns, chanting and processing. Some religions have rules about eating certain foods or fasting on certain days. These rituals are different from everyday life and so they become special. Worship becomes important either at home or at shrines, in temples, churches, mosques or synagogues.

Today there are about 10,000 different religions but nearly 90 per cent of the world's population form the six largest ones: Christianity, Judaism, Islam, Hinduism, Buddhism and Sikhism. These are the religions we will be exploring in this book.

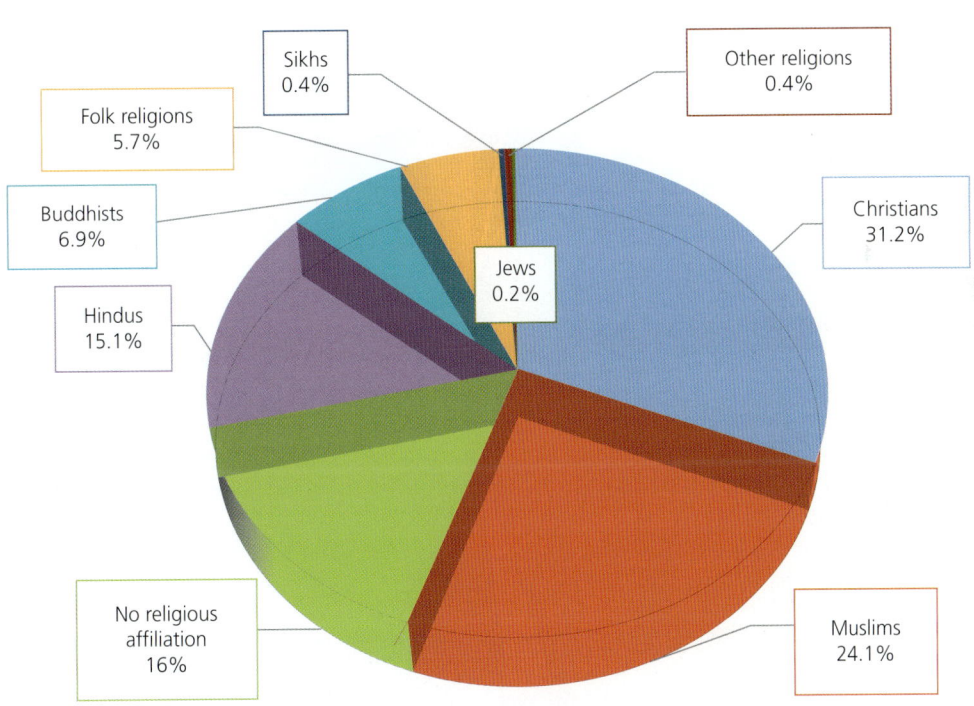

Source: Pew Research Center demographic projections in 'The Changing Global Religious Landscape'.

▲ Statistics from the 2015 survey of the spread of religions worldwide

Religion in the UK

Look at the chart showing what people believe in Britain. The largest group, Christians, may not be a surprise because the UK has been a Christian country for a long time. Half the population still identifies with Christianity. However, the second largest group is those who say they have no religious faith. You might ask whether religion is dying out and, indeed, there are those who say that it is.

Our world view demonstrates what we believe about the world, about who we are and about how we should behave. It gives us context and identity and that is why belief systems are so powerful.

Discuss
- Do you think religious belief will ever die out?
- If religious belief disappears, what comes next?
- How do you think the balance of religious belief will change within your lifetime?

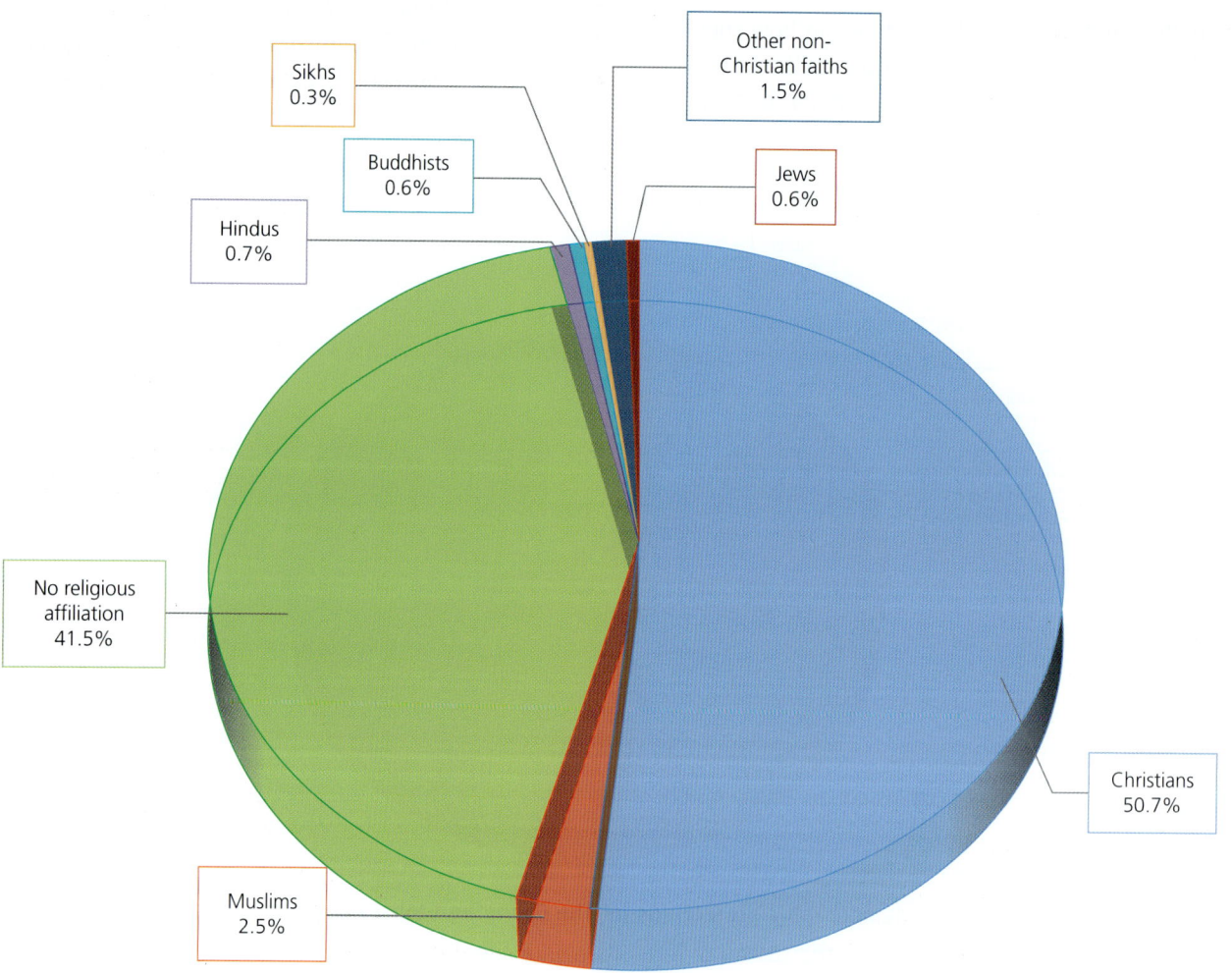

Sikhs 0.3%

Buddhists 0.6%

Hindus 0.7%

Other non-Christian faiths 1.5%

Jews 0.6%

No religious affiliation 41.5%

Christians 50.7%

Muslims 2.5%

Source: *Counting Religion in Britain*, 2018

▲ Statistics from a survey carried out in January 2018 showing the spread of belief in the UK

→ Section A Buddhism

Topic 1 Buddhist beliefs and teachings

Starter: Why do Buddhists not worship the Buddha as a god or God?

1.1 The Buddha

▲ The Buddha

Buddha means 'enlightened one' and is the title given to Siddhartha Gautama (563–483BCE). Siddhartha had a privileged life and was brought up presuming that one day he would follow his father as ruler of the Sakya tribe, a north Indian (modern day Nepal) clan. However, he became a great religious teacher instead, and changed the way people thought about their lives and the world.

Buddhism teaches the importance of committing oneself to three very important ideals, known as the **Three Refuges**:

- the Buddha as the ideal of human enlightenment
- the **Dharma** meaning 'truth' and the teachings which show the way to truth

- the **Sangha**, the men and women who have known this truth for themselves, both past and present, or more broadly the community of all Buddhists.

Siddhartha's early life

The story of Siddhartha's early life, until his enlightenment at the age of 35 when he became the Buddha, is also a parable. This contains some of the most important Buddhist teachings as they were experienced by the young Siddhartha.

Siddhartha was born in 563BCE to King Suddhodana and Queen Maya. There are many stories and legends told about Siddhartha's birth and early life. They are all intended to show how, even before his enlightenment, Siddhartha was destined to be a great spiritual leader. One story tells how Queen Maya was in the gardens of **Lumbini** when she gave birth, painlessly, to Siddhartha – such was the joy of the occasion that all the plants in the gardens burst into flower.

Even more spectacular is the myth that the baby Siddhartha took seven steps in the four directions of the compass and, with each of his steps, lotus flowers sprang up, and fountains and rainbows also appeared. Siddhartha announced, 'I am king of the four directions, this is my last birth!'

Another important sign at Siddhartha's birth was the prediction made by a wise man called **Asita**. He announced that Siddhartha would grow up to be either a great religious teacher, and would give away all his possessions, or a great ruler. His father was terrified that Siddhartha would choose to be a holy man and fail later to rule the kingdom. So, he decided to lavish great luxury on Siddhartha to make him so content that he would never consider a different way of life. So it was that Siddhartha

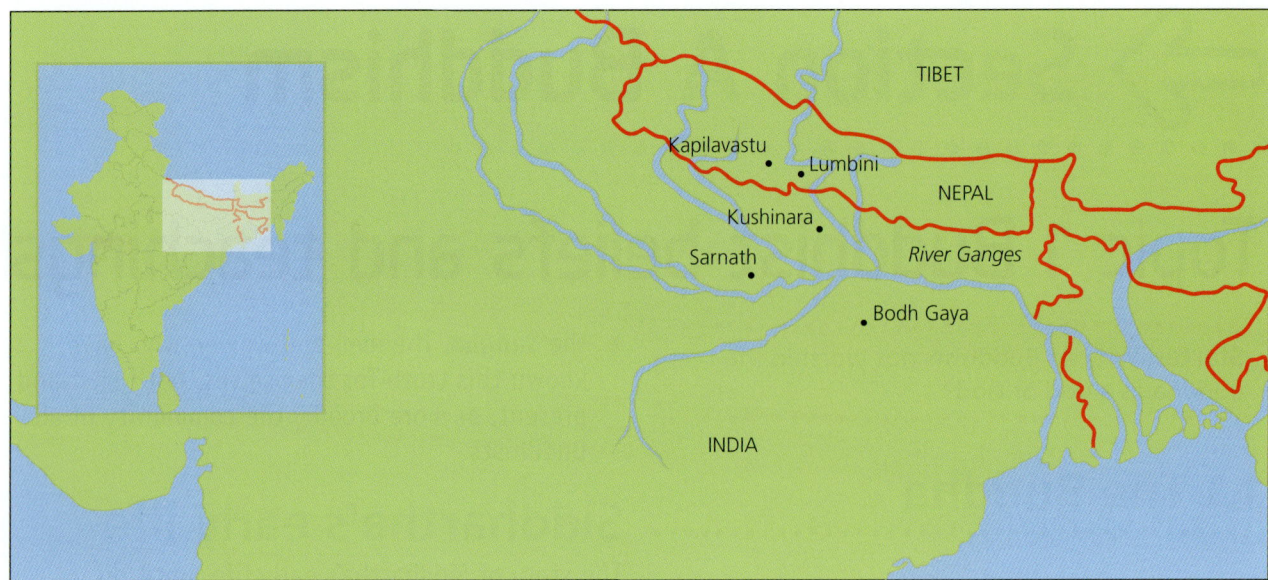

▲ Some places in northern India associated with the Buddha

grew up wanting for nothing. Sadly, his mother died seven days after his birth, but he was brought up by his step-mother Mahapajapati. Even though he was given everything materially he could wish for, this did not stop him thinking about the spiritual nature of the world.

One very important spiritual event in Siddhartha's life was at the annual ploughing festival. As the villagers showed off their skills ploughing up and down the fields, he found his mind suddenly became able to move to a higher level of thought and reality. Without trying, he had learned to meditate – he had a natural talent. While meditating, Siddhartha reflected on the joy of the people at the festival, but also the suffering of the animals who pulled the ploughs, and the worms and insects whose habitations were destroyed by the plough. He discovered he had deep compassion for all forms of life.

The king made sure Siddhartha was fully prepared to rule. Siddhartha was taught martial arts, became skilled at archery and wrestling, and studied music, mathematics and languages. His father made sure that all signs of death and decay were removed from the palace so that Siddhartha would have no need to reflect on religious matters. At the age of 16, Siddhartha married Yashodhara and they had a child, Rahula.

The Four Sights

Siddhartha lived for a further 13 years in the palace after his marriage. Despite his father's plans, inwardly he became increasingly dissatisfied with his life. Finally, at the age of 29, he summoned Channa, his chariot driver, and told him to drive him around the town outside the palace. There, according to tradition, he saw four sights or signs which changed his view of life.

The four sights were:

- an old person
- a sick person
- a dead person
- a wandering holy man.

Channa explained that the first three sights were part of ordinary everyday life from which no one can escape. Siddhartha saw the truth of this clearly, as if for the first time. He realised that his life in the palace could not protect him against old age, sickness and death, but he was intrigued by the holy man. He seemed to have achieved some kind of inner peace. Siddhartha wanted to know how the holy man had done this. So, that night, having said a silent farewell to his wife and son, Siddhartha slipped out of the palace and began his quest for enlightenment.

▲ The four sights seen by Siddhartha

The journey to enlightenment

Now that he had left the palace, Siddhartha got rid of all signs that he was a prince. He cut his hair, disposed of his royal clothes and wore the simple garments of a wandering holy man. He decided to do what many other holy men did by living an **ascetic** life.

▲ The emaciated Buddha

This means giving up all physical pleasures, eating almost nothing and practising some extreme spiritual exercises such as **breath-control**.

Siddhartha lived his ascetic life in the forests and was joined by five ascetics who also practised extreme forms of fasting. At one stage he was living on two grains of rice a day, and was so emaciated that it was said he could feel his backbone through his stomach.

After six years of living this extreme life, Siddhartha had not achieved enlightenment and was near to death. One day a young girl, Sujata, saw Siddhartha and gave him some milk rice to eat. When his five ascetic companions discovered Siddhartha had eaten the rice, they were appalled that he had broken his fast and left him. Siddhartha regained his strength. Remembering his happy experience at the ploughing festival (see page 2), he realised there was another way to achieve enlightenment.

Enlightenment

Siddhartha set off to a forest near the village of Bodh Gaya. Here he found a great fig tree and he vowed he would stay there until he had discovered the truth. This tree would become known as the **Bodhi Tree** ('bodhi' means enlightenment).

Throughout the night, as he sat there in meditation, Siddhartha experienced many temptations. **Mara**, the god of illusion and deceit, tried to stop him meditating by tempting him sexually with his daughters and frightening him with his army of sons who hurled rocks and weapons at the Buddha-to-be. However, Siddhartha understood that Mara represented all the problems which had stopped him from becoming enlightened; these were the **three poisons** of greed, hatred and ignorance. Siddhartha remained fully aware, transforming the three poisons into contentment, love and wisdom. Rocks and arrows turned into flowers and fell at his feet. Mara fled, defeated.

At dawn, at the moment when the morning star rose, Siddhartha experienced the profound peace of freedom from inner obstacles, which Buddhists call enlightenment or awakening. His enlightenment revealed to him the **Three Great Knowledges**:

- The first knowledge was that he had visions of all his many previous lives.
- The second knowledge was that he saw how people's many previous lives and deaths are governed by their actions or **karma**.
- The third knowledge was that of the **Four Noble Truths** and that there is a middle way between the extremes of luxury and asceticism.

The Three Great Knowledges, which became part of the Dharma, gave Siddhartha enlightenment. He no longer desired the life of luxury or the life of an ascetic. He was now called the Buddha or Enlightened One.

Teaching and death

After seven weeks at Bodh Gaya, the Buddha had a vision that all beings have the capacity for enlightenment. Out of compassion, he decided to communicate to others what he had discovered. He

▲ A bodhi tree

travelled to the deer park at Sarnath, where he began to teach the Dharma to all who would listen. The five ascetics returned and they became his first disciples.

After his first sermon, 'Setting in Motion the Wheel of Dharma', the five ascetics experienced what the Buddha had realised and became enlightened themselves. They were also ordained by the Buddha as his first monks or bhikkhus. The bhikkhus became the foundation of the Buddhist sangha or community.

For the next 45 years, the Buddha taught the Dharma to all – rich and poor, young and old, men and women, powerful and weak. He often had long discussions with the Indian priests. He disagreed with them that humans have eternal souls and that there is a God.

At a place called Kushinara, when he was 80 years old, the Buddha fell ill with **dysentery** (a stomach infection) and food poisoning, and died.

Even for an enlightened being, an ageing or ill body can be painful. After his death, the Buddha's awakening was even more profound as he was no longer limited by the physical body. This is **parinirvana**, which is beyond **nirvana**, and is very hard for us to imagine (see page 16). His body was cremated and his remains divided up between eight **stupas** or monuments. Although the Buddha is not worshipped as a god, these monuments became places where his followers could go on **pilgrimage** to think and meditate on his teachings.

When nearing his death, the Buddha was asked who his successor would be. He answered that the Dharma or teaching would be his successor.

▲ The Buddha on his deathbed at his parinirvana. Was this a sad occasion for his followers?

Buddhists worldwide
Since the Buddha's death, Buddhism has developed in Sri Lanka, Burma, Thailand, Cambodia, Laos, Vietnam, Tibet, China, Japan, Mongolia, Korea, in some parts of India, Pakistan and Nepal, and increasingly today in Europe and the USA.

What do you understand? **AO2**

8 Explain the significance of Sujata in Siddhartha's journey to enlightenment.

9 Explain what Mara represented in Siddhartha's mind as he sat under the Bodhi Tree.

10 Explain what knowledge Siddhartha gained at his enlightenment.

11 Explain how Siddhartha's journey to enlightenment is also a parable about the 'middle way'.

What do you know? **AO1**

1 Who was Siddhartha's father?
2 What prediction did Asita make?
3 Describe what Siddhartha experienced at the ploughing festival.
4 Who was Channa?
5 Describe the Four Sights.
6 What is the title of the Buddha's first sermon?
7 What is parinirvana?

What do you think? **AO3**

12 Should all living creatures be treated equally?
13 Was Siddhartha's quest to become enlightened selfish?

1.2 Dharma: The Three Marks of Existence

> **Activity**
>
> 1 Make a list of your ten big questions about life.
> 2 Now compare your list with your neighbour in the class.
> 3 Discuss the questions which are the same (if there are any).
> 4 Discuss the questions which are different.

In the activity, you might have asked questions like 'What is the meaning of life?' and 'Why is there so much suffering in the world?' The Buddha asked these questions too, and his teaching or Dharma helped people to find the answers. The Dharma is also known as the Path of Awakening. By following its teachings, Buddhists hope to achieve enlightenment or understanding of the world, which in turn will give them peace and ultimate happiness.

The Buddha's first three big questions are known as The Three Marks of Existence or The Three Universal Truths. These universal truths form the basis of all other Buddhist teachings.

> The three marks are based on the Buddha's observations of nature. Compare them to your own list of big questions and see if any of the three marks appear on your list.

▲ The stupa or monument at Sarnath, India, where the Buddha began to teach the Dharma

Anicca (impermanence)

▲ Think about these flowers and what is happening to them. What do they suggest to you about our existence?

You will remember that the first three of the sights Siddhartha encountered were all to do with change – sickness after being healthy; old age after youth; death from having been alive.

Anicca means impermanence. Buddhism teaches that everything is impermanent and constantly changing, from stars to trees to mobile phones, and also us – our bodies, our feelings and our thoughts. Ultimately, we cannot stop change. Change is good news, because without change nothing can happen. Through change, things can get better as well as worse.

Siddhartha's father had tried to control life in the palace and to remove all decay and change, but he was unable to do this. What he created instead was a false impression of the world, which Siddhartha instinctively knew was wrong.

Anicca has some important philosophical implications, which the Buddha developed:

- There is no creator God. If everything changes then there can be no eternal being, such as a creator God, who is not subject to change. The Buddha spoke about gods and other types of non-human beings, but they too were subject to the law of change. He did not believe in the traditional God.

- Trying to hold onto people or things, or trying to make situations last forever, causes suffering. Trying to stop change is like trying to stop a train with your feet. All that happens is that you suffer and the train carries on. The Buddha might have liked the story Peter Pan by J.M. Barrie. Peter Pan lives in a place called Neverland where he stays a child, but deep down he is not happy because Neverland is false and an illusion.

If nothing is permanent, then it follows that there is no eternal soul or permanent part of ourselves. This is the basis for the second of the three marks of existence, anatta.

Anatta (no permanent self)

Try to answer the question 'Do I have a soul?' by pointing to yourself – which bit is you? If you point to your head or heart, then you have merely indicated a part of your body. Isn't your foot as much a part of you as your head or heart?

The Buddha argued that although we are made up of many things, there is no fixed self or soul. Our sense of our self and who we are changes through life. Self is an ever-changing flow, like a river. Think of how you have changed as you have grown older.

Anatta is not saying that we do not exist, but rather that we do not exist as a separate self. This can be hard to accept because we all think we exist independently as separate selves. For some people, it might be frightening to think like this. For others, it might give a sense of freedom and of being connected to others and to the world.

Dukkha (suffering)

Even though the Buddha was given every luxury when he lived in the palace, deep down this did not satisfy him. It was only when he saw the first of the Four Sights (see page 2) that he realised that suffering, and our failed attempts to avoid it, are at the heart of what humans do. Suffering is called **dukkha**.

As the Buddha had found out from his time in the palace until his enlightenment, there are different kinds of dukkha:

- First, there is the obvious kind of physical and emotional dukkha, caused when we injure ourselves or fall ill, or fail to get something we hoped for, or – more seriously – when a friend goes away or a loved one dies (as in the picture below).
- Second, there is the suffering of change. Even when life is enjoyable, we know the situation cannot last forever. This can cause anxiety or regret.
- Last, there is a subtle kind of psychological suffering, of being ill at ease with oneself, or having a sense of failure at not achieving one's goals, or a deeper sense that there is no meaning to life. Buddhism teaches that we will not be satisfied and fulfilled unless we are expressing our full spiritual potential.

What do you know? AO1

1 What does anicca mean?
2 What does anatta mean?
3 What does dukkha mean?

What do you understand? AO2

4 Explain why the Dharma is also called the 'Path to Awakening'?
5 Explain two different types of suffering.
6 Explain why Buddhists do not believe in a creator God.

What do you think? AO3

7 Is it impossible for us to escape suffering?
8 Is Buddhism wrong; we do have souls?
9 Is the Buddha's teaching on dukkha a very gloomy view of life or is he just being realistic?

▲ There are many ways which we can experience physical and emotional dukkha

1.3 Dharma: The Four Noble Truths

We have all been to see the doctor at some time in our life. We go because we are ill or worried that there might be something wrong with us. The doctor will usually ask us some questions and then do a number of checks. Finally, she will make a diagnosis and then prescribe some medicine or treatment which will help us. Of course, none of this would be worthwhile unless we take the medicine or receive the treatment as prescribed by the doctor.

The Four Noble Truths is the Buddha's treatment prescribed for spiritual illness and goes through a very similar process to a visit to the doctor. He taught the Four Noble Truths in his first sermon:

- The first Noble Truth recognises that all life involves suffering. This is called dukkha.
- The second Noble Truth diagnoses the cause of the suffering. This is called **samudaya**.
- The third Noble Truth is the prescription which will tackle and overcome the suffering. This is called nirodha.
- The fourth Noble Truth is the process to carry out the prescription. This is called **magga**.

Suffering (dukkha)

There are several different kinds of dukkha, as mentioned on page 8. The first step is to acknowledge that you are suffering and then to reflect on what kind of dukkha you might be experiencing. This is where Buddhist meditation is often very helpful in thinking and reflecting.

The cause of suffering (samudaya)

The next stage is to reflect on what is causing your suffering. The cause of suffering is craving, or sticky attachment, called **tanha**. This is not a healthy desire such as for food and sleep when we are hungry or tired. It is more like a desire to eat too much to overcome feelings of loneliness: the kind of craving that does not satisfy our needs in the end. For example, a new gadget makes us happy for a short while, but soon we get bored and want a newer one.

Tanha links to the three poisons:

- Greed or craving to fill our inner sense of lack with constant sense pleasures, possessions or status, being someone special.
- Hatred. When our greed is frustrated, we want to get rid of things or people we think are the cause of our difficulty. Hatred includes jealousy, destructive anger and revenge: all things which destroy a person's emotional and spiritual life.
- Ignorance of the world as it really is underlies our greed and hatred. If we really understood impermanence (anicca, see page 7) we would give up greed and hatred in favour of contentment and generosity.

The three poisons are also called the three fires. Fire symbolises the destructive side of human nature. In the Buddha's 'Fire Sermon', he describes every aspect of ourselves as burning with tanha – the eye, ear, nose, tongue, body and mind. Buddhism teaches transforming the unhelpful, selfish desires of tanha into helpful, creative desires for the happiness of all, including oneself.

As long as a person experiences tanha, then they will continue to be reborn (**samsara**). Only when tanha is overcome can they be released from samsara and achieve enlightenment.

▲ The three poisons depicted as a cockerel (greed), snake (hatred) and pig (ignorance)

The end of craving (nirodha)

The good news is that dukkha and its causes can be overcome (**nirodha**). The Buddha taught that once craving and attachment ceases so too does suffering and a person is liberated and free to live life fully.

The middle way (magga)

The final stage is action by following the magga, the path to enlightenment. The magga is the middle way between the extremes of luxury and hardship. There is a middle way because extremes do not bring enlightenment, as the Buddha himself found out.

The magga which the Buddha taught is called the **Noble Eightfold Path**; it sets out three areas for everyday living and for training the mind.

The three areas of living are: wisdom (prajna), ethics (sila) and meditation (samadhi). Every description of the magga begins with the word 'right' (see the box below). This is because the right way of achieving the magga takes a great deal of practice and varies from person to person. The right way is also the middle way between extremes, and, as Siddhartha found out, can only be achieved with great effort and determination.

Wisdom
1 Right view means understanding the Dharma, the teaching of the Buddha.
2 Right intention means making a firm commitment to follow the path.

Ethics
3 Right speech means making a moral commitment to speak truthfully, kindly and harmoniously.
4 Right action means making a moral commitment to the **Five Precepts**.
5 Right livelihood means making a moral commitment not to do any job which harms or exploits other humans, animals or the environment.

Meditation
6 Right effort means developing positive mental states such as loving kindness (**metta**), generosity, patience and compassion (**karuna**).
7 Right mindfulness means developing the mind by being aware of the body and its sensations. It also means being mindful of the environment and other living creatures.
8 Right concentration means practising meditation and dwelling on higher states of consciousness, free from the three poisons of hatred, greed and ignorance.

Activity

Right livelihood

Margaret is a 35-year-old senior sales manager of a pharmaceutical (drugs) company. She has a young family, owns an expensive house in the city and earns a six-figure salary. She works long hours, leaving at 7 a.m. and often returning home after her children have gone to bed. Part of her job involves entertaining clients, so several times a week she takes them to expensive restaurants.

She has just received a letter offering her promotion to be one of the vice-presidents of the company. However, now that she has got the offer of the job she has always wanted, she is unsure. It does not feel right. She has begun to doubt whether the business she has devoted herself to for the past 12 years is contributing to society in any meaningful way.

A friend has suggested she talks to you, a Buddhist counsellor, for advice.

Imagine you are a Buddhist counsellor. Choose some of the paths from the Noble Eightfold Path and explain how these might help Margaret think through her life and career choices.

What do you know? AO1

1. What does samudaya mean?
2. What does nirodha mean?
3. What is tanha?
4. Outline the three poisons.
5. What is the magga?
6. What are the three areas of living?

What do you understand? AO2

7. Explain how the three poisons affect everything we do.
8. Explain what 'the right intention' is in the Noble Eightfold Path.
9. Explain how a person might practise 'right speech'.
10. Explain how a person might practise 'right effort'.

What do you think? AO3

11. Is greed worse than hatred?
12. Should a Buddhist never fight in war?
13. Must a Buddhist be a vegetarian?

1.4 Ethical teachings

Usually, when we use the term 'ethics', we mean doing morally good things and avoiding doing bad things. This is true in Buddhism, but as the Four Noble Truths teaches, there is more to ethics than living by moral rules. The truly ethical life according to Buddhism is also about developing or 'cultivating' one's spiritual character.

▲ Cultivating is an important Buddhist idea. It is called **bhavana**. Just as a person cultivates their garden by skilfully planting at the right time and giving the plants the right amount of food, water and sun depending on the seasons and time of day, so cultivating one's spiritual nature takes care, attention and sensitivity to others

Karma

At his enlightenment, the Buddha learned that everything which happens is the result of a preceding cause. For example, if I kick a ball, it moves. My kick is the cause; the movement of the ball is the effect. A seed grows into a tree if the conditions are right. How many conditions are needed for this to happen?

Effect

Cause

▲ Karma: foot-ball

This law of cause and effect is called karma, which means 'action with intention'. Everything we do has consequences, for ourselves and for other people, both in this life and after rebirth in future lives. This is why the Noble Eightfold Path is especially important, as it helps guide us in all the decisions we make throughout life.

There are two kinds of karma:
1 Punna karma – skilful or good actions – those performed with awareness and kindness, which bring about beneficial results for oneself and others.
2 Pappa karma – unskilful or bad actions – those performed with greed, hatred and unawareness, which result in harmful results for oneself and others, and lead to an increase in suffering and dukkha.

The Buddha said about karma, 'The fool, while sinning, thinks and hopes, "This never will catch up with me". But later on there's bitterness, when the punishment must be endured.' (The Dhammapada 4:11). So, karma is inevitable. The Buddha compared it to the wheel of a cart inevitably following on behind the ox which pulls the cart.

Discuss

If all actions inevitably have consequences, does this mean that we can't change the future?

Re-becoming (samsara)

Just as the seasons follow each other in a continuous cycle of birth, death and rebirth, so all sentient life undergoes a constant cycle of birth and rebirth. This cycle is called samsara.

Buddhism teaches that a sentient life is a being which can experience suffering. Sentient creatures include non-human animals, humans, enlightened beings and gods. Rebirth depends on how well a sentient being has lived according to the laws of karma. The Jataka Tales relate how the Buddha, in his previous existence, had lived many times as a non-human animal, such as a monkey and as a deer. Every time, he had always shown great kindness and generosity to others so he was reborn as the Buddha.

The Buddha rejected the idea that there is a permanent unchanging soul, which lives on after death – but he did think that, in some way, consciousness is transferred from one life to another.

In one of his teachings, the Buddha explains that this life and the next one might be compared to lighting a candle from another candle: the second candle or flame is different from the first, but it could not exist without the first candle flame.

▲ The lighting of one flame to another symbolises the cycle of birth and rebirth

The Wheel of Life

Samsara is often represented by the popular Buddhist image of the **Wheel of Life**.

The Wheel of Life is divided into six realms. These realms are inhabited by different sentient beings. These realms and beings can be thought of as actual realms or different aspects of ourselves.

The six realms are:

1 The god world is a state of deep, long-lasting contentment and the higher happiness of reading, music and intellectual thought.

2 The human realm has a balance of happiness and suffering, some craving and some contentment. This balance makes spiritual life easier.

3 The animal world is the state of just wanting to be satisfied with food, sex and home comforts. They have no interest in spiritual life.

4 The hell realm is inhabited by those who live in a continuous state of hatred, suspicion, paranoia, fear and despair. It is hard for them to see beyond their suffering.

5 The hungry ghost realm comprises those who always want more and are never satisfied. If we are addicted, we are like hungry ghosts.

6 The aggressive god world (the titan world) is a competitive state of wanting to succeed against one's rivals. Titans want to grab the fruits of life without sowing the seeds of real happiness.

At the hub of the wheel are the three poisons represented by three animals – a cockerel, a snake and a pig (each biting the other's tail to show how the three poisons are each dependent on each other).

Compassion (karuna) and loving kindness (metta)

When watching the ploughing festival as a child, the Buddha experienced an overwhelming sense of love for all sentient beings (metta or loving kindness). Loving kindness is a natural emotion we all feel at times. It gives us a concern for the welfare of others and we stop worrying about just ourselves.

When we feel metta and come upon someone who is suffering, metta turns into compassion (karuna). Through this, we can support the person who is suffering without becoming horrified and anxious ourselves. We imagine what they may be feeling and thinking, and do our best to help ease their suffering.

In practice, karuna and metta work very closely together. The example the Buddha gives is of a mother saving her child from harm without thinking of her own safety.

Karuna and metta form the basis for The Five Precepts or **pansils** – the Buddhist equivalent to the Jewish and Christian Ten Commandments. The pansils are the foundation for all Buddhist ethics:

- Avoid harming sentient life (such as killing or harming).
- Avoid taking what is not yours (such as stealing).
- Avoid committing any sexually harmful act (such as adultery).
- Avoid harmful speech and saying what is not true (such as lying, slander and gossip).
- Avoid clouding the mind with intoxicants (such as alcohol or drugs).

▲ Which pansil does each picture refer to?

Nirvana and parinirvana

Siddhartha's quest, when he left the palace, was to find out the causes of suffering or dukkha and how to overcome it. Achieving the state of no dukkha is called nirvana. Nirvana literally means 'blowing out', that is, blowing out and being freed from the three poisons of hate, greed and ignorance.

Nirvana is a way of describing an experience which lies beyond thought. It is difficult to imagine it. Buddhists practise meditation to know, directly for themselves, what nirvana is like.

We can imagine that to be without dukkha, nirvana must be a state of utter peace and joy, like when we put down a heavy load we have been carrying for a long time. When the Buddha entered nirvana he also experienced freedom, unconditional love, contentment, energy and fearlessness.

Here is how one Buddhist scholar describes nirvana:

He who has realized the Truth, Nirvana, is the happiest being in the world. He is free from all 'complexes' and obsessions, the worries and troubles that torment others.

Wapola Rahula, *What the Buddha Taught*, page 43

Nirvana is the release or liberation from samsara of the Wheel of Life. At death, once the physical body has passed away, a person who has achieved nirvana enters parinirvana, or final nirvana, and they are not reborn again.

What do you know? AO1

1. What does bhavana mean?
2. What does samsara mean?
3. What does the hub of the Wheel of Life represent?
4. What is karuna?
5. What is metta?

What do you understand? AO2

6. Explain the Buddhist teaching on punna and pappa karma.
7. Explain what is meant by 'sentient life'.
8. Explain how the Wheel of Life may be thought of in two ways.
9. Explain what the Wheel of Life teaches about karma.
10. Explain the purpose of the metta meditation.

What do you think? AO3

11. Do you think Buddhism leads to happiness?
12. Should everyone follow the pansils?

Essay practice

'There is no point in thinking about nirvana if we don't know what it is.' Do you agree? Give reasons for your answer. Show that you have considered more than one point of view.

Topic 2 Buddhist practices and ceremonies

Starter: Why is meditation so important in Buddhism?

As Buddhism spread to different countries, and adapted itself to existing religious practices, people developed different ways of understanding the Buddha's teaching, or Dharma.

From the start, the Buddha had encouraged his followers to think for themselves so it is not surprising that Buddhism should evolve into distinctive forms.

Different Buddhist traditions

Theravada Buddhism

Theravada Buddhism developed mostly in India and today exists mainly in Sri Lanka, Burma and Thailand. It is a way of life developed by the Buddha himself and is the oldest surviving form of Buddhism. Saffron-robed monks and nuns live simply, without possessions, practising meditation, studying and teaching the Dharma.

Buddhism teaches that anyone, including **lay people**, can achieve enlightenment, although some lifestyles, like being a monk, can be helpful if that is your goal. Lay people support the monks and nuns with food, gifts and other offerings (**dana**) to help them survive. This is said to bring each lay person great merit.

▲ Theravada monks on their daily round to collect dana (offerings) from the lay people

Mahayana Buddhism

Mahayana Buddhism, or 'Great Way', developed from the first century CE. It is called Great Way because it supports the idea that Buddhist practice is for the benefit of all beings, not just for one's own happiness. This attitude of compassion is found in the Theravada too, but the Mahayana place great emphasis on it. Mahayana is a broad term that covers a great variety of traditions, largely found in China, Korea and Japan.

The spiritual ideal of the Mahayana is the **bodhisattva**, a person who vows, out of compassion (karuna), to practise Buddhism and forego even enlightenment until every being in the universe knows the peace of nirvana. This is a big task! The point is that it's easy to become selfish or just understand Buddhism with one's head and without kindness – but it's not possible to become a selfish, unkind Buddha.

After they die, many bodhisattvas are worshipped as spiritual beings who help people in their lives. Pictures and rupas of bodhisattvas have many symbols. The bodhisattva **Avalokiteshvara**, for example, has a thousand arms to reach out to living beings to symbolise his compassion for the world. The bodhisattva Tara is often depicted stepping down from her meditation lotus seat as a symbol of helping those in need.

Mahayana also stresses that we all have **Buddha Nature**, meaning that being enlightened is available to everyone and knowable by everyone. It is not exclusively the possession of a special type of religious person, such as a monk.

Each Buddhist tradition has developed its own distinctive forms of worship, practices and ceremonies.

> ## What do you understand? AO2
>
> 1 Explain the key Theravada Buddhist beliefs.
> 2 Explain what Mahayana Buddhists mean by 'Buddha Nature'.
> 3 Explain what a bodhisattva is.

> ## What do you think? AO3
>
> 4 Is it good for there to be different traditions within a religion?

▲ The bodhisattva Tara is popular in meditation to develop compassion. She is depicted stepping down from her meditation lotus seat, because she is always ready to help those in need

2.1 Meditation

Meditation is a key part of Buddhism. The three limbs of the Eightfold Path directly involve meditation – right effort, mindfulness and concentration. Meditation is a way to cultivate the mind. Bhavana means cultivation, as in the metta bhavana: the cultivation of loving kindness.

The Buddha had a gift for meditation. When he was young and attended the ploughing festival (see page 2), he used the rhythms of the plough to focus his mind and see the world in a new way. He trained for many years to develop a clearer, more radiant state of mind and heart, and he still meditated to refresh his mind even after Enlightenment.

At a simple level, anyone can practise meditation by becoming aware of themselves and their surroundings. This is the daily practice of mindfulness.

Meditation is often practised in the lotus position – sitting on the floor with legs crossed and the soles of the feet facing upwards. However, this requires flexibility. You can also practise meditation kneeling or sitting on a cushion or in a chair.

▲ The lotus position

Concentration and tranquillity (samatha)

Samatha meditation is any practice which leads to the cultivation of inner steadiness, well-being and emotional strength. As we meditate, the busyness and clutter of the mind can gradually drift away and calm down.

One form of samatha meditation is mindfulness of breathing. Here are some simple steps for how to practise it:

How to meditate

- Get yourself into an alert, yet relaxed, sitting position, not slumping over.
- Allow your shoulders, stomach and face to soften and relax.
- Now notice your breath flowing in and out. Feel the touch of the air around your nostrils and the breath flowing into your body.
- If your mind wanders into distracted thinking, bring your attention gently back to the breath, focusing on breathing for however long you have set aside, and then open your eyes.

Some people like to use an image or picture to focus on.

Samatha meditation is more than just relaxation. Metta meditation is a samatha practice, as mentioned on page 16. This involves cultivation of well-wishing and love to ourselves and others.

Samatha meditations are about caring for the heart and mind, because this will strongly affect our lives and our sense of well-being and happiness. If practised regularly, the three root poisons begin to transform into generosity, love and awareness.

Insight meditation (vipassana)

Samatha is often used as preparation for the more advanced vipassana meditation. Vipassana means 'insight'. Its purpose is to gain knowledge of the way things actually are. It is best to practise these teachings with guidance from a spiritual master.

In vipassana meditation, you can visualise a buddha or bodhisattva, holding them in mind and reflecting on their qualities. Or you can reflect on teachings such as anicca and anatta, perhaps using images like a fading flower or a personal experience.

Practising vipassana leads eventually to understanding the Dharma, not as a theory or even as abstract thinking, but as direct experience of how things are. There is also a sense of deep relief and liberation.

Imagine what it would be like to be the bodhisattvas Tara or Avalokiteshvara (see pages 18 and 25), who are examples of pure compassion. If you visualise like this regularly it will strengthen your own efforts to be compassionate and loving to everyone you meet in your daily life.

Zen meditation

Zen Buddhism has developed its own distinctive forms of meditation. Zen Buddhists believe that our Buddha Nature can be awakened in quite surprising and unexpected ways.

Koans

One of the Zen methods is the use of **koans**. The koan is usually a short story or a sentence which makes very little rational sense. The problem of sense lies not with the koan but the way we approach it and our mindset. Once we have adjusted our mind, and understood what is being pointed to, then there is a moment of **satori** or 'spiritual awakening'.

Zen teachers sometimes use what might seem quite aggressive forms of teaching – shouting, banging saucepans, interrupting their pupils' answers and even hitting them to make them rethink and look deeper into themselves and find out more about their Buddha Nature.

Zen also teaches that meditation can be carried out in apparently simple everyday tasks such as walking, sitting, arranging flowers, archery and making tea. Much like the samatha breathing meditation, each of these activities can help focus the mind and make the person more aware of their surroundings and their Buddha Nature.

For example, the Zen tea ceremony is widely practised in Japan. A tea-making ceremony can take many hours because every part of it – from laying out the cups to pouring the tea and then drinking it – takes great mindfulness and reveals something about the tea-maker and his relationship to the world.

▲ A Zen Buddhist Master during the tea-making ceremony

Sitting or zazen meditation

Zazen or Just Sitting is one of the most widely practised Zen meditation techniques. The sitter must sit upright and yet be completely relaxed. They might focus at first on the area just below the navel and use the breathing exercise to become calm and full of energy. Then they try to remain alert and aware of whatever arises in the present moment. This isn't as easy as it sounds!

Walking or kinhin meditation

Kinhin is practised between zazen sessions. The person walks in rhythm with their breathing. The left hand forms a fist and the right hand is placed over it; both are held just at the bottom of the rib cage. Walking may be done slowly or at a brisk pace. The aim of kinhin is the same as zazen.

In Japan, from the koan, poets developed the haiku, a seventeen-syllable poem which prompts the listener to think about reality and their Buddha nature:

How marvellous, how miraculous,
I draw water,
I carry fuel.
Quoted in Clive Erricker, *Teach Yourself Buddhism*, page 80

What do you know?

1 Describe the lotus position.
2 What does vipassana mean?
3 Describe kinhin meditation.
4 What is a koan?
5 What does the word satori mean?
6 What is a haiku?

What do you understand?

7 Explain the Buddhist idea of cultivation or bhavana.
8 Explain the purpose of samatha breathing meditation.
9 Explain how a fading flower could be used in vipassana meditation.
10 Explain the purpose of zazen meditation.
11 Explain how a Japanese tea-making ceremony is used in Zen meditation.

What do you think? AO3

12 Do you have to be taught meditation or could someone learn to do it by themselves?
13 Is meditation the same as relaxation?

▲ A Buddhist practising kinhin meditation

2.2 Buddhist places of worship

In the very early days, the Buddha and his monks did not have a permanent place to live and worship. During the rainy season, they created **vihara** or monasteries, which became permanent and were supported by the local people who also came to worship there. A vihara contains bedrooms for the monks, meeting rooms, a library, kitchen, gardens and a cemetery. At the heart of the vihara is the shrine room.

Temples and shrines

The vihara is more than just a place of worship. It is a place for monks and nuns to live a whole way of life, dedicated to Buddhist practice. As much of the time is spent studying and meditating, a vihara or temple usually contains rooms to think, discuss and meditate.

There is no standard design for a Buddhist temple, but most temples or viharas have the following features:

- The shrine room is the most important room in the temple. The shrine contains statues (rupas) and images of the Buddha, bodhisattva and great teachers. These images are not worshipped but are used as a focus for meditation and reflection. These rooms can be highly decorated or very simple depending on the culture and time at which they were constructed.
- Stupas or shrines to commemorate a great teacher or bodhisattva.
- A bodhi tree to remind worshippers of the Buddha's enlightenment.
- A large image of the Buddha placed outside to aid reflection when walking in the gardens.

Although a temple contains a shrine room, shrines may also be found separately, for example outside a temple or near a stupa and most commonly at home. A shrine contains an image of the Buddha or a bodhisattva. The worshipper makes their offerings of candles and incense to this shrine, and they use it as a focus of their meditation.

Monuments (stupas)

When the Buddha died, his ashes were divided up and placed under eight monuments or stupas (see page 5). The stupas were put at significant places in the Buddha's life, including his birthplace at Lumbini, the site of his enlightenment at Bodh Gaya, the location of his first sermon at Sarnath and at Kushinara where he died.

Since then, stupas have been used to store the ashes of great Buddhist teachers and bodhisattvas. They are treated as holy sites and visited by pilgrims. From the earliest of times, pilgrims have circled round the stupa, meditating on the Buddha, bodhisattva or great teacher whose remains it contains.

The creation of the stupa inspired the development of Buddhist art and design. The early Indian stupas were often conical in shape, but in Japan the conical shape developed into the elaborate and highly decorated **pagoda** shape, often with an inverted parasol or umbrella spire on top. The umbrella design is a symbol of royalty, as the Buddha was a prince in his early life.

▲ A Japanese pagoda in Battersea Park, London

Stupa art includes: the animals which the Buddha lived as in his former lives; the eight-spoked Buddhist Wheel of Dharma; the bodhi tree; footprints; an empty throne or saddle.

Stupas may be built in the grounds of a vihara. Often, a miniature stupa is placed in the shrine room of the temple or at home, to commemorate the Buddha or a bodhisattva who is particularly associated with that temple or Buddhist tradition.

Activity

Stupa design

1 Use the internet and find out about a bodhisattva.

2 Using the symbols of this bodhisattva and other Buddhist symbols, design a stupa for him or her.

What do you understand?   AO2

4 Explain two purposes of a vihara (monastery).

5 Explain the significance of a Buddhist shrine for worshippers.

6 Explain why stupas are important for Buddhist pilgrims today.

What do you know?   AO1

1 What is a vihara?

2 Name four things found in a shrine room.

3 Describe the original purpose of a stupa.

What do you think?   AO3

7 Should viharas be as simple as possible with very little decoration?

8 Do stupas encourage Buddhists to worship the dead person?

Worship

Worship or **puja** may take place in the shrine room at the temple or at the shrine at home. Most lay people practise puja at home and at the vihara on special occasions and festivals.

Puja at the shrine

A shrine might contain:

- Buddha images or **rupas**. (See page 24 for their purpose.)
- Seven offering bowls: water for the feet, water for the face, flowers, incense, lamps, perfume and food. Offerings symbolise treating the Buddha as the honoured guest.
- Flowers: traditionally given to an honoured guest but may also be used to aid meditation and as a reminder that everything changes (anicca).
- Candles: the light from candles symbolises the presence of the Dharma and wisdom.
- Incense: creates an atmosphere of peace and calm and represents the good deeds spreading out from the person who performs them into the world.
- A bell or gong: this is rung at the start of puja and at the next stage of a meditation.

The actual practice of puja varies depending on each Buddhist tradition. Typically, at the start of puja, a person will bow three times to the shrine as a sign of humility and respect.

In a vihara a monk or nun might **prostrate** themselves (lying on the ground) in front of the shrine.

The person might perform the **mudra** of respect by holding their hands together then touching their head, lips and chest to symbolise commitment through thought, word and deed.

Worship usually takes place sitting on a cushion on the floor and might involve reciting a **mantra** or **chanting** individually or with others. Mantras and chants are learned by heart as this encourages patience, concentration, effort and determination. These may be followed by times of silence.

▲ An example of items that may be included in a shrine at home

Buddha and bodhisattva images

A rupa is an image of the Buddha or a bodhisattva and might be a picture or a statue. A rupa represents the actual qualities of the Buddha or bodhisattva, and by meditating on it the worshipper gains real insight and knowledge. However, the rupa is never to be worshipped or treated as an idol. The purpose of the rupa is to focus the worshipper's mind and help them imagine the qualities of the Buddha.

Rupas vary enormously from country to country and between different Buddhist traditions, but there are some common characteristics. The Buddha has:

- a dot in the middle of his forehead which represents the centre of energy and wisdom
- a top-knot of hair which was fashionable in India at the time of the Buddha. The flame which emerges from it shows that he was enlightened
- long ear lobes that indicate the Buddha's royal birth.

Not all rupas represent the historical Buddha. Some rupas depict different aspects of enlightenment such as compassion, fearlessness, wisdom and abundance. Other rupas represent bodhisattvas such as Avalokiteshvara and Tara, who can be seen as aspects of the Buddha.

All rupas are images of tranquillity and are designed to calm the worshipper's mind and help meditation. However, this may not always appear obvious. For example, the wrathful Buddha image might symbolise the energy one needs to break through destructive habits or help one overcome fear. This is turn can help create an inner state of peace.

▲ The wrathful Buddha

Symbols

Buddhism has developed a rich artistic tradition. Here are some more common symbols associated with Buddhism:

- The lotus flower is one of the most popular symbols and represents the journey to enlightenment. The flower develops from the muddy waters at the bottom of a pond (ignorance and greed), and then emerges into the sunlight in the most glorious colours (enlightenment of wisdom, love and compassion).

▲ A lotus flower

▲ Why does Avalokiteshvara have so many arms?

● Bodhisattvas are quite often shown stepping down from a throne, as a symbol of generosity and compassion (karuna) to help humankind.

● The bodhisattva Avalokiteshvara is usually depicted with a thousand arms and open hand gestures radiating from behind him as a sign of his love and compassion for all.

● An ancient symbol of Buddhism is the eight-spoked wheel, the Wheel of Dharma or Wheel of Life. The Buddha's very first sermon is called 'Turning the Wheel of Dharma' and the Wheel of Life illustration expresses some of the very basic teachings of Buddhism. It is like a map but instead of showing countries it shows the different states of mind and how Buddhists can move from one state of mind to another. The wheel, like the cross in Christianity or the Star of David in Judaism, is the most widespread symbol of Buddhism.

▲ Why does the wheel have eight spokes?

▲ Why is this bodhisattva stepping down?

● The vajra means both thunderbolt and diamond and is used to symbolise power and determination. In ancient India, the vajra was used as a club in war so, in Buddhist art, came to represent energy and spiritual commitment. It also symbolises that the Dharma, or reality, is like a diamond, indestructible.

▲ What does the vajra symbolise?

Mudras

It is quite natural for us to use our hands to emphasise what we might be saying or to indicate a direction or explain an idea. Most religions have traditions about how a worshipper should hold her hands as an aid to prayer and meditation.

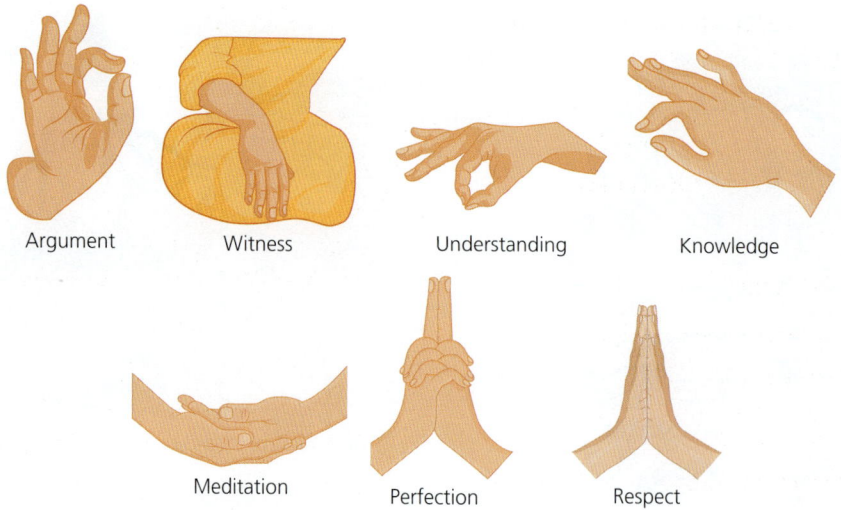

Argument Witness Understanding Knowledge

Meditation Perfection Respect

▲ The mudras (hand gestures) of argument, witness, understanding, knowledge, meditation, perfection, respect

In Buddhism, there are many hand gestures or mudras which are practised in meditation and seen in Buddhist art. One of the first was when the Buddha was being tempted by Mara at his enlightenment (see page 4). The Buddha 'touched the earth' when he called on the Earth to help him fight the temptations he was going through. The witness mudra is used today to indicate a desire not to be distracted from doing right. Another very common mudra is the mudra of respect, often used at the start of puja. The cupped hands represent the lotus flower.

Mental concentration and devotion

A rupa may aid meditation visually; chanting and saying mantras uses the body in a different way to develop mental concentration and devotion. Many people find singing psychologically satisfying, either when singing to themselves or with others. Over the years, Buddhism has developed its own special chants to be used at puja and in meditation.

Chanting

Chanting developed very early on in Buddhism, before the Buddha's words were written down. It was a good way of remembering his teaching, learning it and passing it on. A chant is halfway between singing a tune and singing on a single note. A popular chant honouring the Buddha is:

Namo tassa bhagvato, arahato, samma-sambuddhassa

Honour to the Lord, Arahat, perfectly and completely Enlightened One!

This is repeated three times and is followed by chanting the Three Refuges and Five Moral Precepts (see pages 1 and 15). Often a rosary or string of beads is used to count off the repeated chants.

Mantras

Mantras are short repeated phrases used in meditation to help focus the mind on a particular spiritual quality. The words do not need to mean anything important: it is the power of the syllables when recited properly which gives power. A mantra acts like a tuning fork on the mind by helping it to resonate at the right frequency.

Some mantras have no particular meaning, but when they are chanted, their rhythm lifts the soul to a higher level of awareness.

Each bodhisattva has its own mantra. Perhaps the most famous mantra is Avalokiteshvara's:

Om mani padme hum

Om, the jewel is in the lotus!

It is not the meaning of the words which is important but the syllables themselves. There are many interpretations of this mantra. Some say its six syllables represent the six realms or rebirth which stream into the mind of the person as they recite the mantra.

Activity

Arrange a class debate on the motion: 'We believe that meditation should be compulsory at school.'

What do you know? AO1

1. Describe the use of a rupa in worship.
2. Describe a typical Buddha rupa.
3. Outline what happens at puja.
4. What is the mudra of respect?
5. What do the thousand arms of Avalokiteshvara represent?

What do you understand? AO2

6. Explain the purpose of the seven offering bowls.
7. Explain the difference between a mantra and a chant.
8. Explain the purpose of hand gestures (mudras) in Buddhist worship.
9. Explain what a top-knot symbolises in a Buddha rupa.
10. Explain the symbolism of the lotus flower and the eight-spoked wheel.
11. Explain the purpose of meditating on an angry Buddha rupa.
12. Explain why candles are lit and incense burnt in puja.

What do you think? AO3

13. Is listening to a favourite piece of music worship?
14. Is a mantra useless unless it means something?

2.3 Festivals and ceremonies

Festivals for Buddhists are times when people can show compassion and friendliness to each other and learn more about the Buddha, the Dharma and the Sangha. There are not many festivals in Buddhism and some of its festivals are only found in certain countries. The most commonly celebrated festival is Wesak.

The festival of Wesak

Wesak celebrates the Buddha's two 'birthdays': the dates of his physical birth and his enlightenment. This is why Wesak is sometimes called Buddha Day. It is celebrated at the first full moon in May which, in the Hindu calendar is Wesakha, and is why the festival is called Wesak.

Wesak is a time when Buddhist monks and nuns celebrate with lay people. This helps strengthen the relationship between different members of the Sangha.

There are many customs associated with Wesak.

- People exchange Wesak cards.
- Houses and temples are lit up and people carry lanterns in the streets.
- Lay people make a special effort to visit monasteries and temples where they might water a bodhi tree in the temple grounds.
- Lay people give extra gifts (dana) to the monks and nuns.
- People bathe or wash Buddha rupas in water.
- People spend the day listening to readings from the Buddhist scriptures and learning more about the Dharma.
- Just for the day, many lay people follow the extra rules that are usually only practised by monks and nuns, such as not wearing jewellery and not eating after midday.
- Parents might read stories from the Jataka Tales about the Buddha's former lives.

▲ Bathing a Buddha statue

The 'going for refuge' ceremony

How does one become a Buddhist? The simple answer is by carrying out the Dharma and living according to the Buddhist precepts. However, often it may be that we want to tell others that we have made a commitment to live the Buddhist way and mark the moment. The ceremony for making this commitment is called going for refuge.

A refuge is a safe place which provides shelter and security. People find refuge in positive things such friends, hobbies, sport and music. Some refuges are less positive and more like escapism from real world problems such as drink, drugs, over-eating and over-working.

However, according to the Buddha, none of these refuges helps tackle the problem of dukkha or suffering. The ultimate refuges are the Buddha, the ideal of human awakening, the Dharma, or teaching of the Way to Truth, and the Sangha, the community of men and women, past and present who have understood the Dharma deeply. These are the Three Refuges.

The ceremony of going for refuge means that having studied and thought about Buddhism, a person decides to commit to the Three Refuges and the Five Moral Precepts (the pansils).

The ceremony usually takes place at a shrine.

- The person committing themselves to the refuges and precepts makes three offerings: a candle, a flower and a stick of incense.
- They recite the Three Refuges, also known as the 'three jewels', three times: 'I go for refuge to the Buddha. I go for refuge to the Dharma. I go for refuge to the Sangha.'
- Other members of the Buddhist community are present and will also say the Three Refuges.

The ceremony is just a moment on a journey. In practice, all Buddhists are constantly 'going for refuge' by studying the Dharma, practising the pansils in everyday life, meditating and performing puja, and helping other Buddhists on their spiritual journey.

What do you know? — AO1

1. Give two examples of special things lay people should try and do at Wesak.
2. What are the Jataka Tales?
3. Name the Three Refuges.
4. What are the pansils?
5. Outline what happens at a going for refuge ceremony.

What do you understand? — AO2

6. What is the significance of bathing a Buddha rupa?
7. Explain why Wesak is also called Buddha Day.
8. Explain how Wesak remembers Buddha's various births.
9. Why is light an important feature of Wesak?
10. What does 'going for refuge' mean?

What do you think? — AO3

11. Should there be a distinction between ordained and lay Buddhists today?
12. Is anyone a Buddhist who follows the Buddha's teaching?

Essay practice

'Wesak is not necessary because Buddhists make an effort to follow the Dharma every day.' Do you agree? Give reasons for your answer. Show that you have considered more than one point of view.

Section B Christianity

Topic 1 Christian beliefs and teachings

1.1 The nature of God

Starter: What do you think God is like?

Christians believe that God is above and beyond everything in the physical world. This makes it difficult to describe Him. The language of the early Church was Latin and Greek, so many of the words used to describe Him come from those languages.

A God is OMNIPOTENT

▲ What do you think of when you think of God's power?

The word 'omni' means 'all' and 'potent' means 'powerful'. So, this statement says that God is all powerful and can do all things possible. The Bible contains many examples of His omnipotence, such as in His creation of the world where He said 'Let there be …' and it happened. Everything He does is done effortlessly. He does not need to recharge Himself from an outside source of power because He is that source. Christians believe that God raised Jesus from the dead, showing He has power over death.

They also believe that God has power to save people from the consequences of their sin and its power over them. Through forgiveness, He frees them from God's judgement and from the mental and emotional turmoil that results from sin. Having a God who is omnipotent gives people the confidence to ask Him for help in any situation.

But, if He is omnipotent, does that mean He could make a rock that is so heavy He can't lift it? Can He lie? Although God can do anything, it is important to realise that He does not do anything that goes against His nature or His purpose for the world. He is powerful, but He is good and reliable as well. He is also all-knowing and His power will go hand in hand with His world plan.

> People often ask, 'If God is all powerful, and all good, why doesn't He do something to prevent all the suffering in the world?'

This is a difficult question and it is discussed in Book 1 (*Theology and Philosophy*).

B God is OMNIBENEVOLENT

▲ Why might the rainbow be a symbol of God's benevolence towards the world?

The word 'bene' means 'good' and the word 'volent' means 'willing', so God is willing to be good. His will for Himself is that He is good.

Psalm 119 says that the Law of the Lord is good and Psalm 18 says the way of the Lord is perfect (good). The goodness of God is at the heart of the Christian faith because it underpins everything. It means that, although He is powerful, He will not abuse His power. Even though He knows everything, He will not use that knowledge to harm His creation. His presence will be a source of comfort, support and guidance, rather than one to fear.

However, believing in the goodness of God does not mean believing bad things will never happen. Nevertheless Christians believe that however terrible a situation might be, God is able and will choose to bring good out of it. God's aim is the redemption of the world – to make things right again. He works for the good of His creation in everything He does.

C God is OMNISCIENT

'Scientia' means 'knowing'. There are two ways of thinking about this description of God. The first is that God is able to know anything and everything He chooses to know; nothing is hidden from Him. Since He gave human beings free will, it is argued, God chose to limit His knowledge in order to give humans dignity and free will.

The second is that He knows everything there is to know. This is the traditional view that God knows everything, including what decisions people are going to make and what will happen to them, right up to when and how they will die. Psalm 139 says that God knows people's thoughts even before they think them.

Many people confuse this kind of knowing with something called predestination, which says that God decides the fate of every person and there is nothing anyone can do to change it. Knowing something is going to happen is not the same as making something happen. The omniscience of God means that His wisdom, knowledge and understanding of the world and everything in it, are perfect.

God's omniscience is important to Christians because, if He knows everything about them and their situation, they can trust Him to help them through life's ups and downs.

D God is OMNIPRESENT

This means that God is everywhere at the same time. For example, He is listening to the prayers of people in Australia and to those of people in Europe at the same time. He is outside time and space. Christians take great comfort from this belief, especially in times of trouble or despair. The writer of Psalm 139 asks if there is anywhere a person can go that is outside the presence of God. Then he answers his own question:

'If I go up to the heavens, you are there; if I make my bed in the depths you are there. If I rise on the wings of the dawn, if I settle on the far side of the sea, even there your hand will guide me, your right hand will hold me fast.'

The Bible shows that God can be present in everything to do with human life, and God can interact with His creation whenever and however He likes. Many Christians claim to have felt the presence of God in a particular place or situation. This has given them courage and peace. People often feel His presence particularly strongly in church or in a beautiful place. Such areas sometimes become destinations for **pilgrimage**. The belief that God is omnipresent sometimes makes people more aware of what they are doing, especially if it is something wrong.

What do you know? AO1

1. Outline what Christians believe about the omnipotence of God.
2. Give three examples of God's power.
3. Give an example of God's omnibenevolence.
4. Describe the traditional view that God actually knows everything there is to know.
5. What do Christians say about God's omnipresence?

What do you understand? AO2

6. Explain why some people might say God's power is limited.
7. Explain why belief in God's omnipotence is important to Christians.
8. Explain why the belief that God is omnibenevolent is so important to Christians.
9. How might the belief that God is everywhere influence how a person speaks, acts and thinks?
10. Explain why some people think God has chosen to limit His omniscience.

Activity

Make a colourful diagram to show the meaning of the following words:

- omnipotence
- omnibenevolence
- omniscience
- omnipresence.

What do you think? AO3

11. What would you say to someone who said that God cannot be good because He allows bad things to happen?
12. How would you answer someone who said God cannot be everywhere at once?

1.2 Creation and stewardship

The role of the Word and Spirit

It is no accident that the beginning of the Old Testament, and the beginning of the Gospel of John, highlight the role of the Word and of the Spirit. Both are deeply symbolic of the creative power of God. They show God the Father creating the world through the second and third persons of the **Trinity** (see pages 36–38).

> In the beginning God created the heavens and the Earth. Now the earth was formless and empty, darkness was over the surface of the deep, and the Spirit of God was hovering over the waters.'
>
> **Genesis 1:1–2**

> In the beginning was the Word, and the Word was with God, and the Word was God. He was with God in the beginning. Through Him all things were made. ... in Him was life and that life was the light of men.
>
> **John 1:1–2, 4**

The Spirit (Hebrew: Ruach)

The word for Spirit in Hebrew is often translated as wind or breath. It was the breath of God that gave Adam life (Genesis 2:7). The Spirit is God in action in the world. The writer of Genesis says that God's Spirit was active in the creation of the world, giving it life. The Spirit is also described as 'hovering' over the world. This means that, like a bird hovers protectively over its young, so God's Spirit hovers protectively over His creation.

The Word (Greek: Logos)

The Greeks used this term not only for the spoken word, but for the reasoning that goes on in the mind before it is spoken: the divine plan behind the creation. In other words, when God was project managing it.

Christians believe that the Word applies to Jesus: 'the word became flesh and made his dwelling among us'. (John 1) This verse is important here because it shows that Jesus being fully God was active in the creation of the world. The Word is the intention of God. God spoke and the universe happened.

God's role in creation and responsible human behaviour

> **Discuss**
>
> Christians should always put the interests of the natural world before themselves.

▲ Christian Aid campaigners lobby the government on environmental issues

Christian beliefs about the environment: God's role

Christians believe God created the world, so the world belongs to Him, but He put human beings in charge of looking after it. This responsibility is called **stewardship**. In the beginning, the world was perfect; everything was fit for purpose and the place of humans was established under God's authority.

> God blessed them and said to them, 'Be fruitful and increase in number; fill the Earth and subdue it. Rule over the fish of the sea and the birds of the air and over every living creature that moves on the ground.
> **Genesis 1:28**

> The Lord took the man and put him in the Garden of Eden to work it and take care of it.
> **Genesis 2:15**

There are several places later in the Old Testament where God laid down rules for how this should be done. For example, God says that fruit trees are needed for food and should not be cut down. (Deuteronomy 20:19–20)

Responsible human behaviour

Stewardship involves caring for the world, protecting and controlling it. Over time many people came to believe that this authority gave them the right to exploit the animal kingdom and the environment. It has only been in the last 50 years or so that people have woken up to the fact that they might have been wrong. Warning signals such as global warming and climate change have made us re-think the whole concept of stewardship.

Christians believe that following Jesus means looking at the world through God's eyes. For example, St Francis of Assisi is always pictured surrounded by animals. He tried to persuade the Emperor of his day to create a law ruling that people should provide for animals as well as for the poor and destitute.

Christians also believe they should work hard to undo the damage that has been done to the environment. The Church of England has committed to a target of reducing carbon by 80 per cent by 2050.

Richard Chartres, the former Bishop of London, decided not to travel by plane in order to reduce his carbon footprint. Many others followed his example. He inspired people to think about how they could reduce their own carbon footprints.

In the 21st century, in an interconnected world, practising love of neighbours means that we are committed to mitigate the effects of climate change which will fall disproportionately on the poor and vulnerable in the world.
Richard Chartres

Additionally, Christian environmental charities such as A Rocha run projects all over the world to help protect and restore it.

What do you know? AO1

1 According to John, what was the role of the Word in the creation of the world?

2 According to Genesis, what was the role of the Spirit in the creation of the world?

3 What is stewardship?

4 Give two examples from the Bible of God's rules for being a good steward.

What do you understand? AO2

5 Explain how God wanted humans to care for the planet.

6 Explain how the actions of Richard Chartres set an example to the world.

7 Why are 'logos' and 'ruach' helpful ways of thinking about the creative work of God?

8 Explain what responsible behaviour towards the environment should look like.

What do you think? AO3

9 Do Christians have more of a moral obligation to care for the world than other people?

10 Is caring for the environment a matter of obedience to God or a question of survival?

11 Is caring for the environment an optional extra for Christians?

1.3 The Trinity

▲ Rublev was a Russian artist who lived in the fifteenth century. This beautiful icon, which symbolises the Trinity, hangs in the Tretyakov gallery in Moscow. At the time it was painted, the Trinity represented spiritual unity, peace, harmony, mutual love and humility

The Trinity is God the Father, God the Son and God the Holy Spirit. The word 'Trinity' was not used until the second century although the idea was an important part of Christian teaching in the early Church.

This is a blessing from the first century:

The grace of the Lord Jesus Christ and the love of God and the fellowship of the Holy Spirit be with you all.

The Trinity helps us understand the nature of God.

The oneness of God

Christianity is a monotheistic religion which means that there is only one God. God is one in His essential being and everything that He is and does comes from Him alone. The Godhead of the Father, the Son and the Holy Spirit, is all one; all the persons of the Trinity are one.

The three in one

Christians believe that God is three persons who each share in the fullness of being God; each is fully God but together form only one God. So the Trinity does not mean that there is more than one God. Everything the Father is (Lord, almighty, loving, just, merciful and so on), so is the Son and the Holy Spirit. The Bible tells the story of how God gradually revealed His character to human beings so that He can be known, and He was ultimately known through Jesus, the second person of the Trinity. It also tells the story of His continuing interaction with human lives through the work of His Holy Spirit, the third person of the Trinity.

Here are three everyday things that can help us understand the oneness of the Trinity and also its separateness within it: that God is both one in three and three in one.

The triple ring

You can see from the picture that there are three separate bands and yet it is one ring. The bands cannot be worn by themselves but they are distinct and made of different metals.

A cup of tea

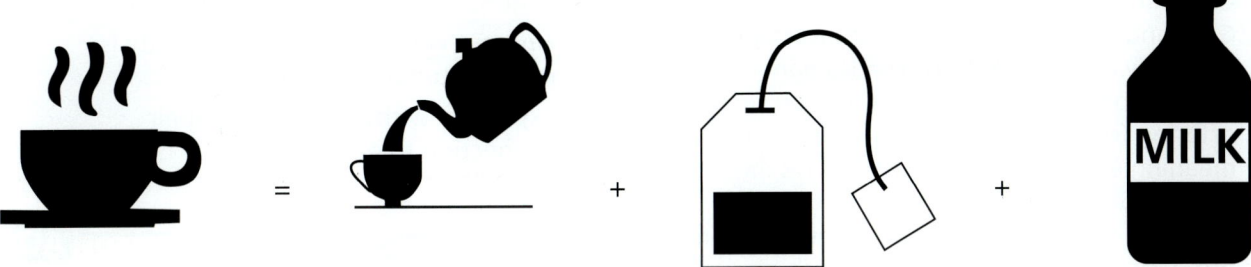

This cup of tea is made of three elements: water, milk and tea, but when you drink it, you are drinking all three together, a cup of tea. You can't take one element out and leave the others once they are mixed. Each element plays a different role, but they are all part of the finished cup of tea.

Ice, water and steam

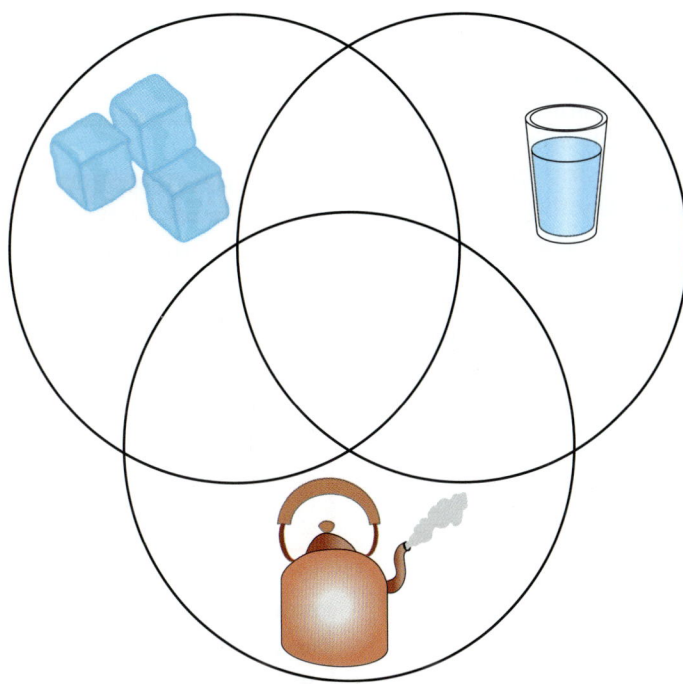

Ice, water and steam are all made of the same thing: H_2O, but at the same time they are all different from each other and serve different purposes.

> ### God the Father
>
> The Apostles' Creed begins with the words:
>
> *I believe in God, the Father almighty, creator of heaven and Earth.*
>
> Fatherhood is seen traditionally as a position of power and authority within a family. People who found tribes and nations are also referred to as fathers, for example, Abraham, Isaac and Jacob. God the Father created the universe and He created human beings. He is the founder of all life.
>
> Jesus referred to God as his father. He taught his disciples how to pray and told them to say 'Our Father'. Christians believe that God is holy but that, like a good father, His power and authority protects His children. In this role, He is seen as the rule giver – loving but strict.

God the Son

Christians believe that Jesus is the 'Son of God' and this belief is called the **Incarnation**. Jesus' divine role was to rescue human beings from the consequences of their sin by offering forgiveness. This forgiveness was not meaningless; it came at the cost of his life. God the Son demonstrated his nature as a God who loves and saves, and through whom ordinary human beings can approach his majestic almighty side.

God the Holy Spirit

The Holy Spirit demonstrates God in action in the world. After God the Son finally left the Earth, human beings needed to stay tuned in to Him. So, God the Son made permanent access to God possible through what Christians term the 'Holy Spirit'. In this form, God influences, guides and speaks to people. The Spirit is literally the 'breath' of God, giving life and power. Christians believe that the Holy Spirit is at work in their lives, enabling them to become the people God wants them to be. The Spirit helps them to pray when they don't know what words to use.

Why is the doctrine of the Trinity important?

- It shows that God as three persons takes an active role in human life.
- It shows that in the Godhead, as the Trinity is sometimes called, there is life in all its fullness.
- It gives both unity – God is one – and diversity – God is three – but all work together towards the same goal.
- It stands as a model for unity within the family, within society and within the community of believers – the Church.

Activity

Look at Rublev's depiction of the Trinity.

1 Find out which person of the Trinity is represented by which figure.
2 Explain how the artist shows their connection to each other.

What do you know? **AO1**

1 Outline what Christians believe about the Trinity.
2 What is the role of God the Father in the Trinity?
3 Describe how God the Son demonstrates the nature of God.
4 What is the 'job description' of the Holy Spirit?

What do you understand? **AO2**

5 Why is the doctrine of the Trinity such a useful way of understanding God?
6 Explain why the doctrine of the Trinity is so important for Christians.
7 Explain how the fatherhood of God is a good way to describe the nature of God.
8 Explain how the work of Jesus was taken up by the Holy Spirit after Jesus' ascension.

What do you think? **AO3**

9 Does the doctrine of the Trinity make it harder to understand God?
10 What might Christianity look like without one of the persons of the Trinity?

1.4 Beliefs and teachings relating to Jesus Christ

Christians believe that Jesus is the Son of God, therefore everything that happened to him during his life on Earth has special significance. Over time, theologians have developed ideas that explain who he is and what his purpose was in coming into the world. He is called Christ because Christians believe he is the long-awaited Messiah or 'anointed one' who has come to rescue them from the slavery of sin. ('Christ' is the Greek word and 'Messiah' is the Hebrew word for 'anointed one'.)

Incarnation

▲ And the word became flesh and made his dwelling among us

Incarnation is the belief that God became human in the person of Jesus. His mother, Mary, is often referred to as the Virgin Mary because she was unmarried. The word 'incarnation' comes from the Latin word 'carno' meaning 'of the flesh'. John wrote that 'the Word became flesh and lived among us.' (John 1:14) When the Bible talks about 'flesh' it means everything to do with the physical life that all living things share. The Incarnation is more than God becoming man; it is God becoming man but keeping His divine nature. That is the mystery – to be both God and man at the same time. The Apostle Paul explained it this way in his letter to the church at Philippi:

> Jesus, who being in very nature God, did not consider equality with God a thing to be grasped, but made himself nothing, taking the very nature of a servant, being made in human likeness.
>
> **Philippians 2:6–7**

When Jesus became human, he threw off the outward glory of being God but kept his power. As the Son, he was never less than God even though he was a human being experiencing physical and emotional highs and lows like any other person. Because he was part of the divine plan for the world, he stuck to his purpose – to bring about salvation through his death. This is described by the gospel writers and Paul as being 'obedient' to God the Father. Being completely obedient meant that he was without sin.

The Incarnation shows God's love for the world by coming down to human level where He could reach the otherwise unreachable people. This is why Christmas is such an important celebration for Christians and a symbol of hope for the world.

Crucifixion

▲ Matthias Grünewald painted this picture. Notice the symbolism of the lamb carrying a cross

The Romans mocked Jesus by dressing him in kingly robes and placing a crown made of thorns on his head. The reed he held was a mockery of the sceptre (staff) held by victorious generals after battle. These symbols show that Christians believe that the crucifixion was part of God's plan for saving the world from the consequences of the evil and sin that had become part of it. Christians say it was ironic that the trappings of royalty given in mockery to Jesus were actually his by right.

The **crucifixion** of Jesus and his **resurrection** from the dead are core Christian beliefs. The account of his death is found in all four Gospels. The cross became the symbol of hope for Christians down the ages.

Jesus' death is seen as a **sacrifice**. He is often described as the 'Lamb of God'. Just as the Passover lamb (see page 136) was killed to bring life rather than death, and freedom rather than slavery, so Jesus' death brought about spiritual life and freedom from the slavery of sin (which leads to death).

Resurrection

Christians believe that on the third day after he was killed, Jesus rose from the dead. By raising him from the dead, God was announcing to everyone that Jesus really was the Son of God. His resurrection was a symbol of God's victory over sin and over death. As a result of the Resurrection, people do not need to fear death because God had overcome it. In doing so, God gave the world new hope for the future and a guarantee of people's own resurrection from the dead.

Two important Christian creeds are the Nicene Creed and the Apostles' Creed. Both say something about the Resurrection:

I look for the Resurrection of the dead and the life of the world to come.
Nicene Creed

I believe in … the Resurrection of the body and the life everlasting.
Apostles' Creed

Ascension

Jesus appeared to his disciples after his resurrection for 40 days, after which he 'ascended' into heaven in a cloud. The cloud symbolises God's presence and it describes how Jesus went back into God's presence to be reunited with Him. We tend to think vertically when we think about heaven – heaven being 'up' – but when Jesus was taken into heaven it simply means that he went from one state of being to another.

Christians believe that Jesus' ascension meant that the Holy Spirit, the third person of the Trinity, could come. He would show people where they were going wrong, speak to God on their behalf and help people to live according the teaching of Jesus Christ. He would keep them in touch with God in a way Jesus, as a human limited in space and time, could not.

▲ A painting of the Ascension by Bernardino Gandino

Atonement

The word 'atonement' means to make amends, to come back into a correct relationship with someone you have wronged. Christians believe that the relationship between human beings and God is broken by sin. Now, as a result of Jesus' death and resurrection, the rift has been mended. If God has the power to raise the dead, He has power to forgive sin. In the Old Testament people offered sacrifices to show how sorry they were. Christians believe that Jesus' death was that kind of sacrifice – a way of taking away all the guilt for what people had done in the past and what people not yet born would do in the future, because human beings can't stop themselves from sinning. Jesus made atonement between God and the world. Christians believe that because of his death, God will forgive anyone who repents.

Activity

Either make a chart to show Christian belief about Jesus or study in more depth one belief about him.

What do you know? **AO1**

1 What is meant by the term 'incarnation'?
2 Outline what Christians believe about Jesus' death.
3 What do Christians believe about the Resurrection?
4 Describe what happened at the Ascension.
5 What does the word 'atonement' mean?

What do you understand? **AO2**

6 Why is the Incarnation often called a 'mystery'?
7 Explain what Christians believe about the Incarnation.
8 Explain how Jesus' death is seen as a sacrifice.
9 Explain how the soldiers' mockery of Jesus in Grünewald's painting might be ironic.
10 Explain the significance of the Resurrection.

What do you think? **AO3**

11 What does the phrase 'the slavery of sin' mean?
12 What do the three paintings in this section show about what people believe about Jesus?

Essay practice

'The Incarnation is the most important belief to have about Jesus.' Do you agree? Give reasons to support your answer. Show that you have considered more than one point of view.

Topic 2 Christian practices and ceremonies

2.1 Different forms of worship

Worship is a deep expression of devotion to God through praise, prayer and reading the Bible. It is when people show their love to God, and give Him glory for who He is and what He has done. It gives people a sense of belonging and identity. You don't have to be in church to worship; you can be anywhere: by yourself or with others, in church, at home, in silence, with music or even when dancing. Worship is important in any religious faith because it shows commitment and devotion to God. It is a sign of what people believe.

Some churches worship God in a formal way within a structure of set prayers and readings. This is called a **liturgy**. People go to church and know exactly what to expect. Other churches have an informal approach. Each service is different

and there is room for spontaneity. The focus of worship is on four main themes:

- adoration – the expression of love for God and the celebration of God's majesty and power
- thanksgiving – gratitude for what God has done
- repentance – saying sorry
- petition – asking God for something for yourself or for others.

The Eucharist or Holy Communion

This is a service which remembers what Jesus' death means. The day before he died he ate a meal with his disciples to celebrate the Jewish

▲ Receiving the bread and the wine during a service of Holy Communion

festival of Passover (see page 136). Jesus used the bread and the wine to explain what his coming death would mean. The bread symbolised his body which would be broken on the cross when he was crucified. The wine symbolised the blood that would pour from his wounds. Water is added to the wine, symbolising the water that came out of Jesus' side when the soldier thrust a spear into it. These symbols are reminders of the horrible and bloody reality of the cross.

> The priest reads the story as a prayer during the service. Part of the story is told when the priest consecrates the bread and wine. For example, when he holds up the bread, he repeats the words of Jesus at the last supper: 'Take, eat, this is my body which is given for you. Do this as often as you eat it in remembrance of me.'
>
> The congregation recites what they believe about Jesus: 'Christ has died! Christ is risen! Christ will come again!'

Christians believe that Jesus' death brought about salvation through the forgiveness of their sins. This is the **new covenant** that Jesus talked about. During the communion service, as they eat the bread and drink the wine, Christians are remembering his death and absorb him into their bodies symbolically. Roman Catholics believe the bread and the wine literally become his flesh and his blood. Sometimes a non-alcoholic drink is offered as well as the wine.

In most churches, the congregation goes up to the rail at the front and kneels down or stands to receive communion. The priest will say something like, 'The body of Christ given for you' while giving the bread. As the priest gives the wine he will say, 'The blood of Christ shed for you.' Each person will respond, 'Amen.'

In some churches, the bread and wine are taken down to the congregation and passed along the rows. In this way, each member of the congregation gives communion to another without

a priest doing it. This shows that everyone is equal in the sight of God.

Communion services are held every week in some churches and less often in others. Clergy will often wear special robes (called vestments), but others wear ordinary clothes.

There are different names for this communion service: **Eucharist**, Holy Communion, Mass, the Lord's Supper. This shows that all Christians believe it is a very important part of their worship. They believe that through it they are blessed and strengthened in their Christian living, and that they are doing what Jesus told his followers to do. It is a way of sharing the very core belief of their faith that Jesus Christ died for them, with everyone who celebrates it wherever they are in the world, those dead, those alive and those not yet born.

What do you know? AO1

1. What is worship?
2. What are the four main elements of Christian worship?
3. Describe what happens in a service of Holy Communion.
4. What other names does this service have?
5. What do the bread and the wine used in communion symbolise?

What do you understand? AO2

6. Explain what Jesus meant by 'the blood of the new covenant'.
7. Why do churches administer the bread and the wine in different ways?
8. Why do people take part in the Eucharist?

What do you think? AO3

9. What do you think is the best way to share and receive the bread and wine?

Liturgical worship

Starter: How might having set prayers and readings be helpful to someone attending a service?

Christian liturgy simply means a pattern to worship, a form of church service, which is used on a regular basis. It is usually set around the sacraments. Sacraments are an outward sign of an inner state of grace. These are important to Christians because they believe they receive special blessings from God in the sacraments. Different kinds of churches have different ideas about what the sacraments are. Roman Catholic and Orthodox churches have seven sacraments, whereas Protestant churches like the Church of England have only two (Baptism and Holy Communion). This is because Jesus commanded just those two. What are sacraments in Orthodox and Catholic tradition, for example marriage, are all practised in the Church of England; they are just not called sacraments.

By using a liturgy, churches feel united with other churches all over the world because they are using the same prayers and hearing the same readings. They value the sense of mystery, historic identity (the communion of saints) and of feeling at home in a particular style of worship. There is a sort of holistic (all-round) spirituality about a liturgy that they say is absent from informal worship. Most churches have a service book.

Typical order of service

Hymns – songs that speak of God's character and love.

Prayers – these are said for the country and the royal family, and for the particular needs of the parish and diocese. A Collect is said (the prayer for that particular Sunday) and the congregation ask for God's forgiveness using the words of the 'General Confession'. Sometimes prayers are sung.

Bible readings – these are set for each Sunday.

The Creed – this is the statement of beliefs about God.

Sermon – a talk usually based on a text or passage from the Bible but it can be about a topical issue. (Children usually have their own Sunday school groups and leave before the sermon.)

Holy Communion – this will often form a part of the service as well with its own prayers and readings.

Informal worship

Some Christians think that traditional religious practices can make it difficult for people to start coming to church, because they feel uncomfortable not knowing what they are supposed to do or say. Informal worship simply means there is no set pattern to the service. There is usually more singing, often led by a band and lead singers, and the clergy wear ordinary clothes. Sometimes the seats in the church are arranged differently, for example in a circle, and some churches set out tables and chairs for people to sit with their friends while they listen to and take part in the service. Members of the congregation will lead the prayers and sometimes even give the sermon.

▲ Informal worship is friendly and inclusive and can be less daunting than more formal services

Individual worship

Christians believe that they can worship God by themselves wherever they are. Christians may have a daily quiet time when they read the Bible and pray or listen to religious music. Children are often brought up to say their prayers before they go to bed. There are also Bible reading schemes which help people understand the Bible while studying independently.

Christians sometimes use religious symbols to help them worship. For example, they could light a candle to remind them of God's presence. Orthodox Christians may look at an icon to focus their thoughts on God, and Roman Catholics might have a crucifix (a cross with the figure of Jesus on it) or a statue of Mary, the mother of Jesus.

Discuss

Which form of worship appeals most to you and why?

What do you know? **AO1**

1. What is a liturgy?
2. What is a sacrament?
3. Outline a typical order of service.
4. Describe how a person might worship by himself or herself.
5. What religious symbols might a person use to help them worship on their own?

What do you understand? **AO2**

6. Explain why sacraments are important.
7. Explain why a church might use a liturgy.
8. Explain why many churches don't use a set form of worship.

What do you think? **AO3**

9. Does worship bring God closer or make Him more remote?
10. Is it more important to live a good life or to worship God?
11. Are the words we say to God more important than what we think as we say them?
12. In order to be a good Christian, do you have to go to church?

Places of worship

Starter: Why do people go to church?

The word church means a community of believers. Early Christians used to meet in each other's homes or outside away from the towns, where they could be private. So the concept of a church being a building evolved after the Roman Empire became Christian. Over the centuries, it has come to mean the building where Christians meet and hold their services. Traditionally, churches were built in the shape of a cross, the symbol of the Christian faith. They are generally built facing east because some Christians believe that when Jesus returns at the end of time, he will come from the east, but there are other reasons and traditions too.

However, not all churches are built like this because they reflect the different ways in which people worship. Some churches don't have clergy, although they do have leaders and pastors. There may be some sort of hierarchy but no ranks such as archdeacons or bishops. Methodists and Baptists meet in a chapel. Other Christian groups may use a school hall or conference centre on Sundays for their services. Since a church is where a group of Christians get together, they say it doesn't matter where they worship.

▲ Cumnor Parish Church in Oxfordshire was built between the twelfth and fourteenth centuries and is a typical English country church

A **chapel** is a room attached to a building. This building can be a church or a non-religious institution. For example, hospitals, airports, prisons and colleges usually have a chapel where people of all faiths can go for quiet reflection and prayer. So too do large houses and palaces. Chapels can also be free standing and be set in their own grounds.

Discuss

Do you think schools should have a chapel for religious worship?

Inside a church

A traditional church will have:

- an altar/communion table where the Eucharist is offered. It is usually at the east end and the focal point of the church.
- a baptismal font
- a pulpit, set slightly above the height of the congregation, from where the priest can give sermons
- a lectern which holds the Bible and from where it is read
- pews or chairs
- candlesticks
- at least one cross or crucifix.

Roman Catholic churches and some Anglican churches have a statue of Mary or one of the saints. Stained-glass windows tell Bible stories and the stories of the saints. They were useful when not many people could read or write. Orthodox, Roman Catholic and some Anglican churches have a confessional. This is a wooden structure, rather like a tall box. It has a partition down the middle with a little window or hatch in it, which the priest opens to hear the confessions of his congregation. The priest sits on one side and the person confessing kneels on the other. Most churches have a pipe organ, although many have a piano as well and a full band of musical instruments.

What is church for?

Churches provide a place for people to worship God.

Many churches involve themselves in local projects.

They might run homework clubs, summer camps, food banks, hospital and prison visiting.

They might help with asylum seekers and the homeless and work with those who are disabled or elderly.

Churches teach people about their faith and to support them in their Christian living.

Churches conduct baptisms, weddings and funerals.

Churches provide a focal point in times of trouble.

Churches are there for the whole community.

Activity

Find examples of as many different kinds of churches as you can and make a collage for the wall. Choose a mixture of interiors and exteriors.

Using these ideas, design a church that you think people would like to go to. Explain your reasons to the rest of the class.

What do you know? AO1

1 What is the purpose of a church?
2 Describe a typical church.
3 Describe the function of the altar, font, pulpit and lectern.
4 What is a chapel?

What do you understand? AO2

5 Explain the difference between a church and a chapel.
6 How can churches help their local communities?
7 Explain the purpose of having a chapel in a hospital or airport.
8 Explain why so a many churches are built to the same or similar design.

What do you think? AO3

9 What are the advantages and disadvantages of worshiping in a church rather than somewhere else?
10 Some people say that too much money is spent repairing old churches. Could the money be spent more usefully?

2.2 Rites of passage

Baptism

Starter: What does it mean to start a new life?

Baptism is a rite of passage marking the beginning of a new life in Christ. In a traditional baptism, a person is fully immersed in water as a symbol that their old self has died. When that person is lifted back up, it is a symbol of their new life: leaving behind a selfish world-centred life and putting God at the centre. It is a response to God's promise that, through faith, the old self has died and a new life begun. Baptism is a washing away of past sin and a commitment to follow principles laid down by Jesus.

In the early church, when a person converted from pagan beliefs to belief in Jesus Christ, they were baptised along with their entire household. It showed that from then on they would live according to Christian values. In a world where Christians were persecuted, this was a very brave step to take. Today, there are still many places where people are not allowed to be Christians, so to convert and be baptised takes a lot of courage.

The use of godparents or sponsors came about under Emperor Nero in Roman times. Christian parents chose friends to take the responsibility of raising their children as Christians, in case they were killed before their children grew up.

Infant baptism

When babies are baptised, they are also named. This goes back to the days when a person converting to Christianity would take a 'Christian' name. This is why infant baptism is often called 'christening'. In Anglican churches the name is written in the register as the child's legal name.

Baptisms usually take place during the Sunday morning service. In old churches you will often see a stone font just inside the door. It was put there to symbolise a person's entry into the Christian faith and into the church community. Today, although old fonts are still sometimes used, a light wooden font with a removable basin is usually placed near the altar, at the front, so everyone can see what's going on.

What happens?

In the Orthodox Church, babies are baptised by total immersion. The priest lowers the child into the water three times. Olive oil, blessed by the priest, is then applied to the baby's forehead, chest, back, hands, feet, ears and mouth. This is the Chrismation and it dedicates the child to living as a follower of Jesus Christ. The child is then dressed in special new clothes as a symbol of new life in Christ. Then the priest, holding the baby, walks three times round the font with the parents and godparents following.

There is a Eucharist immediately after the baptism as the baby is now a full member of the church and is entitled to receive communion.

Some people argue that there is no point in baptising babies – before they are able to understand anything, let alone decide whether they want to be a Christian or not. They say that no one can make promises on someone else's behalf. Others say that baptism shows God's love to children even before they know anything about Him. It shows they are wanted and loved by God right from the moment they are born, and it does not depend on anything they have done. However, it is not a kind of divine passport into heaven. When children are old enough, they must decide for themselves whether they accept or reject the Christian path.

1 The priest, who is normally the vicar but could be anyone who is ordained, welcomes the person about to be baptised if they are old enough to make their own promises, along with his or her sponsors. A baby will be brought by their parents and godparents who will make promises on the child's behalf.

2 The priest asks the parents and godparents whether they will reject evil and follow Jesus Christ. On behalf of the child, they say 'We will.'

8 The priest returns the child to its parents and gives them a lighted candle. This is a symbol that the child has passed from darkness into light. It will be a reminder to them of their duties to the child.

3 The priest then asks them if they will bring the child up in the Christian faith. Again, they say 'With the help of God, we will.'

7 The priest makes the sign of the cross on the child's forehead.

6 The priest prays that God will protect the child from evil.

5 The child is held over the font and the priest pours water over its head saying the child's name followed by the words, 'I baptise you in the name of the Father and of the Son and of the Holy Spirit.'

4 The priest asks the parents to name the child.

Believers' baptism

Many Christians believe that a person should not be baptised until they are old enough to understand what they are doing and to make the promises for themselves. No one is forced into taking this step. It shows that they are serious about being in a relationship with God and to living His way. Some churches have a special pool for baptism, but where such a pool is not available, baptisms can take place in a swimming pool or in a river or in an inflatable pool specially brought into the church for the occasion. Believers' baptism is most common in non-conformist churches (churches that have split away from the Anglican Church), such as the Baptist and Pentecostal churches.

The people being baptised usually make a statement about what they believe and why they want to be baptised. They announce publicly that they turn to Christ and promise to love and serve God for the rest of their lives. They often give their **testimony**, which describes how and why they became a Christian. Then they enter the water one at a time. The minister plunges them backwards fully under the surface, and then brings them up again, as a symbol that their old life is ended and the new one in Christ has begun.

Confirmation

Confirmation is when someone takes on the promises that were made on their behalf when they were baptised as an infant. Every person wanting to be confirmed needs to understand what they are doing, so they complete a preparation course before they take confirmation, usually when they are around fourteen years old. It has to be their decision which they make independently to be a follower of Christ. Girls being confirmed sometimes wear a white veil.

At the ceremony, they repeat the vows made at their baptism – rejecting evil and accepting Christ into their lives. The bishop then lays his hands on each person as a sign of the power of the Holy Spirit coming upon them. The person is then regarded as a full member of the Christian Church.

Traditionally, in the Church of England, only those who have been confirmed may receive Holy Communion. However, nowadays, children who have not been confirmed are increasingly allowed to receive communion.

Confirmation in the Roman Catholic tradition happens when a child is about eight. Girls wear white dresses and veils, symbolising being a bride of Christ. After the ceremony they receive their First Communion.

What do you know? AO1

1 What is baptism?
2 Describe what happens at an infant baptism in an Anglican church.
3 Describe what happens at a typical believers' baptism.
4 What is confirmation?
5 What happens at a confirmation service?
6 What is the role of the godparent?

What do you understand? AO2

7 Explain why the font is usually just inside the door of the church.
8 Why is a candle given to the parents in an infant baptism?
9 Explain what being baptised means in practice.
10 Explain why, in some parts of the world, it is a brave decision to be baptised.
11 Explain why a person might choose to be (a) confirmed and (b) baptised as an adult.
12 Explain the symbolism of the water during baptism.

What do you think? AO3

13 Is infant baptism meaningless?
14 Which is more important, baptism or confirmation?
15 Would you have your child baptised?

Marriage

Starter: Is 'till death us do part' a realistic promise to make in today's society?

Marriage is the legal union of two people as partners. Traditionally this is between a man and a woman and is the official teaching of the vast majority of Christian denominations. Today, two people of the same sex can also be married, but this change in our culture's beliefs is a current area of debate in the Church. Christians believe that marriage should reflect the teaching of Jesus about how people should behave towards each other. A Christian marriage is **monogamous** and for life. Christians believe that marriage was designed and created by God, and that it is a solemn agreement made in His presence.

Marriage preparation

There is always a lot to do to prepare for a wedding. Before the wedding, couples often take a marriage course which helps them to understand the demands and responsibilities of marriage. The leader of the course explains the purpose of getting married:

- to find fulfilment with a lifelong partner and share life's ups and down with them
- to have sex in a safe environment where both partners can feel equally loved
- to have children and bring them up in a Christian home.

Traditionally, the bride's parents made all the arrangements and footed the bill. Today, couples tend to plan their wedding together and finance it themselves. The bride usually wears a white dress and a veil and has bridesmaids, and the groom wears morning dress or a suit. After the ceremony, there is often a party or reception for friends and relations, with food, cake, speeches and dancing. A wedding can take place anywhere so long as an official registrar is present and it is an approved place. All Anglican clergy are official registrars. Christian weddings normally happen in a church.

The marriage ceremony

▲ A traditional Christian wedding takes place in a church

There are four parts to the marriage service:

- The vicar or priest taking the service makes sure that the couple is free to marry, that there are no reasons why they would not be allowed to get married.
- The couple make their vows to each other: 'I take you to be my husband/wife, to have and to hold from this day forward; for better for worse, for richer for poorer, in sickness and in health, to love and to cherish, till death us do part, according to God's holy law; and this is my solemn vow.'
- The couple exchange rings as symbols of their love and faithfulness to each other.
- The vicar pronounces them husband and wife and blesses the union in the name of God.

The actual marriage ceremony is not very long. Couples often have hymns and readings, a talk and prayers. The service starts with the entrance of the bride who is usually escorted up the aisle by her father. A hymn might be sung and then a passage from the Bible or other appropriate book might be read. I Corinthians 13 is a favourite as it is about love. The congregation sits down and the actual marriage takes place followed by anything else the couple want to include in their service. The couple then go into the vestry or side chapel to sign the register, then walk out of the church to triumphal music.

Some weddings, especially in the Roman Catholic Church, include the Eucharist. In the Orthodox Church the service is called 'crowning' and crowns are placed on the heads of the bride and groom. This is a symbol for receiving power from the Holy Spirit to love and care for each other and for any children the couple might have.

The meaning of the vows

Marriage is supposed to be life-long, only broken when one partner dies. This is why the couple each promise to be faithful to each other 'till death us do part'. The vows they make cover the wide range of human experience that people normally expect to have, and they promise to love and cherish each other through any or all of them. The rings they exchange symbolise the love that the couple hope will last and grow for ever, like a circle which has no end or beginning.

> ### Activity
> Look at the marriage vows. In groups, discuss what each promise might mean in practice.

What do you know? AO1

1 What is marriage?
2 Describe the preparations the couple make for their marriage.
3 Describe a typical marriage service.
4 Outline the Christian teaching about marriage.

What do you understand? AO2

5 Explain the purpose of marriage within the Christian faith.
6 Explain the importance of the marriage vows the couple make.

What do you think? AO3

7 Should the clause 'til death us do part' be left out of modern marriage vows?
8 Should marriage be between one man and one woman?
9 How do you think marriage will change in your lifetime?
10 Are all the marriage vows of equal importance?

2.3 Prayer

Starter: Why do people pray?

Prayer is central to a relationship with God, which is why it is so important for Christians. It is a way to communicate with God by talking and listening to Him. Christians believe they are part of a wider family with God as their Father. They follow the example of Jesus, who regularly went off by himself to pray. Christian parents teach their children to pray, just as Jesus taught his disciples. They believe that prayer brings them into the presence of God where they can receive His strength and guidance for their daily lives. They believe that if they ask, God will answer their prayers.

> Prayer is not asking. Prayer is putting oneself in the hands of God, at His disposition, and listening to His voice in the depth of our hearts.
>
> **Mother Teresa**

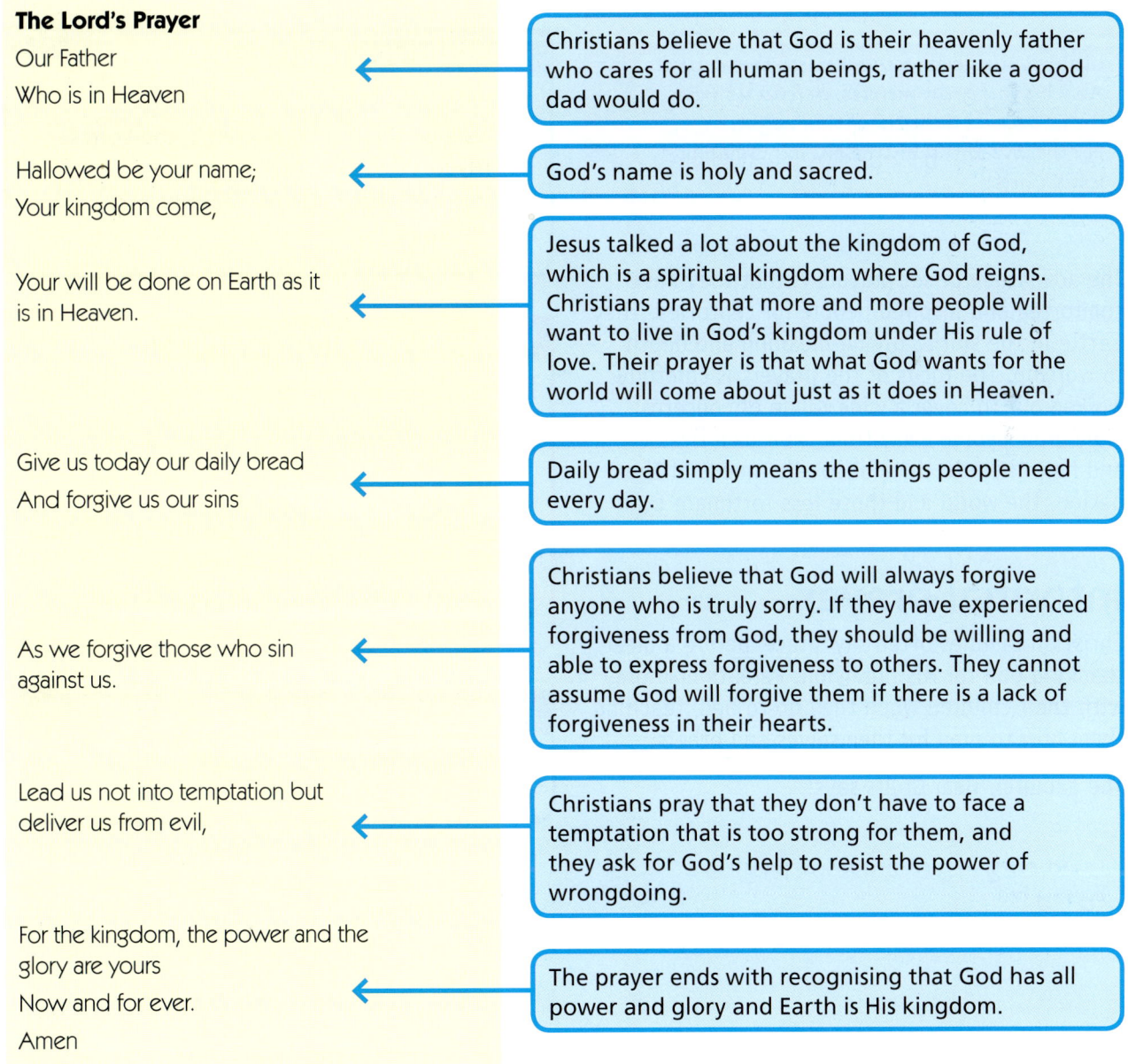

The Lord's Prayer

Our Father
Who is in Heaven

→ Christians believe that God is their heavenly father who cares for all human beings, rather like a good dad would do.

Hallowed be your name;
Your kingdom come,

→ God's name is holy and sacred.

Your will be done on Earth as it is in Heaven.

→ Jesus talked a lot about the kingdom of God, which is a spiritual kingdom where God reigns. Christians pray that more and more people will want to live in God's kingdom under His rule of love. Their prayer is that what God wants for the world will come about just as it does in Heaven.

Give us today our daily bread
And forgive us our sins

→ Daily bread simply means the things people need every day.

As we forgive those who sin against us.

→ Christians believe that God will always forgive anyone who is truly sorry. If they have experienced forgiveness from God, they should be willing and able to express forgiveness to others. They cannot assume God will forgive them if there is a lack of forgiveness in their hearts.

Lead us not into temptation but deliver us from evil,

→ Christians pray that they don't have to face a temptation that is too strong for them, and they ask for God's help to resist the power of wrongdoing.

For the kingdom, the power and the glory are yours
Now and for ever.
Amen

→ The prayer ends with recognising that God has all power and glory and Earth is His kingdom.

Set prayers and intercessions

Some beautiful prayers have been written over the centuries and incorporated into the liturgy of the church. They express people's deepest needs and longing for God. The church also uses a great many modern prayers and prayers made up for a particular situation. This happens during the 'intercessions' where prayers are offered for the needs of the world.

There is a collection of prayers for every Sunday of the year and for every occasion. They are called 'collects' because they are a way of collecting one's thoughts together on a particular Sunday in the church year or in a specific situation. This collect is a popular one to say in the evening:

> Lighten our darkness we beseech thee O Lord
> And by thy great mercies, defend us from
> the perils and dangers of this night;
> For the love of thy only Son, our Saviour
> Jesus Christ.
> Amen

The advantage of set prayers is that they have comforted and inspired people for centuries. They 'settle in the spirit', giving meaning and depth to worship. The focus of the prayers is carefully worked out to cover a wide range of concerns. They draw people away from their own lives and help them to think about the needs of the nation, the world and those less fortunate than themselves.

Informal prayer

Christian families often say 'Grace' before a meal, thanking God for His provision. Parents may pray with their children when they go to bed, teaching them how to pray for themselves and others.

The explorer, Bear Grylls says:

> I start every day on my knees praying by my bed.

Prayers are usually made up rather than taken from a book, although there are many books of prayers that are also used. 'Informal' refers to the setting (not in church) rather than to the prayers themselves. You can use all the prayers in the prayer book while sitting quietly at home, yet still be engaging in informal prayer.

Activity
Find a prayer that you like from the internet or a book of prayers and copy it out. Explain what the prayer is about and why you chose it.

What do you know? AO1

1. What is prayer?
2. Describe the topics covered in the Lord's Prayer.
3. Describe what intercessory prayer is.
4. Describe how set prayers are used in church.

What do you understand? AO2

5. Explain why prayer is important to Christians.
6. Explain the difference between formal and informal prayer.
7. Explain what Mother Teresa meant in her description of prayer.
8. Explain what the Lord's Prayer teaches about prayer.

What do you think? AO3

9. Why is it so hard to forgive?
10. What is the point of praying?

2.4 Pilgrimage

Starter: Is there a difference between a pilgrimage and a journey?

Why do people go on pilgrimage?

The idea of pilgrimage is a very old one. We all associate special events with places and go back to them sometimes because we want to remember what happened there. There are other reasons for visiting a particular place. After 9/11, people wanted to go to the site of the Twin Towers to pay their respects to those who had died.

In the same way, pilgrimage has always been an important part of Christian faith. Christians want to develop their relationship with God and this is often seen as a journey. Going on pilgrimage is a way of joining the outer physical journey with the inner spiritual journey towards God.

Christians make pilgrimages in order to find answers to problems they are facing, or because they want to feel closer to God. They look for forgiveness or refreshment in their Christian lives. Some people visit shrines like those at Walsingham in England, and Lourdes in France, to pray for healing. Both these places are where healing miracles have occurred. The way people travel is also important. Some like to walk so that they can think as they go and take in the world around them. Others ride or run or cycle or use other methods. The journey is as important as the destination.

Others go to be inspired by Saints or by visiting important places in the History of the Church such as Rome. Rome is where the Pope lives. He is the Head of the Roman Catholic church and is based in the Vatican, a city within a city. Pilgrims flock to Rome to receive the Pope's blessing on special occasions such as Easter. They visit important sites all over the city and usually end their pilgrimage by going to see the tombs of St Peter and St Paul, who were both martyred in Rome in the 1st century.

Where do people go?

There are many pilgrim routes and most are ancient. They take people to places made holy by things that happened there. Many places have shrines and relics of holy people.

Canterbury

▲ Pilgrims on their way to Canterbury. This is part of the Old Walk, a 220 mile pilgrims' route from Southampton to Canterbury

Canterbury is the place where St Augustine first brought Christianity to England in 597ce. The king and queen were converted and allowed him to build the cathedral there. It became a place of pilgrimage in 1170. After a long disagreement with King Henry II, Archbishop Thomas Becket was murdered in his own cathedral by four knights who believed they were carrying out the king's wishes. Soon afterwards, the Pope made Becket a saint. His shrine, in Canterbury Cathedral, became the most important pilgrimage destination in England. Later, King Henry VIII destroyed it during the Reformation, but pilgrims still visited where it had stood. They prayed for courage to stand up for what they believed, as Becket had done. Some say they have been healed at Becket's tomb. Canterbury is the starting point for pilgrimages to other places, one of which is the route to Santiago de Compostela in Spain.

The Holy Land

▲ Pilgrims praying on the Via Dolorosa in Jerusalem, Israel. The Via Dolorosa is believed to be the path that Jesus walked on the way to his crucifixion

Christians go on a pilgrimage to the Holy Land because they want to see for themselves where Jesus lived and died, and feel closer to him. They visit the shrine in Bethlehem and remember the humble stable where Jesus was born. They go up to Nazareth where he grew up. They travel round Galilee and stand where he stood when he healed the sick, worked miracles and walked with his disciples. No pilgrimage to Israel is complete without going to Jerusalem because this is the site of Jesus' crucifixion and resurrection.

These two events are at the heart of Christian faith. People visit these holy places to pray and wonder, and to give thanks to God for Jesus. They meditate on what it all means and how it affects their lives.

Santiago de Compostela

Santiago de Compostela, a thirteenth-century cathedral, is the final destination of the Camino de Santiago pilgrimage route. In the ninth century, a hermit called Pelagius saw a mysterious light shining over a Roman tomb in the middle of a forest. It was said that this tomb contained the remains of James, one of Jesus' disciples. Once word spread, pilgrims from all over Europe flocked to the site.

Today, the tomb lies under the altar of the cathedral and still attracts thousands of pilgrims. They queue inside where a small staircase leads up to a statue of St James. They kiss or embrace the statue before descending some steps into the Apostle's Crypt where they are told his remains are kept inside a nineteenth-century silver casket. Pilgrims feel close to God because St James was an actual companion of Jesus. A special pilgrims' Mass is celebrated every day at noon.

Activity

Research a place where Christians go on pilgrimage. Make a presentation to the class, explaining what they might see and do there and why they should go.

What do you know? AO1

1 Where might Christians go on pilgrimage?
2 Describe what a pilgrim might do in the Holy Land.
3 Describe the events that led up to Canterbury Cathedral becoming a famous pilgrimage destination.
4 What would a pilgrim visiting Santiago de Compostela do on their visit?

What do you understand? AO2

5 Explain why Christians make the Holy Land a pilgrimage destination.
6 Explain the importance of Canterbury as a pilgrimage destination.
7 Explain the importance for Christians of going on pilgrimage.
8 Explain how particular places become popular destinations for Christian pilgrimage.

What do you think? AO3

9 Where would you go on pilgrimage?
10 Is there any point in going on pilgrimage?

2.5 Festivals and celebrations

Starter: What is your favourite religious festival?

There is much to celebrate in the Christian Church. Festivals are a reminder of important events and of basic Christian **doctrine**. The big festivals of Christmas and Easter involve a lot of preparation but that is part of the act of remembering as well as it being a happy time. For most families it is an opportunity to get together.

Christmas

This is when Christians celebrate the Incarnation – the birth of Jesus, God made man. It is a time for families to gather together for parties and celebrations, with special foods such as mince pies and Christmas pudding, which are only eaten at Christmas. Primary schools often put on a nativity play and, through TV and radio, charities make appeals for donations. Groups of people go round their local area singing Christmas songs or carols and raising money for good causes. On Christmas Day in churches round the world, people sing traditional carols, which tell the story of Jesus' birth. They listen to prophecies about the coming of the Messiah from the Bible. They hear about Jesus, the light of the world come to shine in the darkness of human hearts, turning them back to God.

The way Christians celebrate is full of symbols:

- Candles represent Jesus, the light of the world.
- Exchanging presents is a way of showing love for people just as God showed His love for the world in sending Jesus.

- The Christmas tree decorated with lights stands for the light of belief in Jesus Christ.
- Christmas dinner is shared by the family and is a celebration of Jesus' presence in the world – a time of rejoicing and feasting on God's bounty.

Holy Week

Holy Week is the week before Easter and marks the events that led up to Jesus' death on the cross. Three particular days are remembered: Palm Sunday, Maundy Thursday and Good Friday.

Palm Sunday

On this day, the crowds were excited about Jesus being in Jerusalem and they welcomed him. The Old Testament prophet Zechariah had prophesied that the long-awaited Messiah would enter his holy city, Jerusalem, riding on a donkey. The Gospel writers record how Jesus did this to show them who he was. People waved palm branches and shouted 'Hosanna!' as they would to welcome a king.

Today, churches give out crosses made of palm leaves as a reminder of Jesus' triumphal entry into Jerusalem and also because he had come to die. People keep them until Ash Wednesday, which marks the beginning of Lent. In some churches, the palm crosses are burned and the priest marks a cross on people's foreheads with the ash.

Maundy Thursday

On this day, Jesus shared the last supper with his disciples. He began the evening by washing their feet as a way of teaching them to live lives of service.

It was also the Passover night and Jesus used the idea of sacrifice to explain that his death would be a sacrifice. It was the first Eucharist. Jesus explained to his disciples that the bread they ate was a symbol of his body that would be broken for them, and the wine was his blood which would be shed for them.

As Head of the Church of England, the Queen distributes special 'Maundy money' to the poor. In some churches, the priest will wash the feet of a few of the parishioners. At the end of the Maundy Thursday evening service, the altar is stripped of its cloth and the candles are blown out to symbolise the coming death of Jesus Christ.

Good Friday

For Jesus, 'Good Friday' began in the Garden of Gethsemane where he had spent all night in prayer before being betrayed by Judas Iscariot. He was arrested and stood trial before the High Priest and then was sentenced to death by Pontius Pilate, the Roman Governor. Christians remember that just as the crowd shouted for Jesus to be crucified, so too must all human beings share that sense of guilt and responsibility for his death. Many churches hold a three-hour service during the hours Jesus was on the cross. The story of the Passion of Christ is read, describing the events that took place on the first Good Friday. In the Roman Catholic Church there are always Masses and people honour the cross by kissing the feet of Christ on a crucifix.

Although Jesus died on this day, it is called 'Good Friday' because Christians believe that through his death, God conquered sin and evil and brought salvation to the world. There is also a tradition of eating hot cross buns for breakfast. These are special spiced buns with crosses cut into them.

▲ Thousands of people congregate in St Peter's Square, Rome, for Easter Mass

Holy Saturday

After sundown on Holy Saturday, the Resurrection of Jesus is celebrated and Easter has begun. A special service takes place and the Easter Candle is lit. Christians recite the vows they made at baptism, sing hymns and have readings and prayers.

Easter Day

This is probably the most important day in the Christian year because it marks the Resurrection of Jesus Christ. This belief, that Jesus rose from the dead and is alive today, is central to the Christian faith.

The priest says, 'He is risen!' and all the people say, 'He is risen indeed!'

Christians go to church to sing joyful hymns, listen to the Gospel accounts of the Easter story and give thanks to God. There is always a Eucharist on Easter Day.

The church is decorated with flowers as a symbol of spring and new life. People give chocolate eggs for the same reason. Jesus' resurrection gives Christians hope of eternal life after death.

Activity

In groups, research the ways different countries celebrate Easter or Christmas.

What do you know?
AO1

1 What is the purpose of celebrating Christian festivals?

2 Describe what happens at Christmas time.

3 Outline how a Christian family might celebrate Christmas.

4 Describe what happened on Palm Sunday.

5 Describe what happens during a church service on Maundy Thursday.

What do you understand?
AO2

6 Explain the significance of the Christmas festival.

7 Explain the importance for Christians of marking Holy Week.

8 Explain why Easter is the most important festival for some Christians.

9 Explain why Good Friday is so called.

10 Explain the symbols used at Christmas.

What do you think?
AO3

11 What do you think the main point of Christmas is now?

12 Do you think the meaning of the Resurrection is still celebrated today?

Essay practice

'Christmas and Easter today are more about us than about God.' Do you agree? Give reasons to support your answer. Show that you have considered more than one point of view.

→ Section C Hinduism

Topic 1 Hindu beliefs and teachings

Starter: Why are there so many different kinds of Hinduism?

1.1 What is Hinduism?

The roots of Hinduism go back thousands of years. Some say that there is no one religion called Hinduism, but that there are many Hinduisms brought together as one, because they all developed in India.

Some Hindus do not think of themselves as 'Hindus' but instead as followers of **Vaishnavism** or **Shaivism** or **Shaktism**. Some forms of Hinduism are plural (worship of many forms of god) and some are monotheistic (worship of one God). However, all these different traditions share many beliefs, teachings and practices.

> In Vaishnavism, Hindus worship Vishnu as God. In Shaivism, Hindus worship Shiva as God. In Shaktism, Hindus worship the Gother Goddess, or **Devi**.

A popular image of Hinduism is to compare it to the Great Banyan tree. The Great Banyan tree has put out many roots and many new trees have grown from these roots. So, although the trees appear separate, they are all connected to each other. In the same way, although there are many 'Hinduisms', they share a common spirituality.

This idea of the 'many and the one' is a constant theme in Hindu philosophy and theology. The 'one' is sometimes referred to as **sanatana dharma** or the eternal truth. The search for truth takes many different paths. Modern Hinduism therefore aims not to judge those of different religious faiths who are following very different paths to the truth.

▲ Hinduism is often compared to the Great Banyan tree (growing in the Acharya Jagadish Chandra Bose Indian Botanic Garden)

Hindus worldwide
- There are around 1.08 billion Hindu followers globally; that is 15 per cent of the world's population.
- Hinduism is the third largest world religion after Christianity and Islam.
- 95 per cent of all Hindus live in India.
- There are 817,000 Hindus in the United Kingdom.

▲ A devotee of Vishnu

1.2 Key beliefs and concepts

Brahman

We know from our everyday experience that all matter is constantly changing. Things come into existence, they decay and they die – but life and the world continue. Hindus believe that, behind all this change, there is one unchanging reality, called Brahman. Everything in the world of change owes its existence to Brahman. Although Brahman is an invisible force, it can be known by observing the beauty of nature through personal spiritual reflection, and by seeing how everything is connected to form a unity – that unity is Brahman, the ultimate reality.

Brahman is the invisible spirit which is the source and origin of everything. It is both personal, as it can be experienced through our own spirit (**atman**), and impersonal, because it is far greater than an individual spirit.

Brahman is often referred to using the mystical word **Aum (or Om)**, a word which represents the deepest vibration or essence of the universe. 'Aum' is said or chanted in **meditation** to connect the worshipper with Brahman.

▲ The Aum symbol represents the power of the universe. It is also the symbol of Hinduism

Brahman and the deities

They call him Indra, Mitra, Varuna, Agni and there is the heavenly-winged Garutman. To what is One, sages give many a title.

Rig Veda

The many gods but the one reality

One day Vidagdha Sakalya asked his teacher, Yajnavalkya, how many gods there were.

Yajnavalkya replied, 'There are 3,300 and 33,000 gods.'

'I know that,' Sakalya said, 'but how many gods are there really?'

Yajnavalkya replied, 'There are 33.'

'Of course, but how many are there actually?' Sakalya continued.

His teacher answered simply, 'Three.'

'Of course,' replied Sakalya, 'but how many are there?'

His teacher answered, 'Two.'

Sakalya asked again, 'But how many are there?'

His teacher answered, 'One and a half.'

Yet again, Sakalya asked, 'But how many are there?'

Yajnavalkya replied, 'One.'

Then Yajnavalkya explained that the numbers he was referring to were not the gods but the powers of the gods to be found in nature. The One power is God or Brahman.

Adapted from Brihadaranyaka Upanishad 9:1

Many Hindus believe that all the various gods and deities are expressions of Brahman, for example:

- If Brahman is the underlying force of nature, then this might be expressed as Shiva, who is the creator and destroyer of creation.
- If Brahman is the source of enlightenment and spiritual insight, this might be expressed in one of the many forms of Vishnu.

Each major Hindu tradition usually considers that their deity or god is the supreme god or goddess:

- In Vaishnavism, Vishnu is God.
- In Shaivism, Shiva is God.
- In Shaktism, Devi or the Mother Goddess is supreme.

A group of blind men have heard that a strange new creature has been brought to their village. None of them have ever met an elephant before. The only way they can find out about it is through touch and from experiences of things they already know about.

The first man held the elephant's trunk. 'This creature is like a thick snake,' he said.

Then the next blind man touched the elephant's ear and exclaims, 'No, the creature is more like a giant fan.'

The man who placed his hand on the elephant's leg said, 'This animal is like a tree-trunk!'

The man who touched the tail thought the elephant was like a rope.

Finally the man who grasped the elephant's tusk said the animal was smooth like a spear.

Sometimes there are tensions between the different Hindu traditions because it does appear contradictory for Vishnu, Shiva and Devi all to be the supreme God. However, as each god represents one aspect of Brahman, there need be no conflict. The popular parable of the blind men and the elephant shows this.

The Rig Veda (one of Hinduism's oldest sacred texts) summarises the Brahman and gods' relationship as:

Reality is one, though wise men speak of it variously.
Rig Veda.

Activity

The many and the one

1 Take an everyday object such as a kettle, mobile phone or table and describe it in three different ways.

2 Read your descriptions to your class or group without telling them what the object is – see if they can work it out.

3 Discuss whether your three descriptions are essentially the same.

4 Now discuss whether all the religions of the world are describing the same ultimate reality.

Atman

Discuss

Are we more than physical bodies?

Activity

Ask yourself the following questions:

- Can you point to yourself?
- How do you think of yourself?
- What makes you more than just a physical body?

For the Hindu, your true self is atman, your spirit, which makes you unique. All living things have atman, but the human atman is the purest form of it.

The atman cannot be easily known, especially when awake, because the mind is thinking about ordinary things and attached to the world of desires. It is only when the desires of the body are overcome, through meditation, that the atman can be free.

In some Hindu philosophy, the atman as spirit is just one particle of the Absolute Spirit of the universe, Brahman.

For the believer, the goal is to become totally aware of one's atman and therefore to experience Brahman. In this state, a person is freed from all desire for the physical world and achieves a state of extreme happiness.

Some Hindu philosophers prefer to use the term jivatman when referring to the individual's atman. The jivatman operates in close relationship with the mind. The mind thinks and acts, and the jivatman reflects. When the two are in perfect harmony, then a person has achieved true happiness.

▲ In one Hindu scripture, the relationship of mind and **jivatman** is described as two birds. One bird is the mind, which thinks and acts; the other bird is the jivatman, which observes the mind

Samsara

Samsara means 'passage' and refers to the process of birth and rebirth over many lifetimes. Samsara is usually known as reincarnation.

▲ What does this picture teach about reincarnation?

Samsara is an entirely natural process. Everyone goes through many changes in life, from being born, to becoming a child, a teenager, a young adult, an adult, an old person and finally reaching death. But at every stage, the person is spiritually the same because their jivatman or soul does not change.

Hindus believe that when a person dies, their jivatman is born again (or reincarnated) into a new body and the samsara process carries on. Samsara only comes to an end with **moksha**. Moksha is when the jivatman is freed from the body and becomes one with Brahman because it no longer desires worldly things.

Moksha

Moksha means liberation or release. Usually, moksha refers to the process when all negative karma has been overcome and the atman is liberated from the cycle of rebirths (samsara) and becomes one with Brahman. This final state is one of pure happiness and total consciousness of God.

Moksha may also refer to any moment of enlightenment when a person grasps the truth that atman is Brahman. In a sense, the whole of life is moksha. What holds us back from achieving moksha is ignorance and attachment to our own selfish desires.

Traditionally, there are four paths to moksha:

- Karma yoga: acting well and doing good works for others.
- **Jnana yoga**: knowing God through the mind and meditation.
- **Bhakti yoga**: devotion to and worship of God.
- **Raja yoga**: meditation and control over bodily/mental desires.

Activity

Write a short story or poem called 'Moksha'. Choose one or two of the moksha paths on which to base your story or poem.

Karma

We observe karma all the time. For example, if I kick a ball it moves. My foot is the cause; the ball moving is the effect. The law of karma simply observes that, in nature, everything has an effect on something else.

For people, the law of **karma** states that everything we do has moral consequences. These consequences can be good as well as bad. Things we have done in the past will affect who and what we are now and in the future. Good or positive karma is created whenever a person acts for the good of another person or for the environment, according to the laws of **dharma** or moral code. Bad or negative karma occurs whenever someone defies the dharma, and acts carelessly and selfishly. One Hindu scripture says that the person who lives a greedy life like a pig will be reborn as a pig.

However, a common mistake is to think that karma means fate. Hinduism teaches that we all have free will, and we can change our karma at any stage by behaving differently.

What do you know? — AO1

1. What is atman?
2. What is jivatman?
3. What is karma?
4. Outline the story of the blind men and the elephant.

What do you understand? — AO2

5. Explain what the story of the blind men and the elephant teaches.
6. Explain the relationship between jivatman and the mind.
7. Explain how samsara or reincarnation works.
8. Explain how good and bad karma are caused.

What do you think? — AO3

9. Is there any evidence to support belief in reincarnation?
10. Do we really get what we deserve in life?
11. Does the parable of the blind men and the elephant make sense to you?

Dharma

Dharma is a very important Hindu idea and refers to the fundamental laws of life and the universe. There are two levels of dharma: the laws of reality and the laws of morality.

Dharma: the laws of reality

This level of dharma teaches that even though everything is changing the world continues to exist. This is because there are some very basic laws of existence which make this possible. These laws are the dharma of reality.

The dharma of reality is often represented by the God Shiva as Lord of the Dance. His dance represents all the constant changes of the universe which is held together by his presence.

Dharma: the laws of morality

As human beings, we experience the laws of dharma as the constant battle between good and evil. This level of dharma is the laws of morality.

One of the great Hindu epic stories, The Ramayana, is about how Rama has to overcome the evil Ravanna in order to rescue his wife, Sita. Rama is assisted on his quest by Hanuman (the king of the monkeys) who symbolises human devotion to God through service and good works.

Every person has moral duties to perform according to their place in society (**varna**) and stage of life (ashrama). This is called **varnashrama dharma**. Varnashrama dharma teaches that a person's moral duties depend on the kind of family they are born into and the nature of their job.

Castes

Families belong to different castes. Traditionally, there are four castes or varnas. In the past, these castes have referred to the different roles people played in society. Over time, some taught others that these castes were fixed, and people could not change from one caste to another. Many Hindu scholars teach that this is wrong and that each caste just describes the different kind of lives we naturally want to live. In modern-day India it is illegal to discriminate on the basis of a person's caste.

The four castes are:

- **brahmins** or teachers/priests
- kshatriyas or leaders/warriors
- vaishyas or traders/skilled workers/farmers
- shudras or unskilled workers.

▲ The four castes or varnas

Teachers have duties to guide their pupils to truth and not to mislead; traders have specific duties to deal fairly and not to overcharge.

Duties are also linked to a person's stage in life. In Hindu teaching there are four **ashrama** or stages of life:

- the student
- the householder
- the forest dweller
- the wandering holy man.

Most people only achieve the first two stages of life, but for some, once the children have grown up and left home, they might choose to become a 'forest dweller' by spending more time alone in meditation, preparing for the next stage of samsara. Only a few choose to give up all their material possessions and live a simple life of prayer and meditation.

The duties or dharma of each ashrama require moral effort. A good student not only studies hard but is also obedient to his parents. At the householder stage, husbands and wives have duties to each other and to their own parents and children. However, life is not simple; sometimes duties clash and it is not clear what a person should do.

Arjuna on the battlefield

The problem of what to do when duties clash is a central theme in one of the great Hindu scriptures, the Bhagavad Gita. In the story, Prince Arjuna, who rules the Pandavas, refuses to fight the enemy, the Kurus, even though as a leader it is his duty to fight.

As Arjuna is taken onto the battlefield in his chariot by Krishna, he looks at the Kuru family and sees amongst them some of his relatives (the Kurus were another branch of the family who had long been in dispute with the Pandavas).

Arjuna's bow falls from his hand – he cannot fight. What looked like a simple battle of good over evil is now complicated, for he knows that if he fights, women will lose husbands, families will break down and the social order will be thrown into confusion. But failing to fight will mean upsetting the higher levels of dharma by allowing evil to triumph over good. Krishna tells him he has to fight.

Discuss

What should Arjuna do? What is his dharma? Should he obey Krishna? Is he a coward if he doesn't fight?

▲ Krishna the charioteer guiding Arjuna in the battlefield of Kurukshetra. Painting located in Shree Jalaram Prarthana Mandal, a Hindu mandir in Leicester

What do you know? **AO1**

1 Give a brief definition of dharma.
2 What is sanatana dharma?
3 What aspect of dharma does Shiva represent?
4 Name two castes (varna).
5 Name two stages of life (ashrama).

What do you understand? **AO2**

6 Explain the relationship of caste, stage of life and dharma (varnashrama dharma).
7 Explain the moral problem which Prince Arjuna faced.

What do you think? **AO3**

8 Does good always triumph over evil?
9 Should it be compulsory for everyone to give up their wealth in old age?

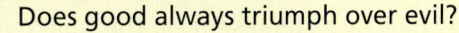

1.3 Manifestations of the divine

Many Hindus are monotheists and believe in **Brahman** or God. However, Brahman has many aspects and this means he can appear and be worshipped in many different forms or gods. These different forms of God illustrate that God is active in the world and that he loves his creation. Depending on one's family tradition, a Hindu is usually a devotee of one particular form of God.

In traditional Hinduism, God is depicted as **tri-murti** or in 'three forms' as Brahma, Vishnu and Shiva. Each represents one of God's cosmic roles as creator (Brahma), preserver (Vishnu) and transformer (Shiva).

Tri-murti

Brahma

▲ Brahma

Brahma represents God the creator. He has four hands symbolising the four corners of the cosmos. He also has four faces representing the four Vedas (the ancient Hindu scriptures). He holds a book as a symbol of knowledge and wears a crown to show his supreme authority.

Vishnu

Vishnu represents God, the preserver of the cosmos. Those who worship only Vishnu as God are called Vaishnavites.

Vishnu is shown in two forms, as the creator and as maintainer of the world. In one image he is dark blue, standing upright with four arms each holding separately a conch shell, discus, mace and lotus flower. He wears a jewel and a curl of hair on his chest.

▲ Vishnu and his avatars

- His four arms symbolise his power.
- The conch shell sounds the mystical word 'Aum', the sound of the universe.
- The discus or shakra symbolises the mind.
- The mace symbolises mental and physical strength.
- The lotus flower symbolises enlightenment and liberation (moksha).

In the second image, he lies asleep on the coils of the snake Shesha, floating on the waters of chaos. A lotus flower appears from his navel from which Brahma emerges and who then creates the universe. Vishnu maintains it until Shiva destroys it.

▲ Vishnu seated on cobras, showing his mastery over the forces of chaos

One of Vishnu's chief characteristics is that he can descend to Earth in various forms, or **avatars**, whenever the world is in danger of being overcome by evil and ignorance. There are ten avatars:

Animal avatars

- Fish
- Tortoise
- Boar
- Half man-lion

Human avatars

- Dwarf
- Parasurama
- Rama
- Krishna
- Buddha
- Kalki

Vishnu will only appear as Kalki at the end of this present age.

Many devotees worship Krishna in his own right as the supreme form of God. Krishna is depicted playing a flute (a symbol of his blissful consciousness of God), with a feather in his hair and as a cow herder. He often plays tricks on people but this shows his love of life and devotion to God. There are many stories about him, from his miraculous birth to his life as a cow herder.

Krishna and the village girls

▲ Krishna entertains the village girls

During one winter, the village girls prayed and offered flowers to the goddess Katayayani, asking in return that she might send them Krishna to marry one of them. Then, every day they would go to the river to bathe, singing about Krishna.

Then, one day, as they bathed, Krishna arrived at the river with some of his friends of the same age. Seeing the girls' clothes he took them and climbed a tree. As he and the boys laughed at the trick he had played on the girls, he called to them, 'If you want your clothes, you will have to come one by one and collect them.'

The girls were shocked and embarrassed and sunk deep into the icy water so Krishna and the boys could not see them. 'You shouldn't have played this trick on us!' they cried. 'Please give us our clothes.'

So, Krishna commanded them to collect their clothes one by one. Each girl tried her best to cover herself. Krishna was pleased with their modesty but told them to bow down to him and confess their sin of having swum in the river without clothes.

The girls did as they were commanded and Krishna took pity on them and gave them back their clothes.

Discuss

What does this story teach about worship of Krishna?

save the world from being destroyed by evil. He invites all his devotees to retreat from the world and go on the path of moksha.

▲ Shiva, Lord of Dance or Nataraja

Shiva

Shiva represents God who transforms the universe. Shiva transforms the universe by creating, preserving and destroying it. Those who worship only Shiva as God are called Shaivites.

Shiva is shown in various forms. One form is Lord of Dance or Nataraja. In this depiction Shiva dances in a ring of fire which surrounds him, symbolising the eternal motion of matter and his power to create and destroy. He beats a drum in one hand which symbolises the rhythm of life and the universe. His foot stands on a dwarf who represents human pride and ignorance. He has one upturned hand that indicates his desire to protect the devotee against destruction.

Another form of Shiva is the yogi in meditation or Maha-Yogi. As a yogi he sits serenely detached from the world with half-closed eyes, his mind focused on God. The third eye in the middle of his forehead symbolises the spiritual eye of a yogi, connecting atman with Brahman. His skin is blue as a reminder that it was he who drank poison to

▲ Shiva, the yogi in meditation or Maha-Yogi

Female deities

Devi

Many Hindus are devotees of Devi the Mother Goddess, or Shakti (meaning power). Devi shares many of the same functions as Shiva and for her devotees she is the supreme deity. Her devotees are called Shaktas.

Her relationship to the male deities is told in the story of the slaying of the buffalo demon Mahisha. In this tale, none of the male deities can kill Mahisha by themselves. Through their collective anger or energies (shakti), they create Devi, who kills the demon using their weapons. This explains why Devi has both male and female characteristics.

Her two main forms are as Durga and Kali.

Durga

▲ Durga

Devi as Durga is depicted having eight or ten hands which symbolise how she protects her devotees. She holds many weapons symbolising her energy, control and role as remover of miseries. She has three eyes which represent desire, action and knowledge.

Kali

▲ Kali

Devi as Kali has a black or blue body with her red tongue hanging out (after drinking the blood of Mahisha). The blood also symbolises the devotees' sacrifices to the Goddess.

She wears a necklace of skulls and holds a severed head and weapons in her other hands. All these represent her uncompromising resistance to evil and ignorance, and victory over death. One hand is raised as a sign of protection. Her frightening features encourage her devotees to turn away from the world of evil and seek moksha.

The word 'Kali' is derived from the term 'Kala' which means time. Time is considered to be the all-destroyer – it destroys everyone, good or evil, and destroys the whole universe too. This is why she is depicted in this horrific manner, as she shows no mercy to anyone.

What do you know? AO1

1 What does Shiva's drum represent?
2 What does Shiva's ring of fire symbolise?
3 What is the purpose of Shiva's third eye?
4 What is a devotee of the Mother Goddess called?

What do you understand? AO2

5 Explain how Devi gained her power.
6 Explain why Durga holds so many weapons.
7 Explain why Kali is so repulsive and fierce.

What do you think? AO3

8 Can only women worship female deities?
9 Should God really be described in human terms?

Murtis

A **murti** is an image or icon, such as a statue or a picture of a god or deity, used in worship and meditation. Murti literally means 'embodiment' as the images capture some of the power of the deity.

Murtis may be richly and expensively produced or simple and cheap; it makes no difference to their significance. The term 'icon' is used because in the Hindu mind the murti is neither just a symbol nor an idol (that is the god itself) but a channel through which the worshipper and the deity find each other.

This two-way process is important. A murti is a way in which Brahman is represented in the form of a particular deity. As it is a channel of God's grace (love), it has to be treated as a supremely honoured guest if the devotee is to receive God's blessing in exchange.

Murtis have a central role to play in **puja** (worship) and bhakti (devotion) to the deity (there is more detail about these terms on pages 73–74).

Essay practice

'There is no ultimate reality. The only reality is this world.' Do you agree? Give reasons for your answer. Show that you have considered more than one point of view.

Many Hindu families have a **shrine** at home with murtis of the family's favourite deity or deities. Each day:

- The deity is welcomed by sprinkling water round the murti and by lighting a lamp.
- Flowers are placed in front of it, incense is burned and the deity is offered food.
- The worshipper sounds a bell to focus her mind on puja and then performs **arti** (see page 75).
- She might also recite a mantra or chant a hymn or maybe practise yoga meditation.
- Finally, the food or **prashad**, which has now been blessed, is eaten by the family.
- At the end of the day, puja is performed again and the murti is put away for the night.

▲ A shrine at home with offerings of food, spices, incense, flowers and light

What do you know? AO1

1 What does the word 'murti' mean?
2 What does the word 'bhakti' mean?
3 What does the word 'prashad' mean?

What do you understand? AO2

4 Explain the purpose of a murti.
5 Explain why a murti is important in worship.

What do you think? AO3

6 Is there a danger that a murti might be worshipped as a god?
7 Can any object be used as a murti in worship?

Topic 2 Hindu practices and ceremonies

Starter: Does worship necessarily mean worshipping God?

2.1 Forms of worship and meditation

Activity

What is 'worship'? Look at these two pictures of Hindus worshipping. Using these pictures, write down as many ideas as you can about what worship is.

▲ A Hindu family shrine inside the home

▲ Lively worship in a temple – singing, drumming, ringing bells

A very important aspect of Hindu worship is meditation. There are lots of different ways of meditating. Bhakti yoga and raja yoga are two examples.

Bhakti yoga worship

Bhakti yoga is the third of four yoga paths leading to moksha (see page 65 for the four moksha paths). Bhakti means loving devotion and worship of God, whatever form that might be – as Brahma, Vishnu, Krishna, Rama, Shiva, Ganesh, Durga and so on. Devotees of the different Hindu traditions have their own special prayers, meditation and forms of worship of their deity. Despite the differences, there are many customs that are practised by all Hindus.

However, bhakti is more than just worship of God at home or in the temple. Bhakti also means living a spiritual and moral life at all times, by loving God and loving others. In the Bhagavad Gita (an important Hindu scripture), Krishna says to Arjuna:

> ... those who participate in this worship fully,
>
> Who have faith,
>
> who are devoted to me,
>
> who have offered their love –
>
> they are most dearly loved by me.
>
> **Bhagavad Gita 12:19**

Raja yoga worship

Raja yoga is the fourth moksha path. Raja yoga, or royal yoga, is not about the worship of God but instead is meditation as a means of freeing the mind from the world. One ancient Hindu text describes the aim of raja yoga as 'the settling of the mind into silence'.

The practice of raja yoga is to make the mind perfectly still, so that it is no longer taken up by ordinary thoughts and mental activity. It requires a lot of effort and practice to achieve this.

The purpose of raja yoga is to overcome the barriers or hindrances to moksha such as: illness, tiredness, doubt, carelessness, laziness, attachment and ignorance. Ignorance is often regarded as the biggest hindrance to moksha and a cause of the other hindrances. Ignorance stops us from seeing the world as it really is, rather than as we would selfishly like it to be.

What do you understand? AO2

1 Explain the aims of bhakti yoga.

2 Explain the purpose of raja yoga.

3 What is the main difference between bhakti yoga and raja yoga?

What do you think? AO3

4 Do you think it is really possible to 'settle the mind into silence'?

There are many aspects to Hindu worship and meditation. The following are some brief descriptions of the most widely practised rituals and of the people who lead them.

Priests and gurus

Every religion has a group of specially trained leaders who conduct ceremonies and are experts in its teachings and interpretations. Many Hindu ceremonies do not need a religious leader, but there are many rituals where a priest is necessary. Hinduism also has a long history of spiritual and learned teachers.

Priests or brahmins are the most senior of the four Hindu castes (see page 66). Today, a brahmin priest is a person of wisdom who conducts the Hindu religious rituals and ceremonies in the temple, at festivals and at marriages and funerals.

A guru is a teacher of wisdom. They have normally spent many years studying and meditating on Hindu scriptures. A guru teaches their pupils to overcome their spiritual ignorance, and is often given the title 'swami' as a sign of respect. Swami Vivekananda (1863–1902) was a particularly

influential **guru** in recent times. He brought Hinduism to the West and worked hard on inter-faith understanding and co-operation.

Puja

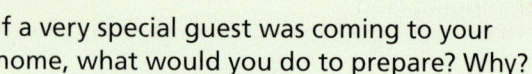

Discuss

If a very special guest was coming to your home, what would you do to prepare? Why?

Puja is the rituals carried out in worship to honour a god or gods, or even to honour a guest or a special event. The word 'puja' means to worship and to honour. There are no set rituals or ceremonies, but lots of people carry out similar types of puja.

Most puja rituals are carried out in front of a murti, but not always. Puja is used to meditate at special moments, such as daily puja at home, at festivals, at the birth and naming of a child, at weddings and at funerals. Puja can be carried out by anyone, but a priest usually carries out puja in the temple where more complicated puja ceremonies and prayers are required.

Darshan, murtis and shrines

Darshan means 'viewing' or glimpsing the deity through a sacred object or holy person. A murti is an image of a deity (either a statue or a painting).

Darshan is a two-way process. For example, when devotees see a murti they experience the blessing of the deity. In return, the deity receives the love and devotion of the devotee. This is why Krishna said to Arjuna that those who worship and love him are 'most dearly loved by me'.

It is important not to think of the murti as an idol or statue which is worshipped, but as a means by which God's spiritual presence is transmitted to the devotee. A murti is always treated with great respect and kept in a shrine, a special place at home or in the temple where it can be looked after properly.

Arti

▲ A priest performs the arti ceremony

The arti ceremony is the central ritual at puja. Arti means 'complete love'. It is performed by waving a lighted candle or lamp clockwise in front of the image of the deity. It is a sign of the devotee's commitment and love to God. Arti is also a way to meditate.

Along with incense, water and flowers, arti is an offering to the deity of the four elements – light (fire), air (incense), water and earth (flowers).

In the temple, the priest performs the arti ceremony five times a day at each stage of the deity's daily routine, from waking up to bedtime.

Havan (fire)

Discuss

What does fire make you think of? Why is it an important religious symbol?

From its earliest days, fire has played an important part in Hindu worship. Fire represents the power of a deity. More importantly, it symbolises the cleansing of mind, spirit and environment.

▲ A fire altar

Havan means 'to offer'. Havan ceremonies always involve a fire offering:

- A fire altar is built and lit.
- Priests and others involved in the ritual sit close to it. The fire is blessed by calling on one or more deities.
- The devotees make their offerings to the fire – this can be an actual offering or one in the mind.
- Prayers and mantras are chanted.

Havan ceremonies can be used at many different occasions such as at a festival or at a naming ceremony. Some people use havan privately to help meditation.

Mantras and japa

Mantras are short repeated phrases used in meditation to help the mind focus on a particular spiritual quality. The words do not need to mean anything important: it is the power of the syllables when recited properly which gives power. A mantra acts like a tuning fork on the mind by helping it to resonate at the right frequency.

Japa is when a mantra is said or chanted many times to a special rhythm. Its purpose is to focus and calm the mind. A person saying the mantra might choose to focus on a particular word and use it to develop their thoughts in that direction.

Some mantras have no particular meaning, but when they are chanted, their rhythm lifts the soul to a higher level of awareness.

Activity

A widely used mantra is the **Gayatri mantra** taken from the ancient Hindu scripture, the Rig Veda. It is dedicated to the power of the Sun as a source of spiritual understanding. The mantra is preceded by saying 'Om' or 'Aum'.

'Om. Let us meditate on that excellent glory of the divine life-giving Sun; may he enlighten our understandings.'

Try repeating the mantra to yourself out loud, silently in your mind when alone and also with others. What effect does each method have on your thoughts?

Bhajans and kirtan

A characteristic of Hindu worship and bhakti meditation is the use of song and dance. **Bhajans** are songs, led by a music group, in which devotees join in. The songs are based on the stories of the gods and teachings of holy people. Bhajans may take place at home, in the temple or at any special place.

A **kirtan** is a chant and slightly different from a bhajan. It is a chant often based on a mantra or repeated phrase that is designed to quieten the mind and connect it to God. A Kirtan may also include dancing and be accompanied by traditional Indian instruments.

Activity

You can find many examples of popular bhajans and kirtans on the internet. Go on the internet and listen to a bhajan and a kirtan. Write down some of your immediate thoughts and reactions after listening to each one. Share your thoughts with others in the class or group.

What do you know?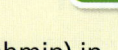

1 Describe the role of the priest (brahmin) in Hindu worship and meditation.
2 What is a guru?
3 What does the word 'puja' mean?
4 What is a mantra?
5 What is meant by 'japa'?
6 What is the Gayatri mantra?

What do you understand?

7 Explain what is meant by 'darshan'.
8 Explain the significance of arti.
9 Explain the purpose of a shrine.

What do you think?

10 Do you think there is any point in saying a mantra if the words don't mean anything?

2.2 Places of worship

Worship at home

Most Hindus perform worship at home once or twice a day. Families are usually devoted to one particular deity. Many Hindu families have a shrine in their home. The shrine might be placed on a shelf in the corner of a room or, if the house is big enough, a whole room could be set aside. The shrine contains images or murtis of the family's favourite deity or deities, along with candles, lights and other decorations.

Everyday worship

Puja or worship is usually performed by one member of the family, often the mother.

- Each day, the deity is welcomed by sprinkling water round the murti and by lighting a lamp.
- She places flowers in front of it, burns incense and offers the deity food.
- She sounds a bell to focus her mind on puja and then performs arti.
- She might also recite a mantra or chant or maybe practise yoga meditation.
- Finally, the food or prashad, which has now been blessed, is eaten by the family.
- At the end of the day, puja is performed again and the murti is put away for the night.

Worship in the mandir

The Hindu name for a temple is 'mandir'. The main function of a mandir is to be the home of one or more deities' murtis or images. It is the place where devotees can experience the presence of the deity. Mandirs often have rooms set aside where local Hindus can meet one another socially.

Mandirs can be very elaborate, with many carvings on the inside and on the outside of animals, humans and deities. The main feature of some of the larger mandirs is a spire or shikhara. The spire has many symbolic meanings. It is tall, like a mountain range, symbolising the meeting realm of the gods and humans on Earth. It also represents the journey of the soul on its way to moksha.

▲ The Khajuraho temples, India

The main porch of the temple contains the vehicle of the deity. In Hinduism, each deity has an animal vehicle which transports them. The vehicle represents some of the deity's spiritual forces. For example, Shiva's vehicle is a bull and Vishnu's vehicle is a serpent.

The main hall or mandapa often has pillars and is used for religious dancing and music. Leading off the mandapa is the inner shrine containing the murti of the deity or deities. (The spire is directly above this room.)

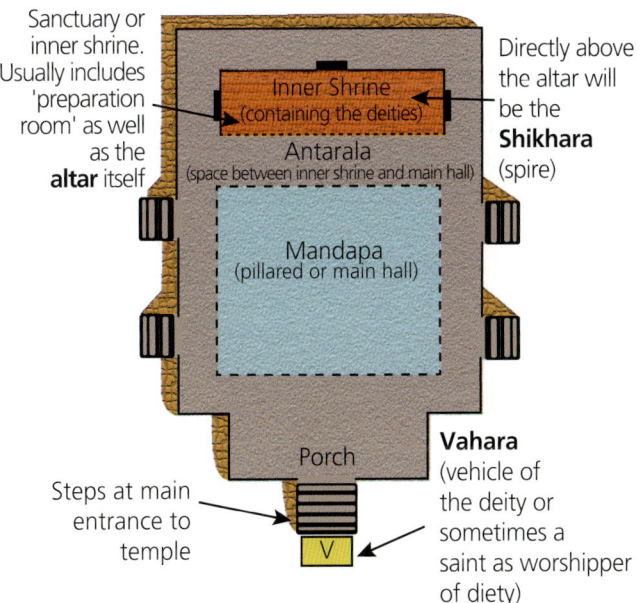

Sanctuary or inner shrine. Usually includes 'preparation room' as well as the **altar** itself

Inner Shrine (containing the deities)

Directly above the altar will be the **Shikhara** (spire)

Antarala (space between inner shrine and main hall)

Mandapa (pillared or main hall)

Porch

Steps at main entrance to temple

Vahara (vehicle of the deity or sometimes a saint as worshipper of diety)

▲ The layout of some Hindu temples

Worship in the temple is very similar to puja at home but it happens more frequently throughout the day and is often more elaborate. Whereas puja at home is carried out entirely by one of the family, in the temple it is the priest's role to perform puja and prepare the murti for the worshippers. At home the murti is treated as an honoured guest and as the temple is the home of the deity, the murti is honoured here as its most important resident.

Everyday worship

- The first puja of the day is for the priest to wake up the murti, bathe and prepare it ready to be viewed by devotees from the mandapa.
- When the devotees arrive at the mandir they take off their shoes to keep the mandir clean and out of respect; each person rings a bell to tell the deity that they have arrived.
- The worshippers make offerings of money, food and flowers. Some people pray by themselves, others in family groups.
- At various times in the day, Hindu scriptures are read by the priest.
- When puja is about to be performed, the priest blows a conch shell and sounds the puja bell.
- The priest then offers the murti incense, fire, flowers and water, and circles the arti lamp in front of it.
- The congregation might then sing hymns or bhajans, accompanied by musical instruments.
- The priest then offers the arti lamp to the worshippers, who place their hands near it so as to experience God's blessings.
- Once the priest has blessed the offerings, the blessed food or prashad is given to the worshippers in return to eat.
- In the evening, the final puja consists of preparing the deity for the night.
- The priest carries out the fifth and final arti ceremony of the day before the murti is undressed and prepared for sleep.

▲ Inside a mandir in Watford, UK

What do you know? AO1

1 Describe a Hindu shrine at home.
2 Outline what happens at morning puja in the home.
3 What does the porch of a Hindu temple contain?
4 What is the shikhara of a temple?
5 What is the mandapa in a temple?

What do you understand? AO2

6 Explain the purpose of evening puja at home.
7 Explain how the murti is treated in temple worship.
8 Explain the meaning of the arti ceremony.

What do you think? AO3

9 Are all the puja rituals equally important?
10 Is there too much focus on the murti in Hindu worship?

2.3 Festivals

Festivals are an important feature of all human societies. There are many Hindu festivals which celebrate stories of the deities, special people and the seasons. They are a time for the local Hindu community to meet and renew friendships. Above all, they remind devotees of their spiritual duties and obligations.

> **Activity**
> Which festival do you enjoy most? Make a list of what makes it special.

Festival of Divali

Divali (or Diwali) takes place in late autumn. It lasts between two and five days and is probably the best known of all Hindu festivals. Divali means 'row of lights'.

People light oil lamps or **divas** which they place on window ledges or by doors. The light commemorates how Rama, the main character in the Ramayana story, was welcomed home – 14 years after he was exiled and had defeated the wicked demon king Ravana with the help of Hanuman, the king of the monkeys. On his return there was no moon, so people lit their oil lamps or divas to welcome him and Sita, his wife, home. The story is a reminder that evil can only be overcome by doing good.

▲ Divali fireworks

Divali also welcomes Lakshmi, the goddess of prosperity, into people's homes. A special puja is celebrated at home in her honour. This is an important family occasion. Gifts and sweets are exchanged, people wear new clothes and the family gather for a large meal. People are also encouraged to support charities. In the evening, fireworks light up the sky in joyful conclusion to the festival.

Festival of Holi

Holi is a spring festival. The festival commemorates the time when the wicked Princess Holika tried to burn alive her nephew Prahlad, who was a child devotee of Vishnu. However, Vishnu descended to Earth in time to save Prahlad from death, and Holika died on the bonfire instead.

On the eve of the festival, a large bonfire is lit in the local community by the priest and special food (such as coconut and dates) is shared. Sometimes these are roasted on the fire and distributed as prashad. Another custom is to bring newborn babies to the fire to receive Vishnu's blessing.

On the following morning, people celebrate the arrival of spring by throwing coloured water and powder over each other.

Holi is also a time of practical jokes, when children are allowed to be cheeky to adults. This is to remember how Krishna often played tricks on people to make them aware of their spiritual journey and love of life. In one story, he threw coloured paint over his sister.

▲ Rama defeats Ravana

▲ Young people throw coloured water and powder over each other at Holi

As a child, Krishna often played tricks on adults and children alike. One day Krishna complained to his mother, Yashoda, that it was unfair that his skin was dark when his sister Radha's skin was fair. Yashoda joked with Krishna that if this was the case, why didn't Krishna smear paint on his sister's face to the colour he wanted it to be. The playful Krishna loved the idea and duly sprayed his sister with coloured water.

Activity

Research another Hindu festival such as: Janmashtami (The Birth of Krishna), Rama Navami (The Birth of Rama), Guru Purnima (Reverence for Gurus and Teachers), Raksha Bandhan, Navaratri or Durga Puja.

Make a colourful poster of the festival you have chosen. Make sure you include details of the main events, some pictures and an explanation of why the festival is important for Hindus.

What do you know? AO1

1 What does the word 'divali' mean?
2 What is prashad?
3 Outline the story of Rama and Ravana.

What do you understand? AO2

4 Explain what light symbolises at Divali.
5 Go back to page 75 and remind yourself about havan. Explain why the fire at Holi has such spiritual significance.
6 Explain why Krishna's tricks help people become more spiritually aware.
7 Explain what the festival Holi teaches about good and evil.

What do you think? AO3

8 Some people think that playing tricks at Holi encourages good relations between people. Do you agree?
9 Should festivals only focus on spiritual matters?

2.4 Pilgrimage

Pilgrimage is the act of making a journey to a place which has special religious significance. In Hinduism these include places such as the city of **Varanasi**, the River Ganges and the Himalaya mountains in India. People who make these journeys are known as pilgrims. Pilgrimage is a sign of religious dedication as it costs the pilgrims time and money. In making the journey, pilgrims have time to reflect on life, and so it is also a time of spiritual cleansing and renewal.

Most Hindu pilgrimages end with a visit to a temple. There are many Hindu temples, but the four most important ones are at Badrinath, Rameshwaram, Puri and Dwarka.

Varanasi

For many pilgrims the experience of entering Varanasi (also called Benares) after travelling long distances and seeing hundreds of pilgrims bathing in the river Ganges and worshipping in the city's many temples is a deeply spiritual moment. This is why Varanasi is the most popular pilgrimage site in the whole of India.

There are several reasons why Varanasi is such a popular pilgrimage destination:

- It is especially important because it is considered to be the dwelling place of Shiva on Earth and so the many images of Lord Shiva in the many temples offer especially significant moments of darshan for the devotee.
- It is an ancient place of learning. Over the centuries it has hosted countless spiritual debates by many wise and learned gurus. Pilgrims can also experience darshan of the wise men and the blessings which their teaching delivers.
- The two tributaries of the holy river Ganges converge at Varanasi. Bathing in the Ganges is a means of purifying the soul on its journey to moksha. Hundreds of pilgrims bathe in the Ganges River.

Ganges River

▲ Pilgrims bathing in the Ganges River

One of the best-known images of India and Hinduism is that of pilgrims standing in the Ganges River, deep in prayer, performing cleansing rituals. The river's spiritual power is its connection with nature and Brahman. According to tradition, it was created by Shiva, and that makes it the most sacred river in India.

The pilgrims believe that bathing in the Ganges washes away sins and negative karma. Some even believe that if they die while bathing, they will receive immediate moksha and be freed from the cycle of samsara for ever.

Badrinath

The ancient city of Badrinath lies 3000 metres up in the Himalayas in northern India. The city and temple are mentioned in several of the Hindu scriptures. The temple of Badrinath is considered to be the most holy of the four great temples in India and is dedicated to Vishnu.

The present temple is about 200 years old and beautifully decorated in many colours. The temple contains many shrines for different deities and gurus. However, its chief attraction for the pilgrim is the one-metre-high black stone murti of Vishnu. The murti is placed under a golden canopy and is accompanied by other images in the shrine, including those of Nar and Narayan (two avatars, or forms, of Vishnu).

▲ The temple at Badrinath is visited by many pilgrims

From ancient times, Badrinath has been associated with Vishnu as the place where he descended in various forms. For pilgrims, worshipping the great murti of Vishnu in the Badrinath temple is an especially significant way of experiencing the darshan or presence of God.

After worshipping in the temple, pilgrims traditionally offer gifts to the temple to honour their ancestors. They then go to wash in the Alaknanda River. Pilgrims are advised to wrap up warm because, at 3000 metres high in the Himalayas, it is cold even in summer.

What do you know? **AO1**

1 What is the other name of Varanasi?
2 Which God is especially associated with Varanasi?
3 Outline two ways pilgrims can experience the darshan of God.
4 Where is Badrinath?

What do you understand? **AO2**

5 Explain why the Ganges River is a very holy place for pilgrims.
6 Explain why the murti of Vishnu at Badrinath is particularly sacred.

What do you think? **AO3**

7 Do you think that bathing in the Ganges literally washes away sin?
8 If someone went on pilgrimage on your behalf, would this be pilgrimage?

2.5 Rites of passage

Life is a journey marked by special moments, such as birthdays, marriages and anniversaries. People usually mark these moments with some rituals, special words and customs, and the giving of gifts and sharing of meals.

Hindus divide a life into sixteen stages or **samskaras** which correspond with an important life event. Each samskara is marked by a special ceremony; these are important in the formation of a person's spiritual development. Some of the important samskaras are: birth, naming, sacred thread, marriage, final moments of life and funeral.

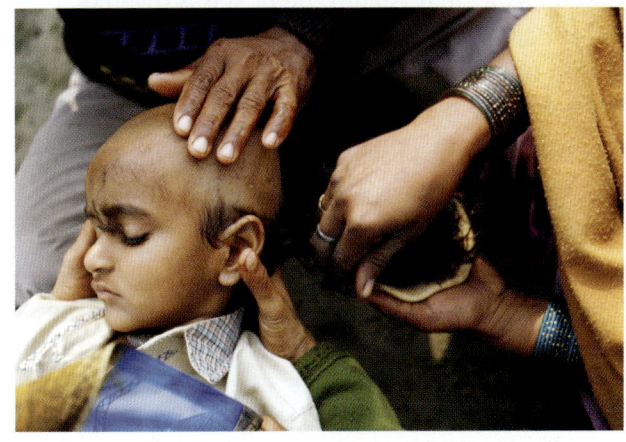

▲ The first haircut – one of the early samskaras

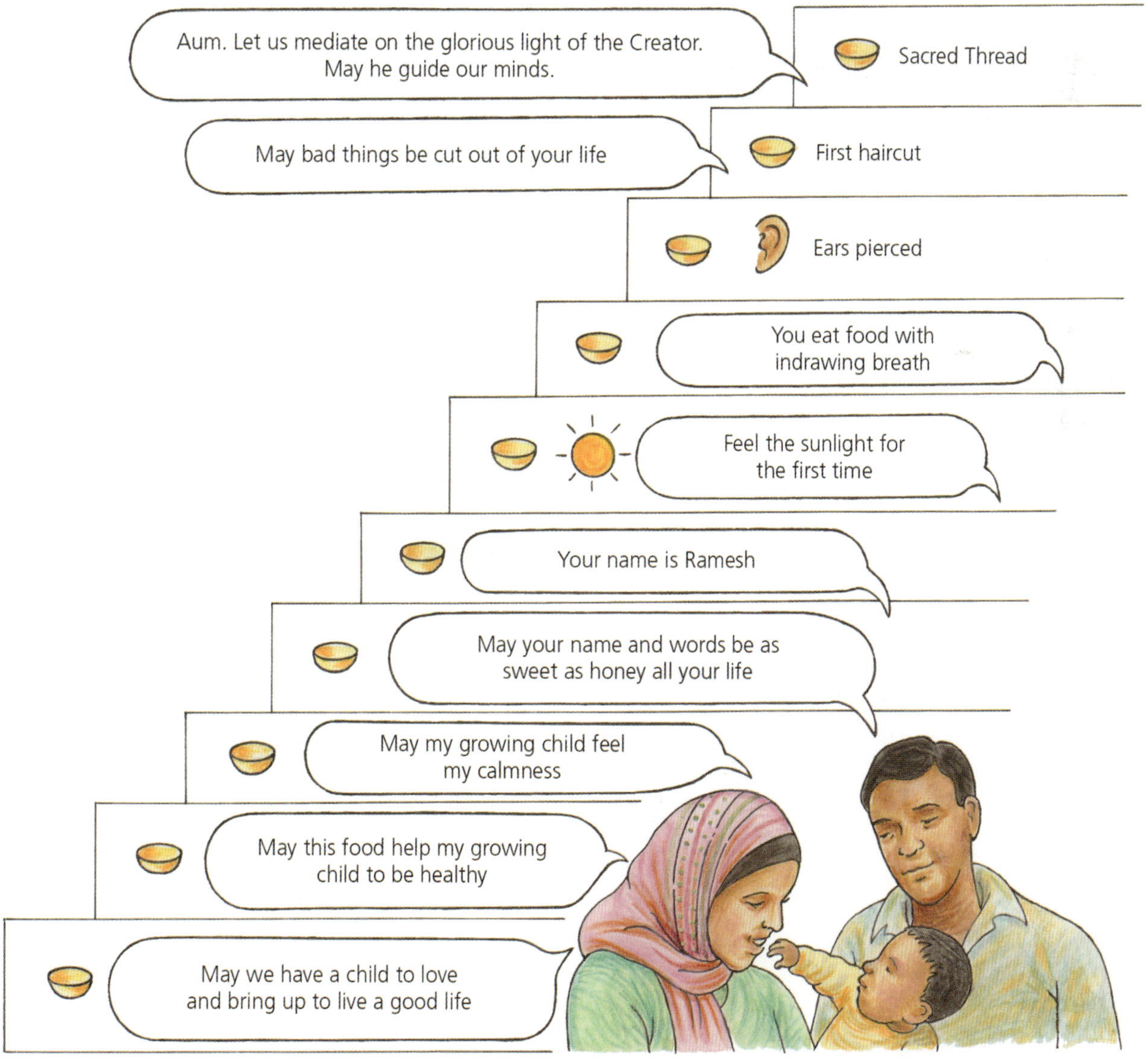

Aum. Let us mediate on the glorious light of the Creator. May he guide our minds.

Sacred Thread

May bad things be cut out of your life

First haircut

Ears pierced

You eat food with indrawing breath

Feel the sunlight for the first time

Your name is Ramesh

May your name and words be as sweet as honey all your life

May my growing child feel my calmness

May this food help my growing child to be healthy

May we have a child to love and bring up to live a good life

▲ The samskaras of childhood

Birth and naming

As soon as a child is born, he or she is given a secret name and their first taste of honey and ghee (a kind of butter). The child's mother says a mantra and begins to feed the child for the first time.

This is the first samskara and is followed, eleven days later, by the fifth samskara, the naming ceremony or **namakarana**.

Naming a child may be done in various ways. First the priest works out a horoscope to see how the planets will affect the child's life. The horoscope tells the parents which letter their child's name should begin with. Then a family aunt will choose a name which is whispered into the baby's ear.

Names may be chosen to reflect spiritual aims, such as the girl's name Jaya (meaning victory) or the boy's name Maadvan (meaning handsome). People traditionally choose at least one name of a Hindu god or goddess, such as Krishna or Lakshmi. This means that whenever the person's name is spoken, it is also honouring God.

The child then goes through four more samskaras until the sacred thread ceremony.

Sacred thread ceremony

After his eighth birthday but before his eleventh birthday, a boy who belongs to one of the three highest castes (see page 66) goes through the tenth samskara, the sacred thread ceremony or **upananyana**. This is a very important stage in his life as it marks his acceptance as a student by a guru. It is like having a second birth as it is the beginning of his spiritual journey as a student rather than a child.

▲ The sacred thread ceremony

The thread consists of three strands (white, red and yellow) as reminders of the boy's three duties to his parents, his teachers and to God.

The ceremony is often held at home. The sacred fire or havan is lit and the father or priest says the Gayatri mantra into the boy's ear as a sign that he has entered into the spiritual life. The thread is placed over his left shoulder and under his right arm by his priest or teacher. The boy will wear the thread all his life; he is now allowed to study sacred scriptures and carry out worship in the shrine at home.

Girls are sometimes honoured in the same way, but it is unusual for them to receive and wear the thread.

What do you know? **AO1**

1 What is a samskara?
2 How many samskaras are there?
3 Which samskara is the birth of a child?
4 Which samskara is the naming of a child?
5 Which samskara is the sacred thread?

What do you understand? **AO2**

6 Explain the significance of the Hindu naming ceremony.
7 Explain the importance of the sacred thread ceremony for a boy's life.

What do you think? **AO3**

8 Do you think it is important to mark certain moments in life with special ceremonies?

Essay practice

'In ancient times, girls were also invested with the sacred thread; there is no reason why they should not be encouraged to participate in this ceremony in modern times.' (Seeta Lakhani) Do you agree? Give reasons for your answer. Show that you have considered more than one point of view.

Topic 1 Muslim beliefs and teachings

Starter: Why is the oneness of God an essential Muslim belief?

1.1 What and where is Islam?

Islam developed in the seventh century CE, in Arabia. In 610CE, a young trader in Makkah (Mecca) called Muhammad received a powerful revelation from God, calling him to preach the oneness of God.

At the time, the Arabian people were worshipping idols or statues of many gods and were failing to worship the one true God. Islam therefore, does not consider that it is a new religion; it believes that Muhammad revived monotheism – the worship of one God – and established it as a powerful religious, spiritual and political force.

After Muhammad's death in 632CE, Muhammad's friend Abu Bakr was appointed his successor or **caliph**. Abu Bakr united the Arabian tribes by persuading them to follow Islam. From then on, Islam spread rapidly into Syria, Persia, Egypt and northern Africa. Under Islam, a powerful empire was formed. Islam is still a major uniting force in the world today.

▲ A map of Sunni and Shi'a Muslims in the world today

Although Muslims essentially share the same beliefs, there are some areas where there are important areas of difference. These differences were caused by a clash over who should lead Islam. The **Shi'ites** believed that Islam should be led by a member of Muhammad's family. The **Sunnis** argue that leadership should be given to the person best suited to govern. Today, 90 per cent of all Muslims are Sunnis.

You will see in this chapter on Islam that many of the key ideas are Arabic words. It is useful but not essential to know them.

1.2 God

The Six Articles of Faith

A literal translation of the word 'islam' tells us a lot about the religion. Islam means to 'surrender' or 'submit' to the will of God. Islam is also linked very closely to another Arabic word, 'salaam', which means 'peace'. Islam is, therefore, a religion of surrender and peace.

'As-Islam'

▲ 'Islam' in Arabic

As mentioned, a person who practises Islam is a Muslim, that is 'one who surrenders' to the will of God. The **Qur'an** (the holy book of Islam) makes it clear that being born into a Muslim family is not enough to be a Muslim – you must surrender yourself through **iman** (belief in God) and **amal** (actions).

A Muslim is one who can say and believe that 'there is no god but God and Muhammad is His Messenger

Muhammad summarised Islam in the following Six Articles of Faith:

1 The oneness of God
2 God's angels
3 God's books
4 God's **prophets**
5 The Last Day
6 The Divine plan.

The Oneness of God

The oneness and unity of God is absolutely central to Islamic theology. All other ideas follow from this belief. The unity or oneness of God is called **tawhid**.

The oneness of God means that He is utterly **transcendent**, meaning that He is outside of both time and space. He is the sole creator of the universe and the controller of its destiny.

However, God is not distant. He is **immanent** or very close to humanity. He knows all human thoughts and is involved in all aspects of His creation. According to the Qur'an, He is closer to us 'than our jugular vein' (Qur'an 50:16).

Anything that undermines the oneness of God is called **shirk**. This might include reducing God to the human level by representing Him in art, claiming that a human is like God or believing that other gods exist and worshipping them. Shirk is often caused by human pride, ignorance and foolishness.

God's omnipotence

God is also **omnipotent**, which means 'all powerful'. God creates all things, therefore everything in the universe owes its existence to Him. God is the 'Absolute'; there is nothing greater than God. This is summarised in the Arabic phrase, 'Allahu Akbar' – 'God is the greatest' – which is used in many Muslim prayers.

'Allahu Akbar'

▲ 'God (Allah) is Greatest'

God's beneficence

Beneficence means goodness. As God is supreme, His **beneficence** means that He is all good, compassionate and merciful.

God's beneficence is most clearly revealed in His involvement with the world and with humans in particular:

- God's first act of beneficence was the creation of the world and giving life.
- His next act of goodness was His creation of humans to look after the world for Him. However, without His generous guidance humans would not be able to do this properly.
- God in His mercy has therefore sent prophets and messengers to guide humans and help them live fulfilled lives.
- His greatest act of beneficence was the giving of the Qur'an, which offers humans ultimate guidance.
- Finally, God's beneficence is that, as a just and fair God, He will reward good people and punish the wicked on the Day of Judgement.

God's beautiful names

In the Qur'an there is a verse which says, 'To Him belong the most beautiful names' (Qur'an 59:24). The Qur'an has many names of God which describe His qualities. These names begin with the word 'the'.

There are 99 names of God in the Qur'an. Muhammad taught his followers to meditate on the names of God. This is why Muslim prayer beads have 33 beads. When some Muslims pray, they pass the beads through their fingers three times, which helps them think about God's 99 qualities. All these qualities are contained in the word **Allah**. Allah is not one of the 99 names nor is it the name for God: Allah is merely the Arabic word for 'God'.

'Allah'

▲ The word 'Allah' (God) in Arabic calligraphy

Some examples of God's 99 beautiful names are:
The Creator, The Maker, The Fashioner, The Mighty, The Praiseworthy, The Wise

'Ar-Rahman'	The Merciful	الرَّحْمَٰنُ
'Al-Khāliq'	The Creator	الخَالِقُ
'Al-Alīm'	The All-Knowing	العَلِيمُ
'Al-Wadūd'	The Loving	الوَدُودُ
'As-Salām'	The Source of Peace	السَّلَامُ

▲ Some of the beautiful names of God

What do you know? AO1

1 What does 'Islam' mean?
2 What does 'Muslim' mean?
3 Name the two main Muslim traditions.
4 What does 'tawhid' mean?
5 Write a definition of monotheism.
6 What does 'omnipotent' mean?

What do you understand? AO2

7 Explain why iman is essential for being a Muslim.
8 Explain what it means to say that God is transcendent.
9 Explain why there can be no pictures representing God (Allah).
10 Explain why it is generous of God to send prophets and messengers to humans.
11 Explain why God has so many names in Islam.

What do you think? AO3

12 How can God be all good when bad people often do far better in this world than good people?

1.3 God's angels

Angels have an important place in Islamic theology. God created angels at the beginning of time to be His servants. They are neither male nor female and are immortal so cannot die. Unlike humans, they do not have free will.

Only angels can come directly into the presence of God. Their chief function is to communicate God's will to humans. Some angels have special roles, for example:

- Jibril (Gabriel) is the chief angel whose role is to deliver God's revelations to the prophets.
- Mikail (Michael) looks after heaven and makes sure the Devil cannot enter it.
- Israfil looks after the Last Judgement and sounds the trumpet to announce it.
- Recording angels keep records of all human actions, which are read out on the Last Day when each person is judged.
- Guardian angels protect the individual against the Devil.
- Iblis/**Shaitan** (Satan) or the Devil was expelled from heaven because he refused to worship God. God has delayed His punishment until the Last Day so until then His role is to tempt and test humans and try to lead them astray.

Humans cannot usually see angels directly but they can sense their presence.

▲ Islam teaches that angels are God's servants who carry out His orders

1.4 God's holy books

There is only one holy book in Islam which is the Qur'an. The **Hadith** (meaning 'story' or 'report') is a collection of Muhammad's sayings and teachings. The Qur'an and the Hadith are the two most important sources of religious authority for Muslims.

The Qur'an

God has sent humankind holy books at various times in history through His prophets. He gave the Torah to Moses, the Psalms to David and the Gospel to Jesus. However, over time, human writers have distorted these books. For Muslims, this is why God sent the Qur'an, His final and complete revelation, to restore the distorted message of His previous books. The Qur'an is the pure Word of God as revealed to Muhammad.

▲ A copy of the Qur'an

Origins of the Qur'an

Muhammad received his very first revelation while he was meditating in the cave on Mount Nur in 610ᴄᴇ (see page 93). To begin with, Muhammad was unable to read or recite what Jibril was showing him, but finally he recited the words.

> ### The first revelation of the Qur'an Muhammad received
>
> Read! In the name of your Lord and Sustainer who created man from a clot of congealed blood, speak these words aloud!
> Your Lord is the Most Generous One –
> He who has taught by the pen,
> who reveals directly things from beyond human knowledge.
>
> **Qur'an 96:1–4 'The Blood Clot'**

This **Night of Power** or Laylat ul Qadr was the first of many revelations which Muhammad received over the next 22 years, in Makkah and in Madinah. Muhammad uttered the revelations and his wife **Khadija** and his friends wrote them down.

As the collection of revelations grew, his followers brought Muhammad the verses for him to check. The verses were later put in a chest kept by his wife Hafsa (along with Aishah, two of many wives he married after Khadija's death). However, the process of putting the 114 surahs or chapters into the right chronological order was cut short by Muhammad's death.

Muhammad's secretary, Zaid ibn Thabit, used the contents of the chest to put the surahs in order. Even so, because many of those who had heard Muhammad deliver the revelations tried to remember the messages by heart, other versions of the Qur'an began to appear in different Arabic dialects.

Eventually, the great Caliph Uthman (644–656ᴄᴇ) rejected all false versions of the Qur'an and established it in the form that we have today. Uthman arranged the Qur'an with the longest surahs at the beginning (with the exception of Surah 1 which is a prayer) and the shortest at the end. Uthman commanded all other versions of the Qur'an to be destroyed.

Main features of the Qur'an

The Qur'an is divided into 114 **surahs** (which means 'portion' in Arabic) or chapters. Unlike the Bible, the Qur'an has very few stories and the surahs are more like a series of thoughts or ideas:

▲ The bismillah prayer in Arabic

- Apart from Surah 1, the Al Fatihah, surahs are all prefaced by the **bismillah**, 'In the name of God, the Compassionate, the Merciful'.
- Surah headings such as 'The Cow', 'The Pen', 'Mary' and so on often refer to a particularly important idea in the surah.
- A verse is called an **ayah**.
- The surahs in the Qur'an are arranged approximately with the longest at the beginning and the shortest at the end.
- The Qur'an may only properly be read in Arabic as that is the language in which Muhammad received it.
- There is only one true Qur'an, in heaven; even Arabic copies are only copies.

Qur'an means 'recitation' and is essentially an oral document to be learned by heart. A person who can recite the Qur'an from memory is known as a **hafiz**.

The Hadith

The Qur'an does not contain any of Muhammad's teaching. The Hadith is particularly useful for understanding the Qur'an and for looking for examples of how Muhammad interpreted it in his teaching. The Hadith and the Qur'an are the foundations of Islamic law or **shari'ah**.

A hadith is a particular saying by Muhammad or story about him. The most influential and trustworthy edition of 700 hadiths was put together by Muhammad al-Bukhari (810–870CE).

The most important and famous hadith is called the Hadith of Gabriel. In this hadith, the angel Jibril (Gabriel) appears to Muhammad and questions him about the fundamentals of Islam. Muhammad sets out:

- the Six Articles of Faith (iman)
- the Five Pillars of Islam
- ihsan (doing that which is beautiful).

▲ Jibril appearing to Muhammad

Qur'an in worship

The Al Fatihah or 'The Opening' is the first surah of the Qur'an and sets out the key principles of Islam. Unlike other surahs, it does not have the usual heading 'In the Name of God, the Compassionate, the Merciful', as this is contained in the surah itself. It is used regularly in prayer as a creed or summary of belief and as a way to meditate.

The Al Fatihah

In the name of God, the Compassionate, the Merciful

All praise be to God

the Lord of the world,

the Most Merciful, the Most Kind,

Master of the Day of Judgement.

You alone do we worship,

From You alone do we seek help.

Show us the next step along the straight path

of those earning Your favour.

Keep us from the path of those earning Your anger, those who are going astray.

The Qur'an must be treated with extreme respect because it is considered a record of the actual words God said to Muhammad. While it is being read, the following customs must be observed:

- There must be no speaking, eating or drinking when reading from the Qur'an.
- Before reading it, a Muslim must wash.
- A Muslim must be in the right frame of mind, with pure intentions (niya).
- When it is being read it is often placed on a small wooden folding bookrest, called a rehal, so that it does not touch the ground.
- When the Qur'an is not being used it must be kept covered with a cloth and placed high up with nothing else on top of it.

▲ A Muslim reading the Qur'an from a rehal

What do you know? **AO1**

1 What is a surah?
2 How was the Qur'an first collected?
3 What role did Hafsa and Zaid ibn Thabit play in producing the Qur'an?
4 What is a hadith?
5 Who created the first trustworthy Hadith collection?

What do you understand? **AO2**

4 Explain the relationship of the Hadith to the Qur'an.
5 Explain why the Hadith of Gabriel is so important in Islam.
6 Explain how the Qur'an is used in worship.

What do you think? **AO3**

7 Do you think God might send another holy book after the Qur'an?

1.5 God's prophets

The Qur'an says God had sent many prophets to human beings before Muhammad. In the Qur'an, 24 prophets are named. Many of them are familiar to Jews and Christians as they are referred to in the Hebrew Bible (**Tanakh**, or Old Testament) and the New Testament. God chooses prophets to deliver his message to the world. Some prophets are also messengers because they deliver God's message in the form of a book or scripture. For example, Adam is a prophet but **Isa** (Jesus) is a prophet and a messenger because the book he delivered was the Gospel.

Islam teaches that all the prophets preached the same six articles of faith (see page 86).

The 24 named prophets in the Qur'an begin with Adam and end with Isa (Jesus). Muhammad is only named a few times in the Qur'an, as the Qur'an is not about him but the words he received from God. He is the final prophet and referred to as the 'seal of the prophets' because the book he had revealed to him, the Qur'an, is pure, complete and final.

All the prophets are male. Some Muslim scholars argue that Mary, the mother of Isa, is a very important figure in the Qur'an. They say as she was visited by an angel, and she set a perfect example of obedience to God's will, she could also be considered a prophet.

▲ Cave Hira on Mount Nur where Muslims believe Muhammad went to reflect and pray

The Prophet Muhammad

Muhammad and the Night of Power

Muhammad was born in 570CE in Makkah. His father died before his birth, and his mother died when he was six, so he was brought up by his grandfather. However, the greatest influence on his early life was his uncle Abu Talib, who brought him up after his grandfather died. He learned to help in his uncle's business and quickly earned the reputation as a trader of great honesty. He was nicknamed al-Amin (the trustworthy) – a title which remained with him for the rest of his life.

In 595CE, Abu Talib arranged for Muhammad to work for a rich Makkan (Meccan) widow and business-woman called Khadija. Not only was she impressed by the young man's skill as a business man, but she also offered to marry him. They married when he was 25 and she was 40 years old.

At this time, Muhammad would often go out to a cave called Hira, just outside Makkah, to reflect and pray. These are the so-called Secret Years of Contemplation. Muhammad began to practise meditation in the desert. He was worried about the increase in poverty and general lack of concern for others in society. This time is called the Period of Darkness because it was a time when life in Makkah was at a moral low point.

Then, in 610CE, when he was 40 years old, Muhammad received his first revelation while meditating in a cave on Mount Nur. This is known as the Night of Power (Laylat ul Qadr), the night when God first revealed Himself to Muhammad.

The revelation was terrifying. The angel Jibril (Gabriel) appeared holding a scroll and instructed him to read it. Muhammad refused. Perhaps he was scared and thought Jibril was some kind of spirit. Jibril commanded him to 'read!' three times. On the third time he placed his hands around Muhammad's waist and squeezed him until the words forced their way into his mouth.

Still shaking, Muhammad returned home to his wife, Khadija, who wrapped him in a shawl. She became his first believer, shortly followed by Ali, his cousin, Zayd ibn Harith, a freed slave and Christian, and Abu Bakr, one of his closest friends. They encouraged him to preach to the Makkans.

Muhammad's message in Makkah

Muhammad's message of the oneness of God did not please the Makkan tribes. They worshipped their many gods contained in the cube-shaped temple called the Ka'bah in the centre of Makkah. The Ka'bah was controlled by the powerful Quraysh tribe. Each time a different tribe came to the Ka'bah, they were forced to pay the Quraysh money. So, Muhammad's message did not please the Quraysh because it undermined their control of the Ka'bah. The Quraysh often attacked Muhammad and his followers.

The migration or hijrah

In 620CE, while preaching outside Makkah, Muhammad met six men from the town of Yathrib who asked him to come and settle an argument between two warring Arab tribes in the city. The new converts promised to accept Muhammad's leadership, worship only God and lead moral lives. This gave Muhammad the opportunity to be able to preach Islam openly without being attacked by the Makkans.

Two years later, in 622CE, Muhammad sent his Muslim followers from Makkah to Yathrib and shortly afterwards he joined them with his friend Abu Bakr. This event is known as the hijrah, or

migration, and it marks the time when Islam became established as a way of life. This is why the Islamic calendar starts with the **hijrah**. The date of the move to Yathrib, or as it was now called Madinah al-Nabi (City of the Prophet), is the year 1 AH or 1 After Hijra.

Muhammad's life and teaching in Madinah

In Madinah, Muhammad developed his idea of Muslim community, or **umma** in Arabic. Umma can refer to local communities as well as to the worldwide sense of Muslim fellowship. Muhammad's life and rule in Madinah have provided Muslims with an example of how to run a Muslim state ever since.

Muhammad's return to Makkah

Despite being accepted and followed in Madinah, there were continuing tensions with the Makkans. In 624CE at the Battle of Badr, the Prophet won a considerable victory against a large Makkan army. Finally, in 630CE, Muhammad made a surprise attack on Makkah with 10,000 men. They circled the **Ka'bah** seven times with no loss of life. The Makkans finally accepted Islam and Muhammad's authority.

The first thing Muhammad did was to cleanse the Ka'bah by removing all the idols of the many gods and dedicating it to the one God.

▲ Madinah al-Nabi (City of the Prophet) – the green dome was built over Muhammad's tomb

▲ The Ka'bah in Makkah

In 632CE, Muhammad gave his Farewell Sermon from the Mount of Arafat and reminded Muslims of their duties. He then returned to Madinah. On 8 June 632CE, (or 10 AH), he died with his head on his wife Aishah's lap (Muhammad had several wives). He was 63 years old.

> All mankind is from Adam and Eve, an Arab has no superiority over a non-Arab nor a non-Arab has any superiority over an Arab; also a white has no superiority over a black nor a black has any superiority over a white – except by piety and good action. Learn that every Muslim is a brother to every Muslim and that the Muslims constitute one brotherhood.

Extract from Muhammad's Farewell Sermon

Activity

Imagine you are one of Muhammad's very first Muslim followers. Write a diary recording and reflecting on Muhammad's life from the Night of Power to his death.

What do you know? AO1

1 How many prophets are named in the Qur'an?
2 Who are the first and last prophets in the Qur'an?
3 What happened to Muhammad in 610CE?
4 What is the hijrah?
5 How old was Muhammad when he died?

What do you understand? AO2

6 Explain why the Quraysh tribe often attacked Muhammad in Makkah.
7 Explain why the year 630CE was significant in Muhammad's life.
8 Why was Madinah important in the development of Islam for Muhammad?

What do you think? AO3

7 Was it right as a prophet for Muhammad to fight?
8 Could these be another prophet after Muhammad?

1.6 The day of judgement and afterlife

Akhirah is the Arabic term referring to the Last Day and the afterlife, judgement and the rewards of heaven and hell. Islam teaches that we only have one physical life. This life on Earth is a test of a person's character to be worthy of a place in paradise where humans can experience true life.

God is always involved with the universe which He has created. On Judgement Day, He will reward and punish people in accordance with their good or evil actions. Every generation has been warned about this and Islamic preaching is often a call to repentance, to show remorse for the wrong we have done.

Akhirah is a sign of God's mercy and justice, especially for those people who have lived good lives but who have not been rewarded in this world. In paradise they receive all the good things which they are owed.

▲ The Prophet has said that the way to paradise will be made easy for those who seek knowledge

At the end of time, all the dead will come alive and God will judge all people according to their deeds (amal) and their intentions (**niyah**). Only God can know who will be rewarded with Jannah (paradise) or Jahanam (hell). Each person is entirely responsible for his or her actions.

Traditional Muslim teaching develops the teaching of the Qur'an and explains what happens when a person dies. When someone dies, the angel Azra'il takes their soul to a waiting place called **barzakh**.

Then, after the world has undergone a great battle between the forces of good and evil, the angel Israfil will sound the last trumpet and everything in the world will die. Then he will sound his trumpet a second time and all bodies will be resurrected and reunited with their souls. Muslims also believe, as do Christians, that Isa (Jesus) will return in his Second Coming when God judges the world.

Then Judgement Day will take place when each person is judged by God according to their record of deeds and intentions. At the Day of Dividing, people will pass along the bridge to Jannah or Jahanam.

The Qur'an describes Jannah as a beautiful garden in which a fountain flows with the most delicious drink served by beautiful women.

Paradise

In gardens of delight they shall enjoy honour and happiness facing each other on thrones: a cup will be passed to them from a clear-flowing fountain – delicious to drink and free from intoxication or headaches: and besides them will be innocent women, restraining their glances, with eyes wide with wonder and beauty.

Qur'an 37:43–48

Jahanam, on the other hand, is a state of perpetual pain and suffering, where God only sends those who have completely rejected or distorted His truth.

Hell

I warn you of the flaming fire. None shall be cast into it but the most wretched, who has called the Truth a lie and turned his back.

Qur'an 92:14–16

Discuss

Are hell and paradise actual places or symbols of our relationship with God after we die?

1.7 The divine plan: God's Will

The Divine Plan, or **Al Qadr**, is that God has commanded or willed all events in the universe. In other words, God is the controller of destiny and knows all things and everything we will do. He knows who will choose good and who will choose evil.

A phrase often used in the Qur'an is 'in-sha' Allah', which means 'if God wills it'. This suggests that God is in control of everything and knows who will be rewarded with paradise or with hell.

The problem of Al Qadr is that if God knows everything in advance, then do humans have any free will or responsibility?

What do you know? **AO1**

1 How are paradise and hell described in the Qur'an?
2 What is the role of the angel Jibril?
3 What does akhirah mean?

What do you understand? **AO2**

4 Explain why angels are important in Islam.
5 Explain the Islamic view of what happens when a person dies.
6 Explain what the Divine Plan is.

What do you think? **AO3**

7 Is it reasonable to believe in angels?
8 Will God reward non-Muslims with paradise at Judgement Day?

Essay practice

'If there was no Day of Judgement then no one would behave well in this life.' Do you agree? Give reasons for your answer. Show that you have considered more than one point of view.

Activity

'I believe that although our bodies are controlled by the laws of cause and effect as everything else in the world, we still are able to choose between good or evil. However, our decisions are limited depending on what choices are available in any given situation. God knows what these situations are and what choices are available for each person; He knows which choices are right and which are wrong. God knows how we will be rewarded or punished on the Last Day.'

'I believe that even though God knows everything we do, He can't know what I intend to do until I do it. What God wills is for each of us to resist evil and to do good, but the choice to do good or evil is always completely our own. As my choices are completely my own, God will judge me on the Last Day entirely on what I have done or have failed to do.'

1 Discuss in your groups what you think free will is.
2 Read the two views above. Explain how the views are different.
3 Discuss in your groups which view you think is better.

Topic 2 Muslim practices and ceremonies

Starter: Why is regular and frequent prayer important for Muslims?

2.1 The Five Pillars

The Five Pillars of Islam are the central teachings and practices of Islam. They are the foundation of the Muslim way of life. They cover all key areas of Muslim life from everyday events, such as prayer and attendance at the mosque, to pilgrimage. The Five Pillars are not optional; all Muslims must do these practices.

All Five Pillars interlink with each other, but at the heart is the Shahadah. This is the belief that God is one and only; He alone is to be worshipped; and Muhammad is His messenger.

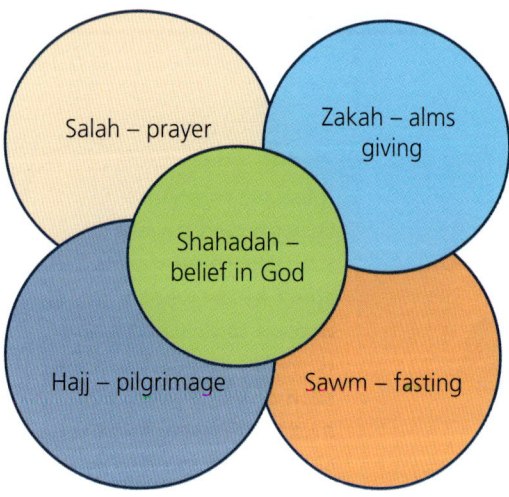

Salah – prayer

Zakah – alms giving

Shahadah – belief in God

Hajj – pilgrimage

Sawm – fasting

▲ The Five Pillars of Islam

Shahadah

I bear witness that there is no God but Allah

I bear witness that Muhammad is the Messenger of Allah.

These are the words of the Shahadah, the central declaration of belief in Islam. Shahadah means 'witness' in Arabic. It is a promise to live in accordance with the two essential Muslim beliefs that there are no gods except God (Allah), and that Muhammad is Allah's messenger. Muhammad said that nothing was more important in his teaching than the Shahadah. A Muslim recites the Shahadah to witness to the oneness of God and to promise to live by God's will.

The Shahadah is used in many forms of Muslim worship and is part of the call to prayer or adhan.

To become a Muslim you need to say the Shahadah in Arabic sincerely in front of two witnesses. However, this is only the beginning. To show true intention, a person must carry out ibadah – worship or servitude to God – by performing the other four Pillars of Islam.

Salah

'Salah' means prayer and is an important means of becoming aware of God; that is why it is the second of the five pillars of faith.

In one story, it is said that, at first, God commanded Muslims to pray 50 times a day! After this, in a vision (called The Night Journey), the prophet Moses suggested that no one would be able to pray so many times and suggested that Muhammad go back to God and ask for fewer prayers. Finally, God decided that five brief moments a day were sufficient. Since then, where possible, Muslims try to pray at the five set prayer times each day:

- before sunrise
- at noon
- mid-afternoon
- at sunset
- before midnight.

Praying frequently means that Muslims are constantly reminded of the presence of God in all that they do. As there are set prayer times, when a Muslim prays they know that they are praying in unity with all other Muslims. They therefore experience what is called umma or Muslim community.

Prayer should take place in a clean place, which is why a prayer mat is often used. The worshipper should turn towards the direction of the Ka'bah in Makkah.

▲ This prayer mat has a built-in compass. Why?

The call to prayer

Allahu-akbar allahu akbar

Allah is the greatest, Allah is the greatest

Ashhadu an la'ilaha illallah [said twice]

I bear witness that there is no God but Allah

Ashhadu anna Muhammad al-rasul Allah [said twice]

I bear witness that Muhammad is the Messenger of Allah

Hayya 'alas salat, hayya 'alas salat

Come to prayer, come to prayer

Hayya 'alas falah, hayya 'alas falah

Come to success, come to success

Allahu-akbar, allahu akbar

Allah is the greatest, Allah is the greatest

La 'ilaha illallah

There is no God but Allah

Prayer time is announced by the person who performs the call to prayer, a **muezzin**. They will do this either inside a mosque or, in some countries, from the **minaret** or tower of the mosque. A muezzin might also announce the prayer time through television or radio, or by a loud-speaker system in the town or market stalls. It is a distinctive sound in most Muslim countries or communities.

The adhan or call to prayer contains the Shahadah. When the muezzin recites the adhan he is therefore making a very public declaration about Islam to Muslims and non-Muslims alike.

The adhan also reminds the worshipper that being Muslim is the means to success, both in this life and in the world to come.

Preparation before prayer

Before prayer Muslims carry out a special cleansing or ritual ablution ceremony. This is called **wudu** in Arabic. Wudu usually comprises washing one's feet, hands and arms up to the elbow, face, nostrils, neck, ears and hair. In hot countries where water is scarce, a form of wudu can be carried out with dust or sand. When wudu is carried out, it is not the washing that matters, but the intention of preparing oneself for prayer. Intention is called niyah in Arabic. Niyah is a very important Muslim idea, not only in worship but in many other areas of Muslim life, such as making ethical decisions and relationships.

▲ A Muslim carrying out wudu

Prayer at home

Many families conduct their five prayers a day at home. Men and women may pray in the same room, but the women usually stand behind or to one side of the men, because men and women should not be distracted by each other. The room should be clean and the family should turn towards Makkah when praying. After wudu, the family go through the set series of prayer movements called **rak'at** or 'bendings'. The prayers at different times of day require a specified number of rak'at.

1 The Niyah - the intention to perform an obligatory prayer. The Takbir - 'shutting out the world'. The allahu akbar recited.

2 Hands are placed across the waist as a symbol of humility. The first surah of the Qur'an (Al Fatihah) is recited, followed by other selected passages from the Qur'an.

3 Ruku - bending. This is a sign of great humility. The person repeats three times, 'Glory be to my Lord, the Magnificent'.

4 Qiyam - standing upright and being aware of God. As the person rises they say, 'Allah listens to the one who praises Him.' When standing the worshipper says, 'O our Lord all praise is for you.'

5 Sujud - full prostration. The worshipper says, 'Glory be to my Lord, the Exalted' followed by the allahu akbar.

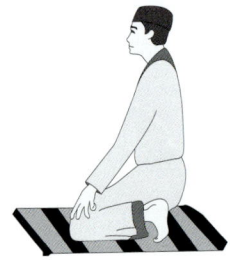

6 Julus - sitting. Prayers are also said for the Prophet, congregation and forgiveness.

7 Salaam - the peace. 'Peace and mercy of Allah be on you.' It is said first to the neighbour on the person's left ,..

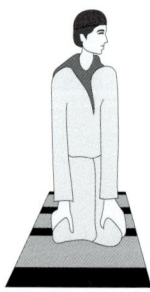

8 ... and then to the neighbour on the person's right.

▲ The rak'at prayer sequence

Personal prayer

Personal individual prayers or **du'a** prayers can take place anywhere and at any time other than the five compulsory prayers a day. Du'a might be to offer thanks, to ask for forgiveness or to request God's help. Some Muslims use a string of beads (sometimes made up of 33 or 99 beads) called subhah to help them pray (see pages 98–99). The beads are passed through the fingers to remember the 99 Names of God.

▲ Muslim prayer beads

Prayer in the mosque

Congregational worship takes place at noon on Jummah (Arabic for Friday) when Muslims meet and worship together. Ideally, all Muslims should attend Jummah prayers. There should be at least 40 adult men in attendance for Friday prayers to be held. They are usually held in the local mosque and led by the **imam** or prayer leader. On entering the mosque, each person will carry out their own personal prayers and rak'at.

Quite often, the imam will give an informal talk before the muezzin recites the formal prayer with the call to prayer. The imam then delivers the formal sermon or **khutba**. The sermon can be wide-ranging but will set out to reinforce some teaching of the Qur'an or the Prophet Muhammad.

The congregational rak'at which follows is done shoulder to shoulder; old and young, rich and poor worshipping together in unity and equality.

Women pray either behind men or in their own separate gallery or hall. At the end of the formal part of **Jummah** worship there is time for those who wish to continue in prayer; some mosques sing hymns and devotional songs.

▲ An imam giving a sermon at Friday prayers

What do you know? AO1

1 What does 'Shahadah' mean?
2 What is ibadah?
3 Describe wudu.
4 Describe rak'at.

What do you understand? AO2

4 Explain the importance of intention or niyah in worship.
5 Explain why Friday or Jummah prayers at the mosque are important for the Muslim community.
6 Explain how the five daily prayers help a person become more aware of God.
7 Explain the key ideas of the adhan (call to prayer).

What do you think? AO3

8 Do you think praying five times a day is too much?
9 Do you think it is better to pray with others or by yourself?

Zakah

Zakah is the compulsory third pillar of Islam and means 'giving to charity'. Muslims believe that wealth and riches are gifts from God, so they must share them. Zakah builds on the two key aspects of Shahadah – witnessing to God in mind and through action. Zakah is therefore also a form of worship, as people consider those who are less fortunate, such as orphans, widows, the poor and the homeless. Zakah may be used to build schools, hospitals, old people's homes and so on.

Adult Muslims must give 2.5 per cent of their overall wealth, after subtracting the minimum amount of money they need to live on, for zakah. In some Muslim countries, zakah is part of the tax system, but for most Muslims zakah is left to a person's individual conscience.

▲ A Muslim giving zakah

Discuss

Do you think that if everyone practised zakah there would be no poverty?

Sawm

Sawm is the fourth pillar of Islam and means 'fasting'. The compulsory time for fasting is during the month of **Ramadan**. Fasting takes place during daylight hours, from sunrise to the end of sunset, and a Muslim must abstain from eating, drinking, smoking and sexual relationships during this time.

Fasting is intended to make Muslims aware of God's presence and His generosity. One of God's gifts is the giving of the Qur'an to the world; the first revelation which God sent to Muhammad occurred on one of the nights of Ramadan which Muslims call 'The Night of Power'. In memory of this great event, people try to read the whole of the Qur'an during the last ten days of Ramadan.

Ramadan is a spiritual act and not intended to cause harm or stress. The rules of sawm state that the following do not have to fast, or may make up for days missed at other times:

- children under the age of 12
- pregnant women and mothers nursing newborn babies
- the sick
- those travelling
- those whose work is particularly physically demanding.

▲ Those that are either sick or pregnant

▲ Children under 12

▲ The elderly

▲ People who are travelling

Ramadan ends with the festival of **Id-ul-Fitr** (see page 107).

The influential Muslim scholar al-Ghazali (1058–1111CE) suggested ten spiritual reasons why fasting and hunger are beneficial:

1 It purifies your heart by making you more aware of yourself.
2 It makes one more aware of God.
3 In overcoming physical desires, it makes one humble and more trusting of God's mercy.
4 It makes one more aware of the suffering of others and their needs.
5 It trains one to overcome and master one's sinful desires.
6 It helps one stay awake and appreciate life.
7 It aids constant worship of God; buying food, preparing and eating it takes away time spent worshipping God.
8 It is physically good for the body not to eat too much.
9 Eating less means that one is not a slave to one's stomach. Fasting means that one desires less of the material world; less time is spent acquiring money to buy food.
10 It makes one more generous to the poor and needy and therefore helps you gain a place in paradise.

What do you know? AO1

1 What does the word 'zakah' mean?
2 How much of their wealth should a Muslim give in zakah?
3 What might zakah be used for in the local community?
4 What does the word 'sawm' mean?

What do you understand? AO2

5 Explain why zakah should be a religious duty.
6 Explain two spiritual reasons for fasting.
7 Why do Muslims try and read the whole of the Qur'an during Ramadan?
8 Why might a Muslim not fast during Ramadan?

What do you think? AO3

9 Which is more demanding: keeping zakah or sawm?
10 Does fasting make you less aware of God?

Hajj

Hajj is the fifth pillar of Islam. It means 'visitation of holy places' such as the Ka'bah (the large cube-shaped shrine in the Great Mosque in Makkah) and Mount Arafat (east of Makkah). Muslims believe that everyone must perform hajj once in their lifetime. Not everyone has the means to go, so others may attend on their behalf. What matters is niyah, or intention.

The origins of hajj go back to the time when Muhammad lived in Madinah. In the year 629CE, Muhammad led a pilgrimage to Makkah where he and his fellow pilgrims circled the Ka'bah, the holy shrine in the centre of Makkah (see page 94). Muslims today go on hajj to imitate the **sunnah** or example of the Prophet. Since Muhammad's first hajj, many more ceremonies have been added to enhance the spiritual journey.

Over the six days of hajj, the ceremonies help the pilgrim to experience:

- the oneness and majesty of God
- the nature of sin and the need for repentance
- Shaitan's (Satan's) temptations
- the faithfulness of the prophets such as Ibrahim (Abraham) and Isma'il
- thanksgiving and sacrifice.

A particularly important part of hajj is that it emphasises Muhammad's teaching that Islam is not a new religion – it continues and renews the message of these prophets:

- Ibrahim's faithfulness was tested by God when He commanded him to sacrifice his son Isma'il (Muslim teaching is that Ibrahim (Abraham) offered Isma'il (Ishmael) not Isaac as the Bible relates). Shaitan (Satan) tempted Ibrahim in three ways, but Ibrahim's strong faith and belief in God's mercy enabled him to resist
- Hajar's (Hagar's) trust in God to protect and provide for her son Isma'il is remembered when the angel Jibril (Gabriel) provided her a well.
- Adam and Eve are remembered, in particular the time when Adam confessed his sins at Mount Arafat when he and Eve had been reunited after their expulsion from paradise (Eden) because of their disobedience. Mount Arafat is also where the Day of Judgement will take place.

The main moments of hajj

Hajj takes place from the eighth day of Dhul Al-Hijjah, a sacred month in the Muslim calendar, and lasts for six days.

1 Preparation

To go on hajj you must be mentally and physically fit, free from debt and able to support dependants at home. Preparation starts in Ramadan, especially after the Night of Power. Men and women get themselves into a state of physical and spiritual cleanliness. Men shave their heads and beards.

On arriving at Makkah, but before entering the court of the Great Mosque, pilgrims must be in a state of **ihram** (religious purity).

- Men wear two pieces of plain white cloth. They may not now shave or cut their hair.
- Women usually wear a plain white garment which must cover their whole body but not the face.
- No jewellery or perfume may be worn.

▲ Pilgrims on hajj, wearing sheets of white cloth

2 Makkah

Once pilgrims enter the courtyard of the Great Mosque, they perform their first significant ceremony called **tawaf**. Pilgrims circle the Ka'bah anti-clockwise seven times. Men may run, and women walk, both saying special prayers at the same time. The desire of many pilgrims is to touch the Black Stone (a stone placed in the eastern corner of the Ka'bah), but for most this is impossible because there are just too many pilgrims to get close to it.

Pilgrims then drink from the Zamzam well in the basement of the Great Mosque and fill their water bottles for the next stages of the hajj.

The well is a reminder of the one Hagar found in the wilderness. In remembrance of her trust in God, pilgrims then carry out **sa'y** by running between the two hills of Safa and Marwah seven times while reciting any verses from the Qur'an they can remember.

Sa'y recalls Hagar's frantic search for water to give to her baby son Ishmael. Today this ceremony is made a great deal easier as the path is covered and air-conditioned! Depending on when pilgrims complete tawaf and sa'y, they continue on to the campsite in Mina or return to their campsites near the Great Mosque, although many pilgrims today use rather more comfortable hotels.

▲ The pilgrimage route in Makkah

3 Mina

Mina is five miles from Makkah. Many pilgrims walk but others may travel by car or coach. Pilgrims aim to arrive for midday prayers and they pray until the last prayers of the day, in the morning they leave Mina and travel to Mount Arafat some eight miles away.

4 Mount Arafat

It is now the ninth day of Dhul Al-Hijjah and all pilgrims must take part in the **Wuquf** Arafat or 'standing' at Arafat. All pilgrims – often over two million of them – stand in prayer on the plain of Arafat and confess their sins from noon to sunset. Wuquf ends when a sermon is preached (this reminds pilgrims that Muhammad gave his final sermon at Mount Arafat).

If the Wuquf Arafat is not performed, then the pilgrim's hajj is invalid. Wuquf is considered by most pilgrims to be the most spiritual and significant moment of hajj.

The ceremonies and events which follow and complete hajj are called 'the unfurling'.

▲ Pilgrims praying at Mount Arafat

5 Muzdalifah

After the sermon at Arafat, pilgrims jog their way to Muzdalifah for a torchlight. At Muzdalifah they pick up 49 or 70 stones in preparation for the stoning ceremony at Mina. In the morning they set off to Mina.

6 Mina

It is now the tenth day of Dhul Al-Hijjah.

The final ceremony of hajj ends at Mina. There are three pillars at Mina, because, according to various Muslim stories, Shaitan tempted Ibrahim to disobey God, then he tempted Hagar to persuade Ibrahim to listen to his reasons, and finally he tempted Isma'il to avoid being sacrificed. They all resisted.

Each pilgrim throws 70 stones at the three pillars to symbolise Shaitan's three temptations of Ibrahim.

Pilgrims celebrate the festival of Id-ul-Adha by sacrificing a sheep or cow in remembrance of Ibrahim's willingness to sacrifice his son Ishmael. The Id-ul-Adha lasts for 2–3 days (see page 107 for more detail on this festival). At the end of the festival, men have their heads shaved and women cut a few centimetres off their hair. Pilgrims are now no longer in a state of ihram.

7 Return to Makkah

On their return to Makkah, pilgrims usually perform a final tawaf of the Ka'bah and sa'y of Safa and Marwa. Some pilgrims visit Madinah to see the tomb of the Prophet, but this is not strictly part of hajj, as hajj is not about Muhammad himself, but rather following his example of hajj.

Those who have been on hajj are now called hajji (men) or hajjah (women).

After his hajj, one convert to Islam wrote that for him hajj was not the end of his journey but rather a beginning because only now had he fully understood what it meant to be a Muslim. Muslims often return from hajj deeply spiritually altered by their experience.

What do you know?   AO1

1 What does 'hajj' mean?
2 What is ihram?
3 Describe tawaf and sa'y.

What do you understand?   AO2

4 Explain how hajj remembers Ibrahim's obedience to God.
5 Explain the religious significance of wuquf.
6 Explain why Hajar is remembered in hajj.
7 Explain why Muslims often find going on hajj life changing.

What do you think?   AO3

8 Which part of the hajj do you think is the most significant?

2.2 Festivals

The Arabic word for festival is **id** or **eid**. Festivals are calculated according to the moon and so can occur at very different times each year. There are many festivals in Islam, such as the Mawlid-al-Nabi (Birthday of the Prophet), Laylat-Ul-Qadr (The Night of Power), Laylat-Ul-Miraj (The Night Journey) and Muharram (New Year). The two most significant festivals are Id-ul-Adha and Id-ul-Fitr.

Id-ul-Adha

On the same day as pilgrims complete their hajj by sacrificing an animal on the tenth day of Dhul Al-Hijjah, Muslims throughout the world join them in the festival of Id-ul-Adha. It is as if the whole Muslim world has participated in hajj itself.

Id-ul-Adha means 'festival of sacrifice'. It commemorates Ibrahim's obedience to God when he was prepared to sacrifice his only son because God had commanded him to do so as a test. God spoke to Ibrahim in a dream (Qur'an 37:100–112) but it was his son who encouraged him to carry out the command. Just at the moment Ibrahim was about to kill his son, God provided an animal for him to sacrifice instead.

Other Muslim stories tell how after Ibrahim had his dream and was passing through Mina, on his way to Mount Arafat, Shaitan (Satan) appeared in the form of a woman. Shaitan tempted him by giving him reasons why he should not obey God's command. But Ibrahim threw pebbles at Shaitan and warned him off. At Mount Arafat, Ibrahim blindfolded himself and cut what he thought was his son Isma'il's throat. But, to his amazement, when he removed the blindfold he found that he had killed a ram and not Isma'il.

Other Muslim stories talk about the three temptations of Ibrahim (see page 106).

For many Muslims, Shaitan need not be an actual demon but a way of explaining the struggle we all have, of overcoming our inner selfish desires in order to remain loyal and obedient to God's commands.

On the festival day itself everyone is encouraged to attend congregational prayer in a mosque or hall or special place outside. After wudu, everyone puts on new or best clothes and performs the rak'at for Id-ul-Adha. A sermon is preached, after which and throughout the day everyone exchanges the greeting, 'id mubarak' ('blessed festival'). Gifts are given and everyone makes the effort to visit friends and family. Muslims are encouraged to invite non-Muslim friends and work colleagues to join in with the festivities.

An important feature of Id-ul-Adha is that families make a sacrifice of a sheep or goat. In the United Kingdom this has to be done by a **halal** butcher. It is traditional, but not compulsory, to divide the animal into thirds for your family, relatives and the poor.

Id-ul-Fitr

The festival of Id-ul-Fitr marks the breaking the fast during Ramadan, usually after 30 days of fasting. It therefore falls on the first day of the month of Shawwal and lasts one, two or three days.

Id-ul-Fitr remembers God's generosity. This is marked by acts of kindness to each other – especially remembering the poor, orphans and the weak.

There is no call to prayer, but everyone, including women, is encouraged to attend congregational prayer in a mosque or hall or special place outside. Before attending these special congregational prayers, Muslims are expected to give as generously as possible to a special ul-Fitr zakah. The custom is that no one should speak to anyone until after the ul-Fitr salat (prayer).

There should be no fasting as this is a time of celebration. Families and friends visit each other and gifts are given, especially to children and between close family members. Often there are large celebrations and festive meals; in some countries, people hold large communal firework displays.

2.3 Rites of passage

In Islamic societies, a stable family, in which every member understands their role and is respectful of each other, is essential for the spiritual and moral welfare of all its members.

Birth

The birth of a Muslim child is not just an addition to the family but also to the worldwide Muslim family or ummah.

At his birth, the head of the family takes the child and whispers the adhan into his right ear, and the command 'to rise and worship' into his left ear. Other ceremonies follow:

- The **tahnik** ceremony is when a very small amount of date or honey is rubbed onto the baby's gums. Prayers are said for the baby and family.
- The **aqiqah** ceremony takes place seven days later when friends and relatives arrive for a big meal in which the baby is given his or her name. The baby's head is shaved and its weight in gold or silver is set aside to give to the poor.

Finally, names given to the child are often those of Muhammad's family or the Prophet himself. Other names might be a combination of the abd (the Arabic name for servant) and one of the names of God. Abdullah, for example, means 'servant of God' and Abdul Karim means 'Servant of the Generous One'. Girls' names might be those of Muhammad's various wives such as Khadija or Aishah. Other names may be qualities mentioned in the Qur'an, such as Barraq (shining) for a boy or Mafazah (great success or salvation) for a girl.

Marriage

The Qur'an's view of men and women is that they are 'equal but different'. Men and women complement each other according to their different natures. The Qur'an says:

> He it is who created you from a single soul, and of the same kind he made his mate that he might find comfort in her.
> **Qur'an 7:189**

> Your wives are a garment for you, and you are a garment for them.
> **Qur'an 2:187**

Muhammad held women in the highest esteem. Muslims look to his own example in his marriage to Khadija and then to Aishah. One of Muhammad's famous sayings is often quoted in this context:

Paradise lies at the feet of your mother.

Traditionally, a woman is responsible for the home and family, and she can work, and in return she can expect, as a right, the protection of her husband. She retains all her own property on marriage.

Muhammad did not believe in the single life. **Nikah** or marriage allows people to express the full range of human experience and particularly sexual love in a stable environment. Marriage is not in the first instance for love, although it is hoped love will follow; marriage is a religious duty:

> Do not marry for the sake of beauty; the beauty may become the cause of moral decline. Do not marry for wealth, since this may become the cause of disobedience. Marry rather on the grounds of religious devotion.
> **Hadith**

A marriage ceremony is primarily a legal moment when the marriage contract is exchanged. Contracts can and do vary according to culture and situation. Modern Muslim marriage contracts in the West reflect the more equal relationships of women and men.

▲ A Muslim bride and groom dressed in traditional wedding clothes in Bangladesh

There are many rituals and ceremonies associated with the marriage day itself which are the result of local traditions. A couple in Britain, therefore, might choose to wear a morning suit and white bridal dress and have a reception or party afterwards. However, the marriage ceremony itself simply comprises the exchange and witnessing of the marriage contract. The contract is written and signed by the bride and groom and by their two respective witnesses, usually the bride's and groom's fathers.

The marriage contract is sealed by the giving of a marriage dowry or **mahr** to the bride from her husband. This is a sign of his commitment to her. This money remains the sole property of the wife as an insurance should she divorce. Often the imam or senior member of the Muslim community will recite verses and a blessing from the Qur'an.

In marriage, the traditional role of the man is to protect and provide for the family by earning money and maintaining the morals of the family in preparation for the Day of Judgement. This means abstaining from alcohol, gambling, stealing or hoarding wealth, and sexual immorality.

What do you know? AO1

1 Name three Muslim festivals.
2 What event does the festival of Id-ul-Adha remember?
3 Describe the aqiqah ceremony.
4 Describe what happens at a typical Muslim marriage ceremony.

What do you understand? AO2

5 Explain the purpose of the festival of Id-ul-Fitr.
6 Explain why certain names are chosen for a Muslim baby.
7 Explain the aims of Muslim marriage.

What do you think? AO3

8 Should a couple marry only if they are in love?

2.4 Mosque

The primary purpose of a mosque is for worship and prayer, though it can also serve other important religious and non-religious functions. It can also be used as a law court, a school or madrassah, or a library. A mosque can also be a place for birth, marriage and death ceremonies, and a community centre for lectures, parties and meetings.

Prayer hall

There is no prescribed layout of the mosque. Mosque or **masjid** (in Arabic) means 'place of prostration' and can be any clean place suitable for worship. The chief feature of a mosque is the prayer hall. This is a large open space with no chairs so that worshippers can perform the rak'at and listen to sermons. There are no special places set aside for officials. Everyone is treated as equals.

▲ A prayer hall in a mosque. Note the ornate niche (the mihrab), pointing the way to Makkah, the stand (the minbar), to the night, where the sermon is preached from and the space to make prayer movements

The prayer hall in a typical mosque has the following features:

- One wall must be orientated towards the sacred Ka'bah in Makkah. This wall is called the **qiblah**, meaning 'direction' in Arabic.
- The wall has a niche or **mihrab** built into it to mark the direction of worship more distinctively. The niche may also have shelves to store copies of the Qur'an.
- Next to the mihrab it is traditional to have a three-stepped pulpit or minbar from where the imam can deliver his sermon.
- Many prayer halls have a domed roof above the prayer hall. This symbolises the universe, the heavens and the oneness of God.
- No figurative art (such as pictures of people and animals) is allowed in a mosque because this is thought to lead to idolatry (worshipping a picture or art as if it is God). There are no pictures of Muhammad because some hadiths say this is forbidden. Instead, Islam has developed a most elaborate and beautiful abstract art, often using calligraphy (writing), mosaic tiles and geometric designs to decorate its mosques.

▲ Mosaic tiles decorating the Shah Mosque, Iran

Minarets and muezzin

The muezzin serves an important role in the mosque. He is chosen because of his good character, voice and ability to ensure the mosque functions properly. At the five appointed times of daily prayer, and for Friday public prayers, he faces the qiblah and recites the adhan. Today, the adhan might be pre-recorded and broadcast through speakers on the minaret or internally throughout the rooms in the mosque.

Having called worshipers to the mosque, the muezzin delivers the **iqama** or 'set up' prayer to summon worshippers to line up for the start of formal prayers in the prayer hall.

▲ A typical mosque has a minaret or tower, from which the muezzin delivers the adhan or call to prayer. Muezzin means 'one who calls to prayer'

Wudu area

It is compulsory to remove your shoes when entering a mosque and to dress modestly according to the local custom. Many mosques have dedicated areas to carry out wudu or washing. In hot countries, the wudu area is often a fountain in a courtyard, usually covered to protect worshippers from the sun.

Women in mosques

In traditional mosques, women usually worship behind men in the prayer hall or in separate galleries. The galleries are usually constructed so that the women can see the men in the main prayer area but they cannot be seen by them.

▲ Children learning about Islam in a madrassah – a religious school at a mosque

What do you know? AO1

1 What does the word mosque mean?
2 What is the quibla?
3 What is the mihrab?

What do you understand? AO2

4 Explain why many mosques have a domed roof above the prayer hall.
5 Explain the symbolism of wudu.

What do you think? AO3

6 Do you think the decorations in mosques help Muslims to worship?

Essay practice

'Prayer should be voluntary not compulsory in any religion.' Do you agree? Give reasons for your answer. Show that you have considered more than one point of view.

Topic 1 Jewish beliefs and teachings

1.1 Beliefs about God

Starter: What is God like?

Judaism is a monotheistic religion. This means that Jews believe in one God, but because He is not like anything else that exists, it is very difficult to describe Him. This is summed up in the word 'holy' which literally means 'separate'. The **Torah**, the Jewish book of the Law (the first five books of Moses in what Christians call the Old Testament), has a lot to say about God. Most of what Jews believe about God comes from the Torah.

▲ God is creator and sustainer of the universe

God is One

In a polytheistic time (where people believed in many gods), Judaism stood out as being monotheistic.

God is always the same, so although He is often described as a warrior, a king or a guide, He is still One God. He unites everything in creation but cannot be separated into different forms. The belief in the Oneness of God is summed up in the **Shema**, the oldest and most important Jewish prayer (see page 129). It is so important to be reverent towards God that observant Jews use 'Hashem', which means 'the name', or write 'G_D', instead of writing or saying 'God'.

God the creator, law-giver and judge

God the creator of the universe

No one created God; He has always existed. As God is outside time, He is everywhere and knows everything. The creation reveals that God is all powerful. As creator of the universe, God must be separate from the world. There is no idea of God being part of His creation (pantheism). God's existence does not depend on anything He has made.

As creator of all, God is above everything He has made. He is the supreme being and because He created the world, God is absolutely different from anything else that exists. This makes Him totally unknowable. However, Jews believe that He watches over the world and cares for everyone in it.

God the law-giver

God gave Moses the Law at Mount Sinai. It revealed the laws and duties all Jews are expected to keep. They are contained in the Torah and are a mark of God's sovereignty and love. Jews believe that everyone has two inclinations: to do good and to do wrong. By giving human beings a framework for how they should live their lives, He is offering them the chance to do good and thus form a closer relationship with Him.

God the judge

God judges according to the Law. He is a God of justice and mercy. His judgement is fair and rewards those who keep the Law. His judgement is also merciful because He gives people the opportunity to repent. At the festival of Rosh Hashanah, Jews remember how God brings out scales to weigh the deeds of each person. In the ten days between then and Yom Kippur (the Day of **Atonement**), people try to make up for what they have done wrong (see page 135).

Shekinah: divine presence or spirit of God

The book of Genesis, the first book of the Jewish scriptures, starts with the words:

> In the beginning … darkness was on the surface of the deep, and the spirit of God was hovering over the face of the water. And God said, 'Let there be light', and there was light.
>
> **Genesis 1:1–2 Tenakh**

▲ The Ark of the Covenant

'**Shekinah**' means the presence of God. There are many places in the Jewish bible that tell of God visiting Earth, not as a physical presence but as Shekinah, although the word itself was coined much later:

- When God guided Jews through the desert after their escape from Egypt, Shekinah was a pillar of fire by night and a pillar of cloud by day (Exodus 13).
- God spoke to Moses through a cloud, but Shekinah does not have to be fire or cloud.
- When God spoke to Elijah, Shekinah was a quiet voice but no less God's presence.

In the **Tabernacle**, and later the Temple, a special area was set aside for Shekinah called the Holy of Holies. The Ark of the **Covenant** was a specially made sacred box that contained the Ten Commandments and represented the presence of God. It was kept in the Holy of Holies. Wherever the Ark went, the people knew God was with them. No one was allowed to touch it because it was so holy. When the candles are lit on **Shabbat**, Jews are welcoming God's presence or Shekinah into their home.

What do you know? `AO1`

1. Outline Jewish beliefs about God.
2. Describe the belief that God is One.
3. Describe the Jewish belief of God as creator.
4. What do Jews believe about God as law-giver and judge?
5. What do Jews believe about God's presence on Earth?

What do you understand? `AO2`

6. Explain the importance of the belief in the Oneness of God to Jews.
7. Explain what the idea of God as creator means to Jews.
8. Explain how the Law gives life.
9. How can God's presence be experienced in the world?

What do you think? `AO3`

10. Is there any evidence of God's presence in the world?
11. What things in today's world do you think God would judge harshly?

1.2 Covenant

Starter: A covenant is an agreement between one or more people or between people and God. Why might you make a covenant with someone?

What does it mean to make a covenant?

A covenant is an agreement. The Jewish scriptures explain how God made a covenant with His chosen people, Jews. He made a covenant with one family, Abraham's, that He would always be faithful to him and his descendants. He would protect them and treat them as His special people. For their part, the descendants of Abraham, the Jews, should remember God at all times, serve Him and keep all His laws.

The covenant and the Jews

Jews are often referred to as the 'Chosen People'. This has been misinterpreted throughout history, leading to many acts of **anti-Semitism**. Being chosen does not mean that Jews think they are better than other people; it means that God has placed an obligation on them and given them a duty to perform. Since the covenant, they were to live according to the Law and be an example to everyone on Earth. God called them a nation of priests, which meant that God would reach out to the world through them.

God made covenants with His people throughout the Jewish scriptures:

- With Adam in the Garden of Eden – God promised to provide what humans need without asking for anything in return.
- With Noah – God promised never again to destroy human beings. God set out seven rules that people were to keep.
- With Abraham – God promised to give him children and a land for his descendants. He also promised to look after them. As a sign of this covenant, all males were to be circumcised.

- With Moses at Sinai – God promised to be faithful to them and protect them. He gave Moses the Ten Commandments which the people were to keep as their side of the covenant.
- With King David – God promised King David would rule Israel.
- With Jeremiah the prophet – God promised a new future with a new covenant that would be written not on stone but on the hearts of His people.

The Ten Commandments

The Ten Commandments appear in two places in the Torah: Exodus and Deuteronomy. The book of Exodus tells the story of how God told Moses to go up Mount Sinai. He gave him the Ten Commandments there, which Moses carved in stone. God told Moses He had chosen the Jews and brought them out of Egypt. They were to be His special people and His treasured possession. In return, the people were to keep the commandments. God had rescued them from physical slavery; now He would rescue them from spiritual slavery by showing them how to live good lives.

At first glance, the Ten Commandments may seem to be ten different things, but they are in fact one thing in ten different forms: 'I am the Lord your God – therefore do this and this but don't do that.' The declaration that 'I am the Lord your God' is the main thing. Before Jews can concentrate on the details, they have to accept who God is.

The first four commandments refer to the relationship between a person and God. This is how people should **worship** and respect God, remembering what He has done for them.

The other six commandments are to do with the relationship between people. They show how God expects a community of His people to behave. If their relationship with God is right, their relationship with each other should be right too.

לֹא תִרְצָח

You shall not murder

אָנֹכִי ה׳

I am the Lord your God

לֹא תִנְאָף

You shall not commit adultery

לֹא יִהְיֶה

You shall have no other gods before Me

לֹא תִגְנֹב

You shall not steal

לֹא תִשָׂא

You shall not take the name of the
Lord your God in vain

לֹא תַעֲנֶה

You shall not bear false witness against
your neighbour

זָכוֹר אֶת

Observe the Sabbath day to keep it holy

לֹא תַחְמֹד

You shall not covet your neighbour's wife

כַּבֵּד אֶת

Honour your father and mother

▲ The Ten Commandments are found on the walls of many synagogues.
(Don't forget Hebrew is read from right to left)

The commandments cover every aspect of human life:

- how people should respect and worship God
- how they should be honest and faithful to each other
- how they should treat each other fairly
- how they should respect human life
- how they should control their thoughts.

The last commandment shows that God looks at the heart and sees a person's motives. However, they are written in two columns of five, indicating that the commandments interact with each other and are of equal importance.

Activity

Make a list of the Ten Commandments. If you like you can write the Hebrew words as well as the English.

What do you know? **AO1**

1 Describe how God made a covenant with Abraham.
2 Outline the covenants God made with His people as recorded in the Jewish scriptures.
3 Describe the covenant God made with Moses.
4 Outline the commandments that relate to God's relationship with His people.

What do you understand? **AO2**

5 Explain the importance of covenant to Jews.
6 Explain the importance of the Ten Commandments to Jewish people.
7 Explain why Jews believe that God is concerned with the way people behave towards each other.

What do you think? **AO3**

8 Which is the most important commandment?
9 If it isn't possible to keep all the commandments, do you think there is any point trying to keep the covenant?

The Shema

The Shema is the only fixed daily prayer in Judaism. It is very important that Jews recite this prayer when they wake up in the morning and before they go to bed at night. The Shema is also the last thing a Jew says before death, and is recited at the end of Yom Kippur (Day of Atonement, see page 135). Jews should cover their eyes when reciting the Shema.

שְׁמַע יִשְׂרָאֵל יְהוָה אֱלֹהֵינוּ יְהוָה אֶחָד

וְאָהַבְתָּ אֵת יְהוָה אֱלֹהֶיךָ בְּכָל־

לְבָבְךָ וּבְכָל־נַפְשְׁךָ וּבְכָל־מְאֹדֶךָ :

Hear, O Israel! The LORD is our God, the LORD is one! And you shall love the LORD your God with all your heart and with all your soul and with all your might.

▲ The first part of the Shema from Deuteronomy 6 in Hebrew and English

The first verse of the Shema is the declaration of the Jewish faith. The passage that follows sets out the specific ways in which that faith should be lived out:

- Love God with everything you are.
- Teach the Shema to your children.
- Recite it when you wake up and when you go to sleep.
- Tie it onto your body as a symbol, usually done by putting the verse in a little box called a **tefillin** and wearing it on your head and arm (see page 128).

▲ An Orthodox Jew wearing the tefillin on his head and his arm

The second part of the Shema describes the rewards of following God's commands – rain in the proper season, good harvests, wine and oil, grass in the fields for the cattle and plenty of food to eat. However, it also says that if people do not keep the commands and worship foreign gods, none of these blessings will come.

The last part of the Shema shows how Jews can remember that God is with them always. Prayer shawls and special vests have tassels called **tzitzit** attached to the corners. The tassels remind the wearer that God is always with them.

The mezuzah

The first section of the Shema is written out and put into the **mezuzah** by the front doors of people's houses.

▲ A mezuzah can be quite plain or very ornate

A mezuzah is a special box containing part of the Shema written on parchment. It is a sign of the Covenant. Written on the back of the parchment is the word 'Shaddai', which means 'Almighty', and is one of the many names for God. Jews were told that they must write down God's Law on the doorposts of their houses. In the past, people actually carved the words of the Shema into the wood. This was not very practical, so instead people began to write the words on a little scroll and tuck it inside a specially made hole in the doorpost. Over time, people designed special boxes to hold the scroll as the boxes could be more easily attached. The boxes can have a simple design or be quite ornate. You can tell if a Jewish family live in a house because of the mezuzah nailed to the right-hand side of their front door. Mezuzahs are also placed on internal walls by entrances to rooms, although they are never put next to a bathroom. This is a visual reminder to the people who live there to obey God's commands. Many Jews touch the mezuzah every time they go in or out of the house as a mark of respect for God's word.

Activity

Design a mezuzah.

What do you know?

1 Outline the contents of the Shema.
2 When do Jews recite the Shema?
3 Describe the ways the Shema tells Jews to live out their faith.
4 Outline how Jews remind themselves to obey God's laws.
5 Describe the system Jews had before mezuzahs were invented.

What do you understand?

6 Explain the importance of the Shema.
7 What could the Shema teach someone about Jewish beliefs?
8 Explain why Jews wear tefillins and tallits.
9 Explain the purpose of the mezuzah.
10 Why do Jews put mezuzahs on the door posts of rooms in the house?

What do you think?

11 Does seeing something to remind you of your faith every day (for example, a mezuzah) lessen or increase its effectiveness?
12 Is it more important to love God or to obey Him?

1.3 The Messiah

Starter: What hopes do you have for the future?

Messiah means 'anointed one'. Originally 'Messiah' was the word used for the anointing ceremony for a king. To be anointed by God meant to be given special powers to carry out specific tasks. There have been many such anointed people in Israel's history:

- The High Priest was anointed so that he could carry out his sacred duties. One of these duties was to offer sacrifices to God on behalf of the people. The book of Leviticus in the Torah sets out in great detail how, why and when sacrifices were to be offered.
- Kings were described as being God's anointed. When Saul, and later David, was chosen to be King of Israel, the prophet Samuel took a flask of oil and 'anointed' him king.

Jewish teaching about the Messiah

The idea of a messiah who would come and lead the Jewish people has always been very important. A major part of the Jewish scriptures records the lives of the prophets. It is in these writings that we find most of the teaching about the Messiah, especially Malachi, Micah and Isaiah – what kind of person the Messiah would be, when he would come, what he would do and so on. However, the Messiah would be a human being, not a divine one. At the time, the Jews' country had been invaded and they had been sent into exile in Babylon (present day Iraq). Many Jews shared the hope for a messiah who would set God's people free and establish his throne in Israel once more.

What the prophets said about the Messiah

Malachi

Malachi prophesied that God would send His messenger who would clear a path for Him and that suddenly, He the Lord would appear in His holy Temple. Malachi likened him to a very strong detergent and to someone who purifies silver by heating it.

What he means is that the Messiah will cleanse Jews of their sin and then establish his kingdom. Before that time, he says that Elijah will appear and he will turn their hearts back to God. This is why Jews always set a place at the table for Elijah at Passover, should he return.

Micah

Micah foresaw a period of peace when the Messiah comes and the beginning of a Golden or Messianic Age.

In this age, people will turn back to God and learn to live in peace. Micah paints a lovely picture of the Torah going out of the Temple in Jerusalem and into the world, symbolising all people living under God's reign and according to His Law. The Messiah would settle arguments between nations, and swords, spears and all the weapons of war would be remoulded into farm equipment for peaceful living.

Micah also prophesied that the Messiah would come from Bethlehem. This was King David's town and as the Messiah would be a descendant of David's, it was appropriate that he should come from here. He would lead the Jews with God's strength and bring about peace.

Isaiah

> For a child has been born to us, a son given to us, and the authority is upon his shoulder, and the wondrous adviser, the mighty God, the everlasting Father, called his name, 'the prince of peace'.
>
> **Isaiah 9, the Tenakh**

Isaiah foretold that the Messiah would reign as king on the throne of David and rule with justice and righteousness forever. He would have God's authority and under his rule there would be peace. He also said that the Messiah would suffer for people's sins.

Has the Messiah come already?

During the Roman occupation of Israel, the Jews renewed their hope for a messiah. They wanted someone to lead them against the Romans and drive their enemy out of the country. There were several revolts led by men claiming to be the Messiah, but they all came to nothing. Jesus of Nazareth was considered to be one of them. After the Romans destroyed the Temple in 70CE, there were more uprisings. The most significant was that of a man called Simon bar Kochba. He was given the title 'Son of the Star', which comes from a prophecy in the book of Numbers in the Jewish scriptures. He was a strong and charismatic leader who rid Jerusalem of the Romans and restarted worship and sacrifice at the site of the old Temple. He set up an independent Jewish state in 132CE, which he ruled for three years before being defeated and killed. The Jews then decided he was not the Messiah.

Modern views about the Messiah in Judaism

In the Middle Ages, Maimonides, a Jewish **rabbi** (teacher of the Torah), wrote a document called 'The 13 Principles of Faith'. The 12th principle was about the coming of the Messiah.

> I believe with perfect faith in the coming of the Messiah, and even though he may delay, nevertheless I anticipate that he will come.
>
> **Principles of Faith 12**

This belief has helped Jews through some very dark times, such as the Holocaust, when those about to die recited it.

▲ A sign on Kingston Avenue in Brooklyn, New York proclaiming that Messiah is coming soon. (Moshiach means Messiah)

Orthodox Jews believe that the Messianic Age is yet to come, when Israel repents and when everyone keeps the Sabbath as it should be kept. Only then will the world be back to what it was at the time of creation. **Hasidic Jews** believe there is one person born in each generation who could potentially be the Messiah. (Hasidic Jews follow a strict religious code and dress in black. They do not cut the hair at the sides of their heads or their beards. Men often wear a black hat.)

Other Jews say that it is impossible to tell when the Messiah will come. Everyone must make up their own minds about it. Many Reform Jews think that the Messianic Age refers to a time of world peace and is not brought in by a specific person, so they do not believe in a messiah as such. Instead, they think that everyone should work towards peace themselves.

What do you know? AO1

1. What is the origin of the word 'messiah'?
2. Outline Jewish teaching about the Messiah.
3. Describe the age of peace that the Messiah will bring about.
4. Outline what Orthodox Jews believe about the Messiah.
5. What do other Jews believe about the Messiah?

What do you understand? AO2

6. Why is belief in a messiah so important to Jewish people?
7. Explain what Jews believe about how the Messiah would change their lives.
8. Explain why Simon bar Kochba was rejected as messiah by the Jews.
9. Explain the phrase, 'they shall beat their swords into ploughshares'.
10. Why are there differing views about the Messiah?

What do you think? AO3

11. How can people help to bring about an age of peace – a Messianic Age?
12. Is it more important for a leader to lead or to be a good person?
13. Is it alright to use any method to bring about peace?

1.4 The world to come

Olam Ha'Ba

Starter: What happens after this life?

Olam Ha'Ba means 'the World to Come'. It is a time when God will bring this world to an end and establish an eternal state of peace, which will last forever. Jews believe that death is not the end but no one is sure what a next life will be like. Some argue that it will be a life in heaven. Others say it will be just like this world but transformed and perfect. What happens after death is in the hands of God. The important thing is to live according to God's laws on Earth and to do one's duty. This is why Jewish people generally spend more time thinking about this life than about a life after death.

> This world is like a lobby before the Olam Ha-Ba. Prepare yourself in the lobby so that you may enter the banquet hall.
>
> **From the Mishnah (first written version of the Oral Torah)**

Jewish beliefs about judgement

There are many differences in Jewish beliefs about life after death and judgement:

- Most Orthodox Jews believe there is only one destination: Olam Ha'Ba. What it is like depends on how you have lived. Daniel, one of the prophets in the Jewish scriptures said that when people died they would wake to everlasting life or everlasting shame. It is their actions that determine their rewards and experience. In other words, all Jews will have a part of Olam Ha'Ba, but each person's experience of it will be different. Some Jews say that life after death will be like this world but transformed and perfect.

- Some Jews believe that if you do not keep God's laws you are cut off from God and from the Jewish community even in the world to come.

- The Hasidic Jews are very pious and some of them believe that the more you enjoy life on Earth, the fewer rewards you will have in Olam Ha'Ba. So some of them limit their pleasures in order to receive a greater reward in the world to come.

What do you know? — AO1

1. Describe Jewish beliefs about Olam Ha'Ba.
2. What do Orthodox Jews believe about judgement?
3. Describe two other views of judgement and the world to come.

What do you understand? — AO2

4. Explain Jewish belief about judgement.
5. Explain why most Jewish people concentrate on life on Earth rather than on the life to come.
6. Explain why there are different views about life after death.
7. Why do some Jews limit earthly pleasure?

What do you think? — AO3

8. What difference would knowing what happens when we die make to the way we live?
9. What is the most important thing about being alive?
10. Is judgement a good or bad thing?

1.5 Mitzvot

Starter: If we did not have free will, would we need rules?

What is mitzvot?

Mitzvot is the plural of 'mitzvah'. They are commandments laid down in the Jewish scriptures. There are 613 of them, divided as follows:

248	365
Positive commands (e.g. 'love God')	Negative commands (e.g. 'do not steal')
Significant because there are 248 bones in a man's body	Significant because there are 365 days in a year

The central mitzvot are the Ten Commandments. Keeping the Law is the aim of every pious Jew. They ask God three times a day to help them keep it:

> O my God, open my heart to Your Torah, and let my soul pursue Your Mitzvot.
>
> **From the Amidah**

The mitzvot fall into two categories: biblical commandments (mitzvot de-oraita), and the rabbinic commandments (mitzvot de-rabbanan). Many no longer apply because they were about the Temple, which no longer exists.

The mitzvot de-oraita (oral mitzvot) were given to Moses by God so that the people could live in the best way possible. So the Law is seen by many Jews as a gift. Orthodox Jews believe the mitzvot are the actual word of God. Those who follow the commandments will be rewarded, but those who disobey or disregard them will be punished.

The mitzvot de-rabbanan (rabbinic mitzvot) were developed over time in order to address new social and political situations as they arose. They are a way of being able to remain Jewish by being close to God even in very difficult situations.

Keeping the mitzvot brings its own reward of a happy and fulfilled life. All adult Jews are responsible to God for keeping the mitzvot. There is a ceremony called **bar mitzvah** when a boy becomes an adult at 13. Girls celebrate **bat mitzvah** at 12 (see page 133).

▲ A boy reading from the Torah at his bar mitzvah (son of the law)

Free will and mitzvot

▲ What moral choices might you have to make today?

If human beings are rewarded for doing right, and punished for doing wrong, they have to be able to choose which they do. Jews believe that when God created humans, He gave them free will so that they could choose whether or not to worship Him.

Humans have two strong desires – to do good (yetzer ha tov) and to do evil (yetzer ha ray). It is their choice to do one or the other. If free will is to mean anything, humans have to live in a world which allows them to make these moral choices.

Adam and Eve had a choice in the Garden of Eden: obey God and refuse to eat the fruit, or disobey God and eat it. If God had already decided that they were to eat the fruit, they would not have had free will and therefore would not have been morally responsible for what they did. In the story, God punishes them, showing that He considered their actions were important because they chose to take them. So He sent them out of the Garden and gave them the opportunity to change.

The Jewish scriptures are full of stories about how humans turn away from God by not keeping the mitzvot. God was patient with them because He believed in their ability to change. Such ability is not possible without free will.

> I have set before you life and death, the blessing and the curse. You shall choose life, so that you and your offspring will live;
> **Deuteronomy 30:19 Tenakh**

The 613 mitzvot are there to help people make the right choices in their behaviour and lifestyle. Keeping them or not keeping them brings consequences that human beings can weigh up for themselves, but their actions will always be their own responsibility.

Mitzvot between people and God

Jews have a special relationship and covenant with God. This means believing in one God and obeying His commandments. The mitzvot are rooted in the belief that there is one God and that His law is true. This is why the first ten mitzvot are about God and can be summarised as follows:

- Know that God exists, that He is One and that there is no other god but Him.
- Have reverence for God's name and remember it is holy. Do not blaspheme or misuse God's name in any way.
- Love God and be in awe of Him.
- Stand for the same things God stands for.
- Pray to God every day and recite the Shema.

The laws between people and God set the rest of the mitzvot in context. Observance of these laws shows that the Jewish people are grateful to God and it gives them a sense of identity. It also means they remember God in their everyday lives. Keeping the mitzvot improves people as human beings, helping them to become good people.

Mitzvot between people and people

Most of the mitzvot are taken up with laws about how people should treat each other, and keeping the laws brings a sense of identity within the Jewish community. The medieval Jewish philosopher, Maimonides, said that mitzvah between people is doubly good, because it fulfils God's command and benefits another person. A religious person who is honest in business and nice to people will inspire others to keep the mitzvot themselves.

The mitzvot are summed up in the command, 'Love God and love your neighbour as yourself.' This does not mean that you put someone else's survival ahead of your own, but that you understand the needs of other people and take their problems seriously.

One rabbi made a list of ways to fulfil this section of the miztvot. He included:

- visiting the sick
- comforting the bereaved
- protecting others from injury
- praising others meaningfully
- feeling joy at the good fortune of others
- welcoming guests into your home.

The mitzvot also say no-one should hold a grudge but look for ways to repair relationships privately.

The mitzvot say that people should show love to everyone but with a special responsibility towards a fellow Jew. They should be especially kind to those who have suffered tragedy, such as widows and orphans.

Activity

Find a copy of the 613 mitzvot and make a list of those you would not find too difficult to keep and a list of the ones you might struggle with.

What do you know? — AO1

1 Describe the two categories of mitzvot.
2 Describe what Jews believe about free will.
3 Describe the role of mitzvot between people and God.
4 Outline how people should observe the mitzvot between each other.

What do you understand? — AO2

5 Why is it important for people to have free will?
6 Explain the purpose of the 613 mitzvot.
7 Explain how keeping the mitzvot brings people closer to God.
8 Explain what it means to love your neighbour as yourself.
9 Explain the importance of making moral choices.

What do you think? — AO3

10 Are our lives too regulated by laws?
11 Which is more important: laws or freedom?
12 Does God's Law ever go out of date?

Essay practice

'It is more important to love people than to love God.' Do you agree? Give reasons to support your answer. Show that you have considered more than one point of view.

Topic 2 Jewish practices and ceremonies

2.1 Worship

Worship in the synagogue

Starter: Why is worship important in religious life?

▲ Inside the Pécs Synagogue, Hungary

The Hebrew word for **synagogue** is 'Beth ha Knesset' (place or house of congregation). It is the place Jews go to worship God together. From the outside, it might look quite ordinary and sometimes the only thing that would tell you it was a synagogue is the Magen David (Star of David).

Services for the Sabbath take place on Friday evenings and on Saturday mornings. The Saturday service can last for two or three hours.

There must be ten adult men (a minyan) present for any service or it cannot happen. The congregation must be dressed modestly and men wear special clothing (see page 128).

Orthodox services are mostly in Hebrew, while other synagogues have a mixture of Hebrew and the local language, for example English. The service can be led by any member of the congregation but there is usually a rabbi present who will generally give the sermon. In Orthodox synagogues, the rabbi is still a man, although that rule may change, but Reform Jews allow women to lead services and to be rabbis. In Britain, the Chief Rabbi is a woman. A **cantor** leads the singing, although no musical instruments are allowed.

The service starts with morning blessings and thanksgiving. This is followed by blessings and psalms, ending with the Song of Moses from Deuteronomy. As the Torah Scrolls are removed from the Ark, the Shema is recited. This is the oldest prayer in Judaism (see page 129). The Scrolls are carried round the synagogue before being laid on the **bimah** and opened at the week's reading. On the Sabbath and festival days, there is a reading from the prophets as well. Then, there are prayers of praise and thanksgiving called the Aleynu – 'Now let us praise the Sovereign of the universe and praise the Creator of the universe ...' Prayers are said for the Queen and the royal family and the service ends with the **Kiddush** (blessing).

Worship at home on Shabbat (Sabbath)

Worship in Judaism is primarily centred in the home. Celebrating the Sabbath is the best example of this practice. Shabbat begins just before sunset on Friday and ends just after sunset on Saturday. It is the law laid down in Exodus 20 that no work should be done on the Sabbath. In observing this law, Jews are fulfilling their dual commandment to remember the Sabbath day and to keep it holy.

Many Jews observe a technology shut-down for the whole of Shabbat, turning off their televisions, computers, laptops and phones. In preparing for Shabbat, the roles of men and women have changed in recent years. Although it is often the women who prepare the home, cleaning, tidying and preparing the food, while the men and boys go to the synagogue on Friday evening, this is not always the case now.

Food for Saturday is often cooked in a slow cooker or using oven timers, as lighting an oven counts as work in many Orthodox households. In the evening, the table is set with the best dishes, a vase of flowers, wine, two special loaves of bread called hallot loaves and candles. The bread is covered with a cloth.

▲ The Shabbat meal is the focal point of the week for Jewish families

Just before Shabbat begins, the mother lights the Shabbat candles and, covering her face, says a special blessing. The two candles represent the man and the woman and lighting them symbolises peace coming into the house.

When those who have been to the synagogue return, the father says the following blessings:

- Over his children: to his sons he says, 'May God make you like Ephraim and Manasseh.' To his daughters he says, 'May God make you like Sarah, Rebecca, Rachel and Leah.'
- He then says another blessing that used to be said by the High Priest: 'May the Lord bless you and keep you. May the light of His countenance rest upon you and give you His peace.'
- Then he blesses his wife from a verse in the book of Proverbs: 'An accomplished woman, who can find? For beyond pearls is her value.'
- The father says a blessing, Kiddush, over the wine and another blessing over **hallot** loaves. This reminds the family that on the Sabbath, God provided a double portion of the wafer-like substance called manna which the Jews at during their wanderings in the desert after the exodus from Egypt.

When all this is done, the family sit down and enjoy the meal together and often sing songs during or after the meal.

Today, the roles of men and women are more flexible. Men often help prepare the house and women often go to the synagogue on Friday evening.

Havdalah

The end of the Sabbath is marked with the Havdalah or separation service. When three stars appear in the sky on Saturday evening, Shabbat is officially over. The time is actually calculated astronomically so it does not matter if it is cloudy. Every family performs a short ritual. First they light a plaited candle and say a blessing over a cup of wine. A spice box is passed round so that the sweet fragrance can stay with everyone over the coming week. Then a blessing is said over the candle flame and the family wish each other a good week: 'Shavuah Tov!' Nearly all the wine is drunk but a little is left to put out the flame.

The importance of Shabbat

Shabbat is important because it brings the family together once a week away from distractions of work and social commitments. It is a day of rest where no work is done, reflecting how God rested on the Sabbath after creating the world. It provides discipline and structure for people's lives and gives them the opportunity to think about God.

Activity

1 In groups, prepare the first part of a Sabbath meal and act out what happens in an average Jewish family. You will need two hallot loaves, two candles and a bottle of wine-coloured liquid (not wine!)

2 Find out why the father refers to Ephraim, Manasseh, Sarah, Rebecca, Rachel and Leah when he blesses his sons and daughters.

What do you know? **AO1**

1 What is a synagogue?

2 Describe a typical Shabbat service in the synagogue.

3 What is Shabbat?

4 Describe the preparations made in the home for Shabbat.

5 What part does the father take in celebrating Shabbat?

6 Describe a Shabbat meal in a Jewish home.

7 Describe the Havdalah service.

What do you understand? **AO2**

8 Explain the importance of Shabbat to Jews.

9 Explain why some synagogues conduct their services entirely in Hebrew and others partly in Hebrew and partly in the local language.

10 Explain why Jews go the synagogue.

11 Explain the symbolism of the two candles lit by the mother at the beginning of Shabbat.

12 Explain the symbolism of the hallot loaves.

13 Why is the spice box passed round at Havdalah?

What do you think? **AO3**

14 Do Jews need to go to the synagogue?

15 Is it more important to live a good life or to worship God?

16 Does worship bring God closer or make Him more remote?

17 Are the words we say to God more important than what we think as we say them?

Prayers

Starter: Why do people pray?

Practising Jews usually pray three times a day: in the morning, in the afternoon and in the evening. Mostly prayers are said at home, but some people go to the synagogue to pray at these times. Prayer is not confined to three times a day – people can pray as often as they like. Praying is important because Jews want to praise and thank God for the things in life that they enjoy, and to pray for people in trouble and for their own needs.

▲ This is a special site for Jews to pray because it is the last standing wall of the Temple in Jerusalem after it was destroyed in 70ce. It used to be called the Wailing Wall because of the centuries of tears shed by Jews longing for the Temple to be rebuilt. They write prayers on scraps of paper and push them into the cracks of the wall

Clothes for prayer

Tefillin: These are two small boxes containing the words of the Shema. One is strapped to the forehead and one to the left arm as a reminder to think about God and His laws. The straps on the forehead are tied in a special knot at the back of the neck, leaving the ends hanging down either side. It reminds the wearer to be loyal to God with their mind. The strap on the arm is wound seven times around the forearm, the wrist and middle finger to remind the wearer to serve God with their strength. Both tefillin act as prompts to pray. In the past, they have only been worn by men, but now, increasing numbers of women want to wear tefillin.

Tallit: This is the large rectangular prayer shawl which men wear during prayer. It is usually white with blue or black stripes. In Reform synagogues, women may also wear the **tallit**. In some Orthodox synagogues, only married men may wear the tallit. The tallit is usually made from wool, cotton or synthetic fabric and has 613 tassels tied to its edges forming a fringe to remind the wearer of the 613 mitzvot (laws). Boys and girls often get their first tallit at their bar or bat mitzvah.

Kippah: This is the head-covering worn by men during prayer. It is a symbol of reverence for God and became common around the second century CE. The **Talmud** says, 'Cover your head in order that the fear of heaven may be upon you.' The cloth and pattern of the **kippah** vary depending on whether a person is Orthodox, Reform or another kind of Jew. The kippah of an Orthodox Jew is often made of suede, while satin is used by many Reform Jews. There is a huge variation in materials and design across the different forms of Judaism. Some have designs on them such as the Star of David. Many Orthodox Jews wear their kippah all the time, except when bathing or in bed.

Tzitzit: In accordance with the Law, the strings attached at the corners of the tallit are knotted into a special pattern called a tzitzit. They remind the wearer of his or her obligations and duties as a Jew. Originally, the tassels were attached to the everyday clothes worn by Jews. Today, people do not wear these kinds of clothes anymore, so the tallit is worn specifically to fulfil the command from the Torah. In Orthodox services you can see people gathering up the tassels and kissing them when the paragraph referring to them in the Torah is read.

The Amidah

One of the prayers is called the silent prayer, the Amidah. This is said standing up. People praying this prayer will take three steps backwards then forwards. Their lips move as they pray but only God can hear them. They want to develop a close relationship between themselves and God, so private prayer is an important part of their day.

Prayers at the synagogue

There are daily prayers in the synagogue. The most common book used for prayer is the **siddur** which is a book of set prayers. They remind Jews of their inheritance – that they are part of an ancient community. The act of praying with other Jews gives a sense of unity not only with each other but with all Jews everywhere. They know that there are Jews all over the world praying the same prayers. The word 'siddur' means 'order' and has the same Hebrew root as '**seder**', the Passover meal. These prayers were collected during the first four or five centuries CE but many reflect ideas from much earlier than that, and have developed up to this day.

The Shema

The most important prayer is the Shema because it summarises and reinforces what every Jew believes about God (see page 112). Jews recite the Shema twice a day, during morning and evening prayers. The prayer reminds them that there is only one God and that they should love Him with all their strength and keep His laws. The first part of the Shema is the part used the most.

> ### The first part of the Shema
>
> Hear, O Israel, the Lord our God, the Lord is One. Blessed be the name of the glory of His kingdom forever and ever. You shall love the Lord your God with all your heart, with all your soul, with all your might. And these words which I command you today shall be upon your heart. You shall teach them thoroughly to your children, and you shall speak of them when you sit in your house and when you walk on the road, when you lie down and when you rise. You shall bind them as a sign upon your hand, and they shall be for you a reminder between your eyes. And you shall write them upon the doorposts of your house and upon your gates.

Activity

Research kippah designs and create your own. Explain what your design symbolises and why you chose it.

What do you know?

1 Describe the daily prayer routine of practising Jews.
2 What is the Amidah?
3 What is the Shema?
4 What is the siddur?
5 Describe what Jews wear for prayer.

What do you understand?

6 Explain why Jews pray.
7 Why is the Shema so important?
8 Explain the significance of the siddur.
9 Explain the symbolism of the tallit and tzitzit.
10 Why do Jews wear a tefillin?
11 What is the significance of the kippah?

What do you think?

12 Is there any point praying?
13 What is the most important religious item worn by Jews?
14 Is it better to pray by yourself or to pray with others?
15 Do people need set times and routines for prayer?

2.2 Synagogue

Starter: What makes a building religious or holy?

Religious features and layout of the synagogue

The ark

The **ark** is a cupboard containing the Sefer Torah. The Sefer Torah is made up of the five books of Moses. In most synagogues the ark is built into the wall that faces Jerusalem. Some arks have beautifully ornate doors while others are plain. The ark is a reminder of the Ark of the Covenant that used to be kept in a very special part of the Temple, the Holy of Holies, in Jerusalem. In many synagogues, the tablets of the Ten Commandments are placed on either side of the ark. Above the ark is the **ner tamid**.

The ner tamid

The ner tamid is the everlasting light, which burns above the ark. It represents the lamp that used to burn in the Temple in Jerusalem. It is a symbol of God's nature and a reminder that the Jewish family will be everlasting. It also symbolises the light from the original **menorah** that stood in front of the ark in the Temple.

The menorah

The menorah is a seven-branched candlestick that has been a symbol of Judaism since ancient times. It was made of hammered gold and originally used in the portable sanctuary set up by Moses in the desert and later placed in the Temple in Jerusalem.

Olive oil of the best quality was burned to light the lamps every day. The menorahs seen in synagogues today represent the one that used to stand in the Temple. They symbolise God's presence, reminding Jews of His creation of the world in seven days. It is also a symbol of wisdom according to the Talmud: the seven lamps point to branches of human knowledge, guided by the light of God.

The bimah

The Torah is read from a special platform called a bimah. It is the centre of the synagogue and often surrounded by a rail. The seating is arranged around it so that everyone can hear the reading and the sermon. The rabbi stands here when they take the service. The bimah is usually made of wood, though in ancient times they were made of stone. When the Torah scrolls are taken out of the ark, they are laid on the bimah and unrolled to the appropriate reading.

Seating in the synagogue

In some synagogues, men and women sit separately, divided by a screen called a **mechitzah**. This is because at the time when Jews worshipped in the Temple, it was thought that men and women should not pray together in case men were distracted. Centuries later, Muslims adopted the same practice and still have segregated worship today. Women were therefore given seats in a gallery away from the men. This practice carried over into synagogues and is still in force within Orthodox Judaism. Not all synagogues have galleries, so some of the seating round the bimah is designated for women, with a screen between them and the men's seats. However, Reform Jews no longer segregate the sexes.

2.3 Law

The Tenakh

Tenakh is the Hebrew word for the Jewish Bible. It contains:

- the Law – Torah
- the prophets – Nevi'im
- the writings – Ketuvim.

The T, N and K put together make up the word TeNaKh, hence its name.

For Jews, the most important part of the Tenakh is the Torah, where the Law is written. There are five books in the Torah – Genesis, Exodus, Leviticus, Numbers and Deuteronomy. Here the Law or Mitzvot (see page 122) is explained in considerable detail. It covers laws about the way to celebrate festivals, how to lead lives that are pleasing to God, how, what, why and when to offer sacrifices and many other laws. Orthodox Jews try to keep as many laws as they can. Reform Jews believe that what is written in the Tenakh may have been how Jews lived in the past, but many of its laws are not relevant today.

The Talmud

Between 200 and 500CE, Jewish rabbis began to make a collection of teachings that had been handed down orally since the time of Moses. It is made up of two parts: part one is called the **Mishnah**, which is the oral teaching of the rabbis. Part two is called the **Gemara**. The Gemara is a commentary on the oral laws. It gives a lot of extra detail about the laws in the Torah and advice on how individual laws can be kept. Together, the Mishnah and Gemara form the Talmud. The Talmud is often referred to as 'the oral law' because it describes laws that were passed down by word of mouth from rabbi to rabbi.

The Torah in worship

The Torah that is kept in the synagogue is called the Sefer Torah. It is handwritten in Hebrew on animal skin and attached to large rollers. There are no vowels or punctuation and it takes practice to read it. The Sefer Torah is kept in the ark and is the focal point of worship. It is also where all Jewish teaching and customs originate. It is wrapped in richly embroidered cloth, and bells and decorations hang from it.

When the Sefer Torah is removed from the ark at the beginning of a service, it is processed around the synagogue before being placed on the bimah. A portion is read each week. The person reading it uses a special pointer called a yad because people are not allowed to touch the parchment.

The Torah is so important that if it is torn or damaged, it has to be buried, so enormous care is taken of it. At the end of the service, the Torah is held up and a prayer is said before putting it back in the ark. Many of the prayers used during the service are taken from the Torah including the Shema, which is from Deuteronomy.

▲ This Torah scroll has been taken from the ark and is being processed round the synagogue

What do you know? **AO1**

1 Describe the ark and the ner tamid.
2 What is the bimah and what is it used for?
3 What is the menorah and what do Jews remember when they see it?
4 What are the Tenakh and the Talmud?
5 How is the Torah used during worship?

What do you understand? **AO2**

6 Explain the symbolism of the ner tamid.
7 Explain the significance of the menorah.
8 Why do some Jewish synagogues separate men and women?
9 Explain the importance of the Tenakh and the Talmud to Jewish people.
10 Why is the Torah treated with such respect?

What do you think? **AO3**

12 Should men and women sit separately during religious services?
13 What is the most important feature in a synagogue?
14 Do you think places of worship need anything other than chairs to sit on?
15 Do religious symbols and ritual keep faith alive?

2.4 Rites of passage

Starter: What would be the most important rite of passage for you?

The three main rites of passage in Judaism are birth, bar or bat mitzvah and marriage. All mark significant life events and add to the richness of Jewish life.

Birth ceremonies: circumcision (brit milah)

The birth of a baby in Judaism is celebrated as a gift from God. Girls have a naming ceremony in the synagogue, but for boys it is different. God told Abraham that all males should be circumcised as a sign of the covenant He made with him. **Circumcision** is the removal of the baby boy's foreskin and is a ritual in both Judaism and Islam as both religions claim their descent through Abraham. The ceremony is performed by a **mohel**, a person medically and religiously qualified to do it, on the eighth day after birth and nearly always at home. It is a great honour to be chosen to be the 'sandek', the companion of the child and the one who holds the baby during the ceremony. Traditionally, he either holds the baby across his knees or thighs, or hands the baby to the mohel. The ceremony ends with the Kiddush over a glass of wine.

Bar and bat mitzvah

When a boy reaches the age of 13, he is considered responsible for keeping the mitzvot himself. The 'bar' in bar mitzvah means son, so he has literally become the son of the mitzvot. The occasion is marked with a ceremony in the synagogue and relations and friends attend. Before the day, boys must study and prepare for it carefully. On the day, boys wear the tallit and tefillin for the first time.

Orthodox Jewish girls have a smaller ceremony called 'bat chayil' which means 'daughter of worth'

when they are 12. In Reform synagogues, girls become bat mitzvah (daughter of the mitzvot) and take on more of the same responsibilities as boys, such as reading from the Torah. Like boys, they can wear the tallit.

Preparation includes learning to perform domestic tasks at home (because home is the centre of Jewish life) and being able to read Hebrew reasonably fluently. During the ceremony, boys and/or girls will be expected to read aloud from the Torah for the first time in public. The importance of this rite of passage is that boys and girls make it their own responsibility to observe the mitzvot.

After the ceremony, there is a party with a special meal.

▲ What might this girl be feeling right now, as she reads the Torah in the synagogue for the first time?

Marriage

▲ Comment on what you see in the photo

Most of Jewish teaching on marriage is in the Talmud, which explains how to find a partner, how the wedding should be conducted and how the husband and wife should treat each other. Like most traditions, there are two stages to marriage: the engagement or **kiddushin**, and the wedding or nisuin.

Huppah

During the ceremony, the couple stand under a canopy called a **huppah**. Sometimes this is a tallit, as in the picture. The huppah is a symbol of their future home together. It is open on all sides as a sign of hospitality and the couple are led up to it by their parents. The bride circles the groom seven times, like the Jews circled Jericho before the walls came down. This symbolises the destruction of hurtful barriers between the couple. The rabbi then gives a talk about what it means to be married. The rabbi says a blessing over a cup of wine from which the bride and groom both drink.

Ketubah

The rabbi then reads the **ketubah** or marriage contract, which is signed by two witnesses before the ceremony. Traditionally, the ketubah outlines the rights and responsibilities the man will take in relation to his wife. This was to protect the wife. It essentially specifies an amount of money to be paid to the wife should the marriage come to an end. She would also be entitled to clothing and other essentials. It is written in Aramaic because

it dates from the second or third century BCE, when the common language in Israel was Aramaic.

Then the groom puts a ring onto the first finger of his bride's right hand. The rabbi and the guests recite the seven blessings that they hope God will bestow on the couple. Finally, the groom crushes a glass with his foot. This reminds them that just as the Temple was destroyed in 70CE, so they should be prepared for times when life gets tough. After that the couple are officially married. Everyone shouts 'Mozel tov!' – 'Congratulations!'

What do you know? **AO1**

1. What takes place on the eighth day after a boy is born in a Jewish family?
2. Describe what happens at a bar or bat mitzvah.
3. Outline what happens at a Jewish wedding.
4. What is a huppah?
5. What is the ketubah?

What do you understand? **AO2**

6. Explain why Jewish boys are circumcised.
7. What is the role of a sandek?
8. What is the significance of the bar mitzvah ceremony?
9. Explain why the ketubah is signed and read at Jewish marriages.

What do you think? **AO3**

10. Which is the most important Jewish rite of passage?
11. Which is the most important symbol at a Jewish wedding?
12. Are 12 and 13 too young for bat and bar mitzvah?

2.5 Festivals

Starter: What festivals does your school observe and why?

Although Shabbat is the most important festival and celebrated every week, the Jewish calendar has 26 big festivals which run right through the year. Festivals:

- provide a sense of community through worshipping and praying together
- remind people of their religion
- keep people in touch with their roots and shared heritage
- are usually happy occasions when families get together, and people often buy new clothes and send greeting cards to family and friends.

Rosh Hashanah is the Jewish New Year celebration, with Yom Kippur following, usually ten days after, in September and/or October. The dates are not fixed because Jews follow a lunar calendar which changes from year to year. These festivals are central to the Jewish year. Jews who do not celebrate other festivals will usually try to get to the synagogue for these. They are an important time to think about life, the past year and the one to come.

Rosh Hashanah

Rosh Hashanah means 'head of the year'. The Talmud says that God writes down a person's good and bad actions from the past year and decides what sort of year they will have. People greet each other with the words, 'May you be inscribed (in the Book of Life) for a good year.' It is a day of accountability, so Jews spend a lot of time thinking back over what they have done and what they should have done. They make peace with each other and many people visit the graves of their relations. Every day during this festival, the **shofar**, a ram's horn, is blown 100 times in the synagogue. The shofar sounds like weeping as the people weep for their sins. Tradition says that on Rosh Hashanah, God forgave Adam his sin.

▲ An example of the shofar horn

As well as a service in the synagogue, families carry out traditions at home. At the Rosh Hashanah meal, people dip special round pieces of hallot, and pieces of apple, in honey and ask God to give them a sweet year. After the meal, they might go outside to where there is running water and throw crumbs into the water. This casting of crumbs symbolises the casting away of their sins. It is called **tashlikh**.

This leads into the ten days of repentance, or 'ten days of returning', between Rosh Hashanah and Yom Kippur. During this time, everyone must try to make amends for what they have done wrong and say sorry to those they have hurt. Judaism teaches that unless a person has asked forgiveness from someone they have wronged, God will not forgive them.

Yom Kippur

Yom Kippur ends the days of repentance, and God's decision regarding the year ahead for each person has been sealed in the Book of Life. Yom Kippur is sometimes called the Shabbat Shabbaton (the ultimate Sabbath). Jews turn from asking each other for forgiveness to asking God for forgiveness, usually by fasting.

In the Jewish scriptures, Yom Kippur is referred to as the Day of Atonement. In ancient days, a goat without any defects was brought to the High Priest. He would place his hands on the head of the goat, symbolically transferring the sins of the people to the goat. The 'scapegoat' would then be sent into the desert carrying the sins away. The High Priest would enter the Holy of Holies on this day only, to beg God to forgive His people.

On the day

Yom Kippur begins at sunset, but before it starts, the meal must be eaten. Then the candles are lit and the 25-hour fast begins. The father blesses the children so that their names may be sealed in the Book of Life. Parents and children ask each other for forgiveness for any hurt they might have caused over the past year. The following day, everyone goes to the synagogue where they pray for several hours, asking God's forgiveness. Some people wear white to symbolise purity. At the evening service, Jews cancel promises they made to God but that they know they will not be able to keep. The prayer they use is called the Kol Nidre.

Pesach (Passover)

Pesach happens in the spring. It is when Jews remember the night of the tenth plague – when the angel of death passed over Egypt and killed all firstborn males, but Jewish homes were spared. Jews remember how Pharaoh let them go and Moses led them out of Egypt, in what became known as the Exodus. They are reminded of God's power and His special covenant with His people. It is an important festival because it celebrates national freedom, identity as a nation under God and family unity.

Preparations for Pesach

Everything containing yeast has to be removed from the home. Yeast makes bread rise. During the Exodus there was no time for this, so Jews ate unleavened bread (without yeast). Matzot, the flatbread, is the only kind Jews are allowed to eat at Pesach.

Seder wine

Jews drink four glasses of wine during the Seder meal to remember the four promises God made to Moses: to bring Jews out of captivity, to welcome them with an outstretched arm, to make them his people and to be their God.

A door is always left open and a place laid for Elijah, in the hope that he will return and announce the return of the Messiah at Passover. A fifth glass of wine is poured.

At Pesach, it is tradition for the youngest child to ask why this day is special and for the oldest person to read the story of the Exodus.

The Seder meal

Beitza: a roasted egg, a symbol of new life after Egypt. It is not eaten.

Charoset: a mixture of fruit, nuts and spices that represents the mortar used by the slaves in making bricks.

Karpas: parsley and a spring vegetable are signs of new life. They are dipped in salt water which symbolises the tears of the slaves.

Maror: bitter herbs such as lettuce or horseradish represent the bitterness of slavery.

Zeroa: roasted shankbone represents the lamb that was killed on the night of the Passover. It also represents all the lambs sacrificed in the Temple before it was destroyed in 70CE.

Hanukkah – the festival of lights

▲ What might these boys be thinking as they look at the Hanukkah candlestick?

160BCE

Hanukkah is a minor festival all about hope and the presence of God. It is a winter festival; the light shining in the dark winter evenings is deeply symbolic. Hanukkah has its origin in something that happened over 2000 years ago: the Syrian Greeks had invaded Israel and worship of God was forbidden on pain of death. At last, under the leadership of Judas Maccabeus, the Greeks were thrown out of Jerusalem and the Temple could be rededicated to God. But there was a problem. There was only enough oil to keep the lamp in the Temple burning for one night. However, they lit it anyway and to everyone's amazement it burned continuously for the eight days it took to get more oil.

On the day

At Hanukkah, a special candlestick is used which has eight candleholders. The candle in the middle is lit first, and the other seven candles are lit from this candle. On the first evening one candle is lit, on the second two are lit and so on until they are all alight. Remembering the oil that did not run out, oil is used in cooking special foods such as latkes and loukoumades. They represent the cakes eaten by the men in Judas Maccabeus' army. People have parties to celebrate the festival and give presents to each other. Traditional songs such as this one are sung:

My refuge, my rock of salvation!
It is a pleasure to sing Your praises.
Let our house of prayer be restored.
And there we will offer You our thanks.

A traditional Hanukkah game is played with a four-sided spinning top called a dreidel. A letter is carved on each side of the dreidel. Together they stand for the words: 'A great miracle happened there.' In Israel, the last word on the dreidel is 'here'.

Activity

Design a greeting card for one of the festivals explored in this chapter. Think about what is remembered and celebrated at the festival and incorporate those ideas into the design and wording.

What do you know? **AO1**

1 Outline what the festivals of Rosh Hashanah and Yom Kippur are about.
2 What is the origin of Yom Kippur?
3 Describe how Jews keep Yom Kippur.
4 Describe how Rosh Hashanah is celebrated.
5 Outline what Jews remember at Pesach.
6 Describe how Pesach is celebrated.
7 What do Jews remember at Hanukkah?

What do you understand? **AO2**

8 Why are the festivals of Rosh Hashanah and Yom Kippur serious occasions for Jews?
9 Why are Rosh Hashanah and Yom Kippur central to Judaism?
10 Explain the significance of the Seder meal at Pesach.
11 Explain why Pesach is an important festival for Jews.
12 Explain why Hanukkah is a festival of hope.

What do you think? **AO3**

13 Is any Jewish festival more important than the others?
14 Is keeping festivals the best way to learn about your faith?
15 Is Yom Kippur more important today than Passover?

2.6 Dietary and food laws

Starter: Does it matter what we eat?

What we eat says something about who we are. People from different countries eat different things because of what is available to eat in different parts of the world, and because of what they believe. Jews observe laws about what they can and cannot eat, and about food combinations and preparation. This is because the Torah laid down clear instructions about it. Keeping these laws reminds Jews of their faith and of their covenant with God. However, the way Jews observe dietary laws varies widely.

Kashrut in Orthodox and Reform Judaism

▲ A kosher McDonalds in Beit Shemesh, Israel

Orthodox Jews will only eat food that has a reliable kosher certificate and they will never eat in a restaurant unless it has Orthodox certification. They will probably not eat in the house of anyone who is not an Orthodox Jew. They see the keeping of **kashrut** laws as a fundamental part of their faith. To them, it is showing solidarity with Jews all over the world as they live as God's covenant people.

Reform Jews differ in how they observe kashrut. Some find remembering that spirituality and all things physical are not separate in the eyes of God is helpful

in their daily living. They like the way that such thinking transforms each moment from the mundane to the special. Other Reform thinkers believe that the early Mosaic and Rabbinical laws about priestly purity, diet and dress, have no relevance today. They think that these laws are a barrier to practising their faith, rather than helping them.

Kosher

Kosher means suitable or pure and refers mainly to food. Kosher food has its origins in the very foundation of the Jewish nation after Moses had led the people out of Egypt. As a nation under God, they had to be different from all the other tribes who lived around them and worshipped pagan gods. One of the ways they became different was through the food they ate and, more importantly, what they did not eat.

Trefa

Food that is not kosher is commonly referred to as **trefa**. Trefa means 'torn'. The commandment in the Torah forbids the eating of any animal whose flesh has been torn by other animals. The Torah lists a huge range of food that is trefa. Jews are allowed to eat meat from animals that chew the cud and have cloven (split) hooves. Beef and lamb for example, are kosher foods but pork is trefa. Fish with scales, fins and backbones are kosher, but shellfish are trefa. Some birds may not be eaten, for example owl, vulture and swan. Kosher birds include goose, duck and chicken. Insects are forbidden, so great care has to be taken to remove them from vegetables such as cabbage or lettuce.

Blood is a symbol of life and therefore sacred to Jews, so it too is trefa. All animals have to be slaughtered in such a way as to drain the carcass of blood. This ritual method is called shechitah and is performed by a shochet, a person who is specially trained. Many people say that the quick, clean cut across the throat is the most humane way to slaughter an animal.

Kashrut laws

Kashrut is the Jewish law that deals with food that can and cannot be eaten. It also deals with the way food is prepared, what foods can be eaten together and what cannot. It also has something to say about the clothes Jews wear, for example, women may not wear men's clothing and vice versa. Mixed-fibre cloth may not be worn, and wool and linen may not be sewn together.

One kashrut law in particular has a huge impact on life in a Jewish household and community: the rule that meat and dairy cannot be cooked or served in the same pots and pans, and cannot be eaten together. There can be up to six hours between the consumption of meat and being able to eat anything with dairy in it, for example chocolate or ice cream.

When preparing a meal or clearing up afterwards, Jews have to keep the dishes separate. Dishwashers can be a problem unless they have separate trays or you can run them with separate meat and dairy loads. Most Jewish kitchens have two sinks and two sets of cutlery, crockery and utensils, so that meat and dairy can be prepared separately. Glass is the only thing that can be used for both meat and dairy. Synagogues have two kitchens, one for dairy and one for meat.

Jews observe kashrut laws:

- out of obedience to the Torah
- to mark themselves different from other nations
- to keep themselves holy.

Kashrut is not kept for hygienic reasons, although some argue that there are health benefits from doing so.

▲ With so much processed and pre-packaged food, labelling becomes very important when looking for kosher food

Activity
Write a menu for a Jewish family. All the ingredients must be kosher.

What do you know? **AO1**
1 What do the terms 'kosher' and 'trefa' mean?
2 What is the origin of kosher?
3 What type of meat and fish products are kosher?
4 What are kashrut laws?
5 What do Orthodox Jews believe about kashrut laws?
6 How do Reform Jews differ from Orthodox Jews in how they view kashrut laws?

What do you understand? **AO2**
7 Explain why kosher rules are important to the Jewish people.
8 Explain how keeping meat and dairy separate affects Jewish life.
9 Explain why Jewish people keep kashrut laws.
10 Explain why some Jews are less strict about making sure everything is kosher.

What do you think? **AO3**
11 Is keeping kashrut the most important thing about being Jewish?
12 What food laws would you create for today's world?

Essay practice
'Jewish food laws are irrelevant in today's world.' Do you agree? Give reasons to support your answer. Show that you have considered more than one point of view.

Section F Sikhism

Topic 1 Sikh beliefs and teachings

1.1 God's nature

Starter: What is God like?

Mul Mantra

The Mul Mantra is the most important piece of Sikh writing. All their teaching is rooted in it and it is what keeps Sikhs going in their daily lives. The Mul Mantra is the opening hymn of the **Guru Granth Sahib**, the Sikhs' holy book, and it is the prayer all Sikhs say every morning (see below). It is their '**Japji**' (morning prayer).

What does the Mul Mantra teach that is so important?

1 **God is truth.**
   'Truth is the beginning, Truth when time began, Truth even now and for always.' In other words God has always existed. He is outside time so He does not change like we do. God sees everything in its proper perspective, unlike us who only understand things within the context of time.

2 **God is creator.**
   Sikhs believe that God designed and created many universes and that they have no limit. They believe that everything on Earth evolved:

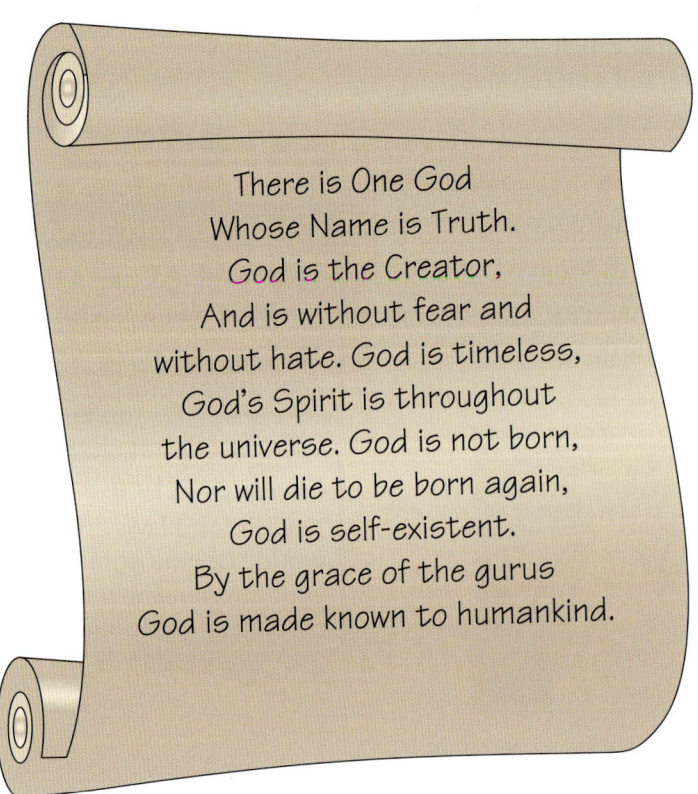

There is One God
Whose Name is Truth.
God is the Creator,
And is without fear and
without hate. God is timeless,
God's Spirit is throughout
the universe. God is not born,
Nor will die to be born again,
God is self-existent.
By the grace of the gurus
God is made known to humankind.

air, water, lower forms of life, plants, fish, birds, animals and human beings.

3 **God exists completely in Himself.**
He does not intervene in the lives of human beings, nor does He come to Earth as an avatar or incarnation. That is why Sikhs do not worship images of God because they are the work of human hands and not God.

4 **God can be known in a personal way.**
This can be through prayer and meditation even though God is beyond His creation. Sikhs repeat the name of God and meditate on it in a practice called Nam Japna. They use lots of different phrases in their meditation – here are a few of the most popular ones: Sat Naam – the Eternal Reality, Akal Purakh – the Eternal One, and **Waheguru** – Wonderful Lord. His names reflect His character and hurt no one and according to the last **guru**, Gobind Singh, there are over 900 of them.

5 **God is directly accessible to all human beings.**
This is through the teachings of the gurus. The gurus were men who taught the people about God (see pages 148–150).

'The True One is not far from us but resides within us.' (Guru Arjan)

6 **God is not exclusive to one religion or people.**
No one can claim the monopoly on the truth. Different religions might come to God via different paths but they are led to the same truth.

What do you know?

1 What is the Mul Mantra?
2 Outline what Sikhs believe about God.
3 According to Sikh tradition, how can God be known to human beings?
4 What are the most popular names Sikhs use to address God?
5 Where might you find the Ik Onkar displayed?

What do you understand?

6 Explain how Sikhs believe they can know God.
7 What does the Mul Mantra teach about the nature of God?
8 'God is self-existent', that is He exists completely in Himself. Explain what is meant by this phrase.
9 What does it mean for God to be timeless?
10 Explain why Sikhs do not worship images of God.

What do you think? **AO3**

11 Is there any evidence of God?
12 What is the most important characteristic of God?
13 What might be the problems and advantages of seeing God as a mystery?

▲ These letters read 'Ik Onkar', which means 'One God'. Sikhs believe that there is only one God and He is the only one to be worshipped. You will often see the words displayed in Sikh homes and nearly always in the gurdwara where Sikhs worship

Human life as an opportunity to unite with God

In Sikhism, the main aim of life is to unite with God, but what does this mean?

- Sikhs teach that everyone has a divine spark in them that wants to be part of God. They say that there are lots of opportunities in life to do this and everyone has to be on the lookout for anything that might distract them from it. How you live your life is therefore very important.
- If a person follows their religion properly, whatever it might be, they will get back to God.
- We have seen that everything evolves and the soul is no different. It evolves and becomes purer and purer through many lifetimes. Then it can reunite with the 'Supreme Soul'.
- In practice, this means that Sikhs work hard at the relationships they make and at the work they do. They give up their time and money unselfishly, they study the **gurbani** (teachings of the gurus) and they meditate.

Gurmukh: being God-centred and eliminating the ego

Gurmukh is a Punjabi word and means to be God-centred. Sikhs aim to become closer to God in three main ways:

- through meditation on the names of God
- through concentration on the shabad – the hymns in the Guru Granth Sahib
- through following the teachings of the gurus.

Gurmukhs have achieved this. In a way, it means such people have truly met with the guru inside themselves. They are calm and focused, and live good, clean lives which support the spirit and do not work against it by giving in to the ego. The ego (**haumi**) is that selfish part of us which puts pleasing ourselves first. This stops us thinking about God and means we are more likely to indulge our senses, live selfishly and give in to the worst human desires such as envy, greed and anger. A person who has given in is called '**Manmukh**'.

Gurmukhs, on the other hand, have turned their faces towards the guru and in the lives they lead show everyone that they are the kind of people all Sikhs should try to become. They scrupulously follow the gurus' teaching to the letter and their lives are inspired by God. They are so close to God that you could say that they and the words of the gurus have become one. They are said to have 'bathed in the pool of truth' and truth fills their minds. Their actions are always good, their lives are free of human attachments, and pleasure and pain no longer bother them. They have concentrated so hard on the word of the gurus that they have successfully burned away their egos.

However, this does not mean that they have abandoned their responsibilities or live like hermits away from other people. It means that they rise above the natural pull of the world and give their lives in service (**sewa**) to others.

▲ Gurmukh: What do you think it means to bathe in the pool of truth?

Karma and rebirth

> As she has planted, so does she harvest; such is the field of karma.
>
> **Guru Granth Sahib**

Sikhs believe that all a person's actions have consequences, some good and some bad. **Karma** is the word that describes this. It is your karma that determines what life form your soul moves to next. The soul lives through many existences such as plants and animals before being born into a human body. This shows the importance of human life. Humans are the only beings who know the difference between right and wrong.

If there is still work to be done to bring your soul into close union with God, your karma will cause you to be reborn. If you have led a particularly bad life, you might even return as an animal. On the other hand, if you live a life of meditation on God and the teachings of the gurus, in service to others and in obedience to the word of the gurus, your karma will allow you to achieve **mukti**.

Mukti

Mukti means freedom from the cycle of birth, death and rebirth. Mukti is union with God. Sikhs believe that the barriers to achieving mukti are five specific things called the five vices:

- lust
- anger
- pride
- greed
- worldly attachment

They believe that a materialistic view of the world keeps a person out of touch with God and too attached to worldly things. It makes them self-centred rather than God-centred. The gurus teach that everything to do with the world is an illusion (maya), not in the sense that people and things are not real, but that they do not last. Only God is eternal.

Activity

Make a diagram to show the things that Sikhs believe prevent us from achieving mukti and those things that help.

What do you know? **AO1**

1 Describe what Sikhs believe about the divine spark.
2 Outline what steps Sikhs can take to unite with God.
3 What does the word 'gurmukh' refer to?
4 How can a person become gurmukh?
5 Describe the kind of life a gurmukh might live.
6 What are karma and mukti?
7 Outline what Sikhs believe about life and death.

What do you understand? **AO2**

8 Explain why it might take many lifetimes for a person to be united with God.
9 Explain why it is important for Sikhs to become gurmukh.
10 Explain how a person's ego stops them thinking about God.
11 Explain why working towards a good karma is so important for Sikhs.
12 Explain the Sikh concept of mukti.
13 Explain what Sikhs believe about reincarnation.

What do you think? **AO3**

14 Does belief in reincarnation make you more likely to lead a good life?
15 Is it more important to keep trying to lead a good life or to succeed?

1.2 Service to others

Guru Gobind Singh and the Khalsa

Starter: Why are names important?

Guru Gobind Rai was only nine when he became guru in 1675. (He took the name Singh later.) His father, along with other Sikhs, had been **martyred** because he refused to give up his Sikh faith. However, Guru Gobind Rai had help from wise older Sikhs and he learned military strategy along with studying the sacred texts of the gurus. By the time he reached his 30th birthday, he knew Sikhism demanded some radical redirection to deal with the Sikhs' situation. They needed a strong leader to unite them to overcome their persecution and encourage a sense of identity and belonging. Some argue that the wearing of **the Five Ks** (see page 166) started here. Certainly his creation of the **Khalsa** laid the foundation of Sikhism as it is practised today.

The creation of the Khalsa

It is 1699 and time for the spring festival of Vaisakhi. Guru Gobind Rai lives in Anandpur, which is in the Punjab region of India. He invites Sikhs from all over India to come to Anandpur. They assemble in a large open space. Gobind Rai stands in front of his tent facing the crowd. He has a long curved sword (khanda) in his hand and he holds it aloft crying out in a loud voice, 'I need a head! Will any of you loyal Sikhs give me your head?'

There is an astonished silence as everyone looks at one another nervously. Then one man raises his hand and comes forward. 'I will give you my head,' he says and goes with the guru into the tent. The flaps close behind them, hiding them from view. The crowd wait. Those nearest the front hear the swish of the sword and the sound of something heavy hitting the ground. The guru returns, his sword dripping with blood. He waves it aloft again.

'I want another head!' he roars.

This time there is a longer wait for someone to respond before another man steps forward. He too goes into the tent with the guru. Again the guru returns with a blood-stained sword.

'And another head!' he cries as the blood drips down the blade and onto the grass.

Three more men offer their lives to Guru Gobind Rai. The crowd shuffle about trying to see what is happening. Why has their guru killed all these men, they ask each other, but no one knows.

A silence falls as everyone wonders what will happen next. The last volunteer has disappeared into the tent and there is a long pause. Eventually, the guru comes back out to face the crowd once more, but this time he has with him the five men who had willingly offered their heads, alive and unharmed. There is a gasp from the crowd.

Dramatically, Guru Gobind Rai throws back the flaps of his tent to reveal the carcasses of five goats. Instead of chopping off the heads of the five men, the guru had cut off the heads of five goats. Each man had believed he was going to his death.

Now gone were the clothes they had been wearing that morning. Instead they were all dressed the same: they wore turbans on their heads, tunics of the same colour, each tied round the waist with a cummerbund.

'This,' announces the guru, 'is the kind of self-sacrifice in the name of love I want from my leaders. These five men will form my "Khalsa" – the company of the pure. These five brave people are my "Panj Payares" – my five beloved ones, my blessed ones!'. They live the truth of the hymn, 'If you wish to play the game of love, come my way, with your head on the palm of your hand' (Guru Granth Sahib (GGS) p.1412).

The crowd roars their approval but the guru waves his hand for silence. 'I and my Panj Payares and any future man in my Khalsa will be as brave as a lion so from now onwards we shall take the name "Singh" and "Kaur". I am no longer Gobind Rai but Gobind Singh – the lion-heart!'

Again the crowd roars their approval. Guru Gobind Singh calls for a large iron bowl. In it he mixes sugar and water and stirs it with his sword. He gives each man some of the amrit (the sugar–water mixture) to drink and after they have all drunk, he sprinkles the rest over their hair and on their eyes. The five men declare that the Khalsa and victory belong to God. This baptism ritual will become known as the 'amrit ceremony' and every Sikh entering the Khalsa will go through it.

*

Note: There is more than one version of this story. In one, the five people are actually killed and brought back to life and in another, Guru Gobind Singh asks for volunteers and there is no bloodshed at all.

The names Singh and Kaur

The origin of the Sikh names, 'Singh' for men and 'Kaur' for women, goes back to this event. The forming of the Khalsa was the beginning of a new era of equality. In India, society was divided horizontally into castes or classes. Higher castes did not mix with those in lower castes. Particular occupations were associated with the different castes so it was a divided hierarchical society. The Khalsa changed all this. Under Khalsa rules, people would no longer be identified and classified by their job or the family they were born into. Instead, everyone would become an equal member of the Sikh community. For this reason, all men would be given the name 'Singh', which means lion, and women would be given the name 'Kaur', meaning princess. Their names would show the world they were equal. Today, Sikhs are given these names at their Khalsa ceremony when they are old enough to take the responsibilities of Sikh faith themselves.

Activity
Imagine you were one of the five men who offered your head to the Guru. Write an account of your experience.

Equality of all human beings

Starter: Do we live in an equal society? What does it mean to be treated equally? Should everybody be treated equally? Does being treated equally mean being treated in the same way?

Sikhs believe that all people are equal because they believe that God created the world and all humanity. People should not be divided because of race, gender, faith, ability, job or address. It is what people do that counts.

The gurus rejected the idea that some people were more superior than others. In a caste-based society this was radical thinking.

Sikhs have two main ways to demonstrate that all people are equal:
1   through having the same names – Singh and Kaur
2   through the langar.

The **langar** is the kitchen attached to every **gurdwara**. Following the example of the gurus, it is open to anyone who is hungry. No one is turned away. Sitting together and eating the same food from the same bowls is a powerful expression of equality. As one Sikh put it:

Sikhism is all about equality, this is why you go to the Gurdwara and eat Langar. It's not just a free meal for you to enjoy. It's a symbol of equality and respect of all faiths and backgrounds. We sit on the floor to eat the same meal, at the same level. No one is better than anyone else.
From https://putasinghonit.wordpress.com/

▲ 'Recognise there is but one race of all human beings.' (Guru Gobind Singh)

In Sikhism, men and women play an equal part in worship and leadership. The initiation ceremonies are the same for women as they are for men. In marriage, women are considered equal and child marriages are banned. In the Punjab a woman may not marry until she is 18 and a man until he is 20 years old. Both Sikh men and women are allowed to remarry if they are widowed.

The Guru Granth Sahib contains the writings and thoughts of other traditions as well as those of Sikhism. The teaching of Hindu and Muslim holy people were similar to that of the gurus and are therefore included in the holy text. The foundation stone of the Golden Temple in Amritsar was laid by a Muslim. The four doors, one on each side of the Temple, are to show that people are welcome from all corners of the world. Sikhs believe that truth can come from any religion.

Activity

In groups, research the work of Sikhs today in which their belief in equality is put into practice. Make a short presentation to the class.

What do you know?

1 Make a flow chart of the events that you think most likely led to the formation of the first Khalsa.

2 Describe the situation before Guru Gobind Singh invited all Sikhs to his home.

3 Describe the first amrit ceremony.

4 What do the names Singh and Kaur mean?

5 Describe the ways in which Sikhs show that everyone is equal.

What do you understand?

6 Explain why Guru Gobind Singh began the Khalsa.

7 Why did Guru Gobind Singh choose the Panj Payares in such a dramatic way?

8 What was the purpose of the amrit ceremony at the end?

9 Explain why Sikhs have the names Singh and Kaur.

10 Explain how the langar is a symbol of equality.

11 How might the Golden Temple be a symbol of equality?

What do you think?

12 What things would you be prepared to give up your life for?

13 Are Singh and Kaur good names?

14 What is true courage?

15 What is the best thing about the Khalsa?

16 Do you think all humans are equal?

The gurus

Starter: Who do you look up to?

Who were the gurus?

Sikhism is based on the lives and teaching of the gurus. A guru is a spiritual teacher or guide. The word 'guru' is a combined word: 'gu' means dark and 'ru' means light. So a guru is one who leads their followers out of the darkness of ignorance into the light of wisdom and spiritual knowledge – enlightenment. Sikhs believe that God spoke through the gurus and that their teaching is directly from Him. They are all equally respected and honoured but they are not worshipped.

Each of the gurus added wisdom and insight into the Sikh faith, and contributed to the formation of the Sikh community in different ways. The word 'Sikh' means learner or disciple, so Sikhs follow the example and teachings of the gurus. There were ten gurus in all, the last one being Guru Gobind Singh. It was he who declared that there should be no more human gurus. Instead, the gurus' teaching should be written down. The book containing their wisdom and teaching (gurbani) is called the Guru Granth Sahib. The ten gurus lived in northern India between the mid-fifteenth and the very early eighteenth centuries.

First guru – Guru Nanak (1469–1539)

Guru Nanak was born into a high caste Hindu family. His father worked for a Muslim businessman and they were reasonably well off. There are many stories about miraculous things that happened during his childhood. They include a time when he was deep in meditation in a field and a cobra slithered alongside him. It raised its head but instead of attacking him, it shielded him from the hot midday sun.

Another story, which reveals Guru Nanak's kindness, tells how his father gave him some money to spend wisely in town and he spent it on food for a holy man who had not eaten for four days. His father accused him of wasting his money, but Guru Nanak said there could not be a better way to spend it.

The stories show that even as a child, Guru Nanak was special. He had a deep concern for the inequalities in life, especially among people. He was immensely compassionate towards the poor and was always bringing them home so that his mother could provide a meal for them. This was the forerunner of the langar.

When he was about 16, he married and worked as a storekeeper for the local Muslim governor. He had two sons called Lakmi Das and Siri Chand. Life continued normally for him until one day, when he was 30, he had an experience that would change his life forever.

There is no Hindu, no Muslim.

He was taking his morning bath in the river when he was swept up into the presence of God in a trance. For two days his friends assumed he had drowned but on the third day he reappeared and explained what had happened. He went home, sold all his possessions and travelled around India spreading his new teaching that everyone is equal in the sight of God. He taught that there is only one God, that He is the creator of all and that He loves all people. Everyone should live as members of the same family even if they belong to different religions.

His companion was a Muslim called Mardana, who was a musician. He played a stringed instrument called the rebeck while Nanak sang poems that spoke of his spiritual insights. When he came to Kartarpur, a town on the western banks of the Ravi River, he established a settled community. Everyone followed a programme of worship and work. Guru Nanak composed 974 of the hymns that are in the Guru Granth Sahib.

Second guru – Guru Angad (1504–52)

Guru Angad became guru in 1539 after Guru Nanak died. His name originally was Lehna and he had met Guru Nanak while on a pilgrimage to a Hindu shrine. Lehna became one of the guru's closest followers. The story is told that one day, wearing his best clothes as was fitting to visit the guru, Lehna went to Kartarpur. Just outside the town, he came across some people who were gathering grass to take into the town for the cows. He saw a large bundle of wet muddy grass waiting to be transported, so he hefted it up onto his back and carried it into the town, getting very dirty in the process. Guru Nanak said that his bundle of grass was a crown to honour the best of men. This was only one example of Lehna's love and devotion. Guru Nanak chose him as his successor.

Guru Nanak changed Lehna's name to Angad which means 'my limb'. This shows how important it was that the message carried on through the gurus stayed the same. Guru Angad wrote down many of Guru Nanak's hymns and some of his own too. They were written in the Gurmukhi script, which is the written version of Punjabi. He also started schools so that children could learn to read. He loved sport and encouraged Sikhs to take part in sporting events. He said that God liked a healthy body and mind.

Third guru – Guru Amar Das (1479–1574)

Guru Amar Das is remembered for three main things:

1 He sent people out to spread the Sikh faith, 22 of whom were women.
2 He held Sikh gatherings at the same time as key Hindu festivals to make Sikhs choose between Sikhism and keeping the Hindu rituals.
3 To further the gurus' ideal of equality, he started the langar – the kitchen attached to every gurdwara. He refused to see anyone unless they had first eaten in the langar.

Fourth guru – Guru Ram Das (1534–81)

Guru Ram Das founded the city of Amritsar, which became a very important place for Sikhs. He also wrote many hymns. The most famous is the Lavan, which is sung at weddings.

Fifth guru – Guru Arjan (1563–1606)

Guru Arjan built the Harmandir – the Golden Temple in Amritsar. It became an important place for Sikhs to come to worship. The symbolism of the structure of the Temple reinforced people's understanding of what it means to be a Sikh.

He also created the first collection of hymns and writings of the gurus. Some were his own work and some were written by Hindu and Muslim holy men. The collection was known as the **Adi Granth** and it was kept in the Golden Temple.

Guru Arjan was the first guru to be martyred, showing all Sikhs that their faith was so important it was worth dying for.

▲ The Golden Temple at Amritsar

Sixth guru – Guru Hargobind (1595–1644)

Guru Hargobind was guru at a time of unrest and persecution of Sikhs by the Moghul emperors. He is sometimes referred to as the Warrior Guru. He carried two curved swords (kirpans) which would later form part of the **Nishan Sahib** (Sikh flag). The swords stood for spiritual power, which was God's truth, and worldly power, which meant fighting oppression and injustice.

Seventh guru – Guru Har Rai (1630–61)

Guru Har Rai extended the Sikh practice of service to include giving medical treatment to the sick.

Eighth and ninth gurus – Guru Har Krishen (1656–64) and Guru Tegh Bahadur (1621–75)

Guru Har Krishen was only five years old when he became guru and he died of smallpox three years later. His successor, Guru Tegh Bahadur, was guru at a time of great persecution. Sikhs were being told by the Moghal emperors to give up their faith or face huge fines. Many schools and gurdwaras were closed. Hindus were also being persecuted as well as many moderate Muslims, so they and their leaders also went to Guru Tegh Bahadur for guidance. The guru believed that everyone had the right to worship freely and he refused to give up his faith. History records that he told the Muslim emperor that if the emperor succeeded in converting him to Islam, then everyone would follow suit. The emperor summoned him to Delhi where the guru was tortured for many weeks, forced to watch his companions being executed and eventually beheaded when he would not convert. He is revered by Sikhs today for sacrificing his life for his faith.

Tenth guru – Guru Gobind Rai (1666–1708)

He later changed his name to Guru Gobind Singh in line with the new name given to all Sikh men.

Guru Gobind Singh is remembered for four main things:
1 Starting the Khalsa in 1699. This united every Sikh in common aims: to fight injustice, to seek God and to live as equals among all people.
2 Encouraging Sikhs to wear the Five Ks.
3 Saying that all Sikh men and women should take the names Singh and Kaur respectively.
4 Declaring that he was to be the last human guru and that from then on the teachings of the gurus would be written down. The Sikh scriptures, which Guru Arjan had put together and which Guru Gobind Singh had revised, would be in a book – the Guru Granth Sahib. Worldly authority would now rest with the Khalsa; spiritual authority would rest in the scriptures.

Activity
Research the life of one of the ten gurus and make a short presentation to the class.

What do you know? **AO1**
1 Describe the role of a guru.
2 Outline how Guru Nanak founded Sikhism.
3 What important things did guru Nanak realise about God and about life?
4 What example did Guru Angad set that future Sikhs might follow?
5 What contribution did Guru Gobind Singh make to Sikhism?
6 Outline the basic message of the gurus.

What do you understand? **AO2**
7 Explain the significance of Guru Nanak's experience in the river.
8 Explain why the second guru's name was changed.
9 Explain the importance of Guru Amar Das' creation of the langar.
10 Why is the image of Guru Gobind Singh as a warrior such an important one for Sikhs?

What do you think? **AO3**
11 Which of the ten gurus impresses you most? Why?
12 Which guru sets the best example?
13 Was one guru more important for Sikhism than the others?

Guru Granth Sahib

Starter: What makes a book holy?

The history of the Guru Granth Sahib

The Guru Granth Sahib is a collection of the teachings and hymns of the gurus. Guru Angad began putting together some of his poems and those of Guru Nanak so that their teaching and philosophy should not be lost. Over the next hundred years, other gurus added to the collection. Guru Arjan put them together in a book called the Adi Granth, which he kept in the Golden Temple at Amritsar. For the first time, the teachings of the gurus were available to the public and could be read in the Temple. It provided a benchmark for other copies which could now be checked against the Adi Granth. This encouraged those who copied it and those who taught it to be consistent.

Now there was a framework for Sikh daily life which helped to unite them. The tenth and last guru, Gobind Singh, added some of his father's hymns. He then decreed that from his death onwards there should be no more human gurus but only the written words of the gurus. The new and final collection was called the Guru Granth Sahib, which means 'from the guru's mouth'. It is written in the Gurmukhi script which is the written form of Punjabi.

The Guru Granth Sahib contains 1430 pages consisting of over 5000 shabads or hymns. They are arranged into 31 musical groupings called ragas. Every copy of the Guru Granth Sahib is exactly the same so that it does not matter which copy you are using, the hymns will be set out in exactly the same way and in the same place on the page. The words form a continuous line without gaps across the page.

Sikhs believe that the Guru Granth Sahib contains the actual words spoken by the gurus so it carries absolute authority. In worship, only the original version is used, although it has been translated into other languages. Prayer, meditation and worship are based on it.

▲ The Guru Granth Sahib being read in the Golden Temple at Amritsar

The contents of the Guru Granth Sahib

- It contains the writings of Hindus and Muslims as well as those of the gurus. However, all the writings are sacred. As already mentioned, this demonstrates that Sikhs believe no one has a monopoly on the truth (see page 141). Truth comes from more than one faith or world view. God's love and grace is open to everyone.
- It contains instructions on how to live a responsible, good and meaningful life, not just within the Sikh community but in the world community. Guru Arjan likened the Sikh scriptures to a plate of food: 'In the plate are placed three things, truth, contentment and meditation ... whoever eats this food will be free from sorrow.' (Guru Granth Sahib, page 1429)

The shabads in the Guru Granth Sahib are not all the same length. Some run for pages and others are only a few lines long. Sikhs take a small part at the beginning and at the end of the Guru Granth Sahib for their daily readings and prayers. The opening shabad is called the Mul Mantra.

Respect for the Guru Granth Sahib

The Guru Granth Sahib is treated with the kind of respect a king would deserve:

- It rests on a **takht** (throne), under a **palki** (canopy).
- It is covered with a beautifully decorated cloth called a romala.
- The granthi, the person who reads from it, sits on a low stool and a special fan called a **chauri** is wafted to and fro, as for a king.
- It is always kept in a gurdwara, whether that is a separate building for public worship or a private home. Gurdwara is actually the name of a special room which houses the Guru Granth Sahib.
- When it is not in use, it is ceremonially closed (Sukhasan).
- Sukhasan also takes place after sunset when it is moved to another special room in the gurdwara. A soft light is left on all night.
- Whenever it is moved it is covered with a romala and carried on a special cushion on the head. The Sikh who carries it acts as its hands and feet. It is always carried with great pomp and ceremony in festivals and travels in its own special vehicle.

▲ What do you see in this picture?

Sewa – Service

Starter: What does it mean to serve others?

Sikhs try to live their lives by following three basic rules:

1 Nam Japna – remembering God
2 Kirat Karni – earning a living honestly
3 Vand Chakna – sharing what they have with those less fortunate (sewa).

The Guru Granth Sahib says that there can be no worship without performing good deeds.

> A place in God's court can only be attained if we do service to others in this world...Wandering ascetics, warriors, celibates, holy men, none of them can obtain mukti without performing sewa.
>
> **Guru Granth Sahib**

What is sewa?

Sewa is one of the most important parts of being a Sikh. It means serving the community in which you live, both the Sikh community (Khalsa) and the non-Sikh community. All Sikhs are expected to give up some of their time, skills and energy to help others. Wherever gurdwaras are set up, they provide a centre for this service to others but this is only the starting place for a life spent in service because sewa means much more than this. Sewa can be put into three categories: maan, taan and dhan.

Taan: physical service

This is practical service to the community. It can be done in a variety of ways depending on a person's skills. Many gurdwaras offer free medical services to those who cannot afford them, so if you are a doctor or a nurse, you might give your service in this way. Taan could mean helping to build or maintain the gurdwara in your local town, mowing someone's lawn or repairing the plumbing in the home of an old age pensioner. On 25 March, Sikhs gather together at the Golden Temple in Amritsar to cleanse the tank of water that surrounds the Temple.

The tank is emptied and thousands of people clear the silt from the bottom, then fresh water is pumped back into it. This is also Taan.

Maan: mental/intellectual

Sikhs believe that as you serve God, you will become like Him and live according to His will. An important part of sewa is the service offered to God, not through actions but through words and thoughts. This is maan. Maan can be reading the Guru Granth Sahib and meditating on it. It can be reading the stories of the gurus to your children or talking about your faith at school. Sikhs do not try to convert others to their faith, but instead concentrate on what religions have in common. Helping others to understand the teachings of the gurus is all part of maan. It also means sharing in someone else's grief and pain and showing compassion.

Dhan: material service

This is service to humanity through giving time and money to charity. Guru Amar Das introduced the idea of 'daswandh' which is giving up one tenth of your surplus wealth to help others. One charity is Sikh Relief, which covers a huge range of needs such as disability and medical aid, caring for the elderly and caring for the environment.

Another large Sikh charity is Khalsa Aid which was founded in 1999 and is based upon the Sikh principle: 'Recognise the whole human race as one'. Its aim is to provide humanitarian aid in civil conflict zones and disaster areas around the world.

In September 2017, Khalsa Aid were among those helping the plight of the Rohingya Muslim refugees in Bangladesh.

These people are arriving in a desperate state. I have never seen anyone so relieved for a drink of water. They have no money to pay for public transport to the refugee camps. Local rickshaws have increased their rates because of the heightened demand so we have organised transportation to take families safely to the refugee camps.

Amarpreet Singh, Khalsa Aid director

Activity

1 There are many charities such as Sikh Relief, City Sikhs and Khalsa Aid. In groups, research one of the many Sikh charities. Describe what it does and show how it fulfils the teaching of the gurus on sewa.

2 Find out about the life of a Sikh called Bhai Kanhaiya who lived in the seventeenth century. Show how his actions get to the heart of sewa. Ask your teacher for a copy of his story.

What do you know? **AO1**

1 What is 'sewa'?

2 Describe the three kinds of sewa.

3 Give examples of how Sikhs might offer each different kind of sewa.

What do you understand? **AO2**

4 Explain the Sikh teaching on sewa.

5 Explain how 'maan' is sewa.

6 Explain how the principle of seeing the whole of the human race as one can be lived out in sewa.

What do you think? **AO3**

7 How could you offer sewa in your daily life at school?

8 Is serving others more important than worshipping God?

9 Is one of the three forms of sewa of more importance than the others?

10 Is sewa the most important part of being a Sikh?

Community and worship

Starter: What are the advantages and disadvantages of living in a community?

Community and worship are as one to Sikhs, as they each grow out of the other. After Guru Gobind Singh started the Khalsa, Sikhs developed a strong sense of community living. They were responsible for each other, they helped each other and they worked together to try to create the kind of society that would be pleasing to God. We have already seen how important reading and meditating on the Guru Granth Sahib and service to others are to Sikhs.

Code of conduct

Guru Gobind Singh told his followers that to belong to the Khalsa meant obeying a strict code of conduct. Over the years, what should or should not be included in this 'rahit', or code, has changed many times and there have been disputes about it. At the beginning of the twentieth century, a group of Sikhs got together and spent 15 years working on an acceptable version. It was published in 1945 and called the Rahit Maryada.

Living as a community means being responsible for your actions within it. To enter the Khalsa a Sikh must go through Amrit Sanskar, the initiation ceremony, take the name Singh if they are men and Kaur if they are women, and agree to wear the Five Ks (see page 166). Many women wear all Five Ks including carrying a kirpan. Some even wear a turban although most wear a scarf to cover their long hair. These mark them out as being part of the Sikh community. In addition, they agree to follow certain rules that affect their lifestyles. Since Sikhs are supposed to live in harmony with nature, they may not paint their nails or cut their hair. Body-piercing for wearing ornaments is also forbidden. Sikhs should not gamble, smoke tobacco, take drugs or drink alcohol.

Kirat Karna

Apart from these very specific laws, there are more general rules to do with how a person makes a living and how children should be brought up. This is called **Kirat Karna**. Integrity is central to Sikh teaching. Sikhs may not have jobs that exploit or abuse other people. Underlying all of these rules is the teaching that all people are equal.

Work should be for the good of society as well as for the family or individual. The kind of work does not matter – whether it is manual, agricultural, professional or social. As long as it is honestly earned, wealth does not matter; it is being obsessed by wealth that is wrong.

▲ Sikhs should balance work, charity and worship

Living as a community also means worshipping as a community. Sikhs aim to draw closer to God and to their own freedom from the continuous karmaic cycle (birth, death and rebirth according to individual karma) by:

- reading the Guru Granth Sahib
- understanding the gurbani (teachings of the gurus)
- praying and meditating.

This is why the gurdwara is central to community living. Meeting together to worship reinforces a sense of community and common purpose. This collective worship is reinforced by worship at home by oneself or with family. Private worship can include the following:

- saying the morning and evening prayers
- reading the Gukta, a book containing a small collection of hymns
- listening to religious programmes on the internet
- radio and television
- studying the gurbani.

These all strengthen individual identity within the Sikh community.

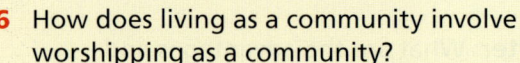

What do you understand? AO2

6 How does living as a community involve worshipping as a community?

7 Explain the importance of private worship.

8 Explain the importance of Kirat Karna.

What do you think? AO3

9 What would be suitable and unsuitable occupations for a Sikh to have?

10 Should a person's religion lay down guidelines for how they should live?

11 Is worshiping God more important than work and charity?

12 Is it wrong to be rich?

Essay practice

'A person's religion is what determines how they live.' Do you agree? Give reasons to support your answer. Show that you have considered more than one point of view.

What do you know? AO1

1 What are Sikhs not allowed to do?

2 Describe the kind of jobs Sikhs are encouraged to do.

3 What kind of jobs should they avoid?

4 Describe how Sikhs draw closer to God.

5 Describe how Sikhs balance work, charity and worship.

Topic 2 Sikh practices and ceremonies

2.1 The gurdwara – 'the doorway to the guru'

▲ The Guru Nanak Gurdwara in Bedford

What is a gurdwara?

The gurdwara is where Sikhs go to worship God. The Rahit Maryada says that Sikhs should visit the gurdwara as often as possible because it is the place where they can study the gurbani (teachings of the gurus). Sunday is the principle day for **diwan** (worship) in the UK, but Sikhs may go whenever they want to. Gurdwaras vary in style enormously. Some are very simple buildings while others are grand and ornate. The Nishan Sahib (the saffron yellow flag bearing the **khanda**, the sign of the Khalsa) flies outside.

▲ The Nishan Sahib

The name 'gurdwara' means 'doorway to the guru' because its purpose is to house the Guru Granth Sahib.

> Through the Gurdwara, the Guru's Gate, one obtains understanding. By being washed through the Word and the congregation one becomes pure.
> **Guru Granth Sahib 730:1–2**

Guru Nanak built the first gurdwara in Kartarpur in 1521. The iconic gurdwara is the Harmander Sahib or Golden Temple, built by the fifth guru. It has four doors into it to show that people from all four points of the compass are welcome.

The role of a gurdwara in the Sikh community

A gurdwara is somewhere:

- to learn spiritual wisdom
- for religious ceremonies
- for children to learn about their faith, customs and traditions
- for people to gather – like a community centre. Historically, gurdwaras were often used as places to practise martial arts and offer medicines. Today, they are social centres as well, where trips for the elderly are organised, and lessons in karate, football and music take place. The gurdwara offers food, shelter and companionship to those who need it.

The diwan hall

The diwan hall is where worship and ceremonies such as weddings and naming ceremonies take place. Everyone is welcome even if they are not Sikh but certain conventions must be respected. Once inside the gurdwara, shoes must be removed and men and women have to cover their heads.

Visitors are given a shawl or a headscarf. The hall is a big, open, carpeted space with the takht (the throne upon which the Guru Granth Sahib rests) as the main focus at the front.

The book is placed on the takht under a canopy called a palki and is covered with an ornate cloth called a romala when it is not being read. A person called a granthi waves a special fan called a chauri over the book during ceremonies and services. Chauris were used to fan Indian kings in the past and this is where the practice originates. Chauris are symbols of respect and authority for this reason. The Guru Granth Sahib has its own special room in the gurdwara where it is kept when not in use. When it is moved, it is carried above the head as a mark of respect.

There are no symbols, bells or statues to distract worshippers in the gurdwara, although there may be pictures of the gurus or of other famous gurdwaras, such as the Golden Temple at Amritsar. There are no priests or religious leaders either. Gurdwaras are managed by a committee. Men and women are considered equal and a granthi may be either gender, provided he or she can read Gurmukhi.

Worship (diwan)

On entering the diwan hall and removing their shoes, Sikhs walk to the front and bow down in front of the Guru Granth Sahib, touching their foreheads to the ground in respect and submission to its teaching. They do not worship the book but respect its teachings. Only God is to be worshipped. They might make an offering of food or money.

If worshippers need to move about in the gurdwara, it must always be in a clockwise direction. The hall is divided by a central aisle and men sit on one side and women on the other. They sit on the floor cross-legged, making sure their feet do not point towards the takht as that would show disrespect. The raghi or music group usually sit to one side of the takht. The singing of hymns is a large part of Sikh worship, as the Guru Granth Sahib is arranged musically.

Each gurdwara has a granthi who organises the daily services and reads from the Guru Granth Sahib. They must be trained to look after the Guru Granth Sahib properly. They are expected to be full members of the Sikh Khalsa and live according to its ideals.

There are rules for special ceremonies but there is no prescribed order of service.

What happens in a typical Sikh service?

1 **Presentation of karah parshad, the holy sweet:** this will be brought into the hall and placed near the Guru Granth Sahib, ready for sharing at the end of the service.
2 **Greeting:** an appointed Sikh bows to the Guru Granth Sahib then turns to greet the congregation with the words:

   Waheguru ji ka khalsa, Waheguru ji ki fateh.

   (The khalsa owes allegiance to God, victory belongs to God alone.)

3 **Kirtan (hymn-singing):** the morning service begins with the singing of one of the shabads (hymns) written by Guru Nanak – 'Asa Di Var'. Then more hymns are sung from the Guru Granth Sahib accompanied by musical instruments. Kirtan helps worshippers concentrate more on God and less on themselves. They can focus their thoughts and emotions on God, which is the goal of Sikh worship.
4 **Sermon:** these talks are usually based on an event or theme in Sikh history.
5 **The singing of the Anand Sahib:** this is a song written by Guru Amar Das, the third guru.
6 **Ardas (prayer):** the congregation stands facing the Guru Granth Sahib and prayers are said. The word 'Waheguru' is repeated often. It means literally 'praise to the Guru' and is the Sikh word for God.
7 **Hukam:** this is when the Guru Granth Sahib is opened at random and the first hymn at the top of the left-hand page is read. The text is thought to be a relevant lesson for that particular day.
8 **Karah parshad:** the sharing of ceremonial food ends the service. Parshad is made from water and equal quantities of flour, sugar and clarified butter. The first five portions are given to the Panj Payares (five Sikhs representing the first members of the Khalsa) and after them it is served to everyone else, regardless of rank.

The langar

The langar is a free food kitchen and there is one attached to every gurdwara. Langar is also the word used to describe the communal meal that is served there.

Service is central to Sikh practice and the gurdwara acts as a place of worship and a centre for service to others. Everyone is welcome at the langar, regardless of who they are, their religious faith or their caste. This prevents richer congregations showing off by preparing lavish feasts.

The food is always vegetarian and the same food is given to everyone. This ensures no one is excluded for religious dietary reasons. A typical meal will include chapattis, dahl (lentils), rice, yoghurt, vegetables and rice pudding.

All food is prepared in the langar. Large gurdwaras can serve meals for over 1000 people. The Golden Temple in Amritsar feeds around 100,000 people every day and at least double that at festivals.

▲ Everyone receives a hot meal in the langar

People sit in lines facing each other down the langar with a long cloth between them. There is often more than one pair of lines. Men and women sit together and everyone sits on the floor to show that all are equal. Servers walk up and down on the cloth with dishes of food. Families take it in turns to help prepare, serve and clear up. This service is part of sewa. While preparing langar, helpers should recite God's name to keep themselves free of stress and bad thoughts.

Activity

Working in groups, imagine you have just taken over a building to convert into a new gurdwara. You want to make it a really useful community centre to serve your area. Draw up a plan of what you would do.

What do you know? AO1

1 Describe what you might see in a typical gurdwara.
2 Outline a typical Sunday service.
3 Describe how people behave in a gurdwara.
4 What is the Nishan Sahib?
5 Describe what happens in the langar.

What do you understand? AO2

6 Explain the role of the gurdwara in the community.
7 Explain why there are four doors into the gurdwara.
8 Explain the importance of the langar.
9 Why do Sikhs go the gurdwara?
10 Explain the symbolism of the takht, the palki and the chauri.

What do you think? AO3

11 Should every religious community have a langar?
12 Should men and women always sit separately in religious services?
13 Do places of worship need specially trained leaders?

2.2 Prayer, reading and meditation

Starter: Why is worship central to religious practice?

Nam japna – meditating on the name of God

In the Guru Granth Sahib, there are many different names given to God. Nam japna worship is repeating these names for God over and over in reverent prayer.

> If I had 100,000 tongues, and these were multiplied twenty times more, with each tongue, I would repeat, hundreds of thousands of times, the Name of the One, the Lord of the Universe.
>
> **The words of Guru Nanak in the Guru Granth Sahib 7:6–7**

> You are my Father, and You are my Mother. You are my Relative, and You are my Brother. You are my Protector everywhere …
>
> **Guru Granth Sahib 103:12–13**

Waheguru is the most commonly used name and it means 'Wonderful Guru, or Lord'. It is found 16 times in the Guru Granth Sahib. When Sikhs use it in private prayer and meditation, they are expressing the reality of God and His ultimate power.

Sikhs believe that although God is 'Inaccessible, Infinite, Eternal and Primordial', He is also personal and close to you like family. The language is poetic but Sikhs say meditating on God's mystery brings them to closer understanding.

Hukam – reading the will of God from the Guru Granth Sahib

Hukam is the divine will. Hukam is usually used to refer to the hymn that is read after the Ardas prayer is said. The passage for the service is chosen by opening the central section of the Guru Granth Sahib at random and is considered by Sikhs as the divine 'command of the guru' for the day. People can also take hukams as guidance in a specific situation or in answer to a problem.

Hukam is a basic idea in Sikhism. Sikhs believe that everything in the universe is ordained by God and nothing happens outside His will. A common saying in Punjabi is that without His will, '... even a leaf on the tree would not move'.

Akand Path – the continuous reading of the Guru Granth Sahib

▲ Reading the Guru Granth Sahib right through during a celebration. A small group of Sikhs take it in turns to read

During festivals and on special occasions, the Guru Granth Sahib is read from beginning to end without interruption. The 1430 pages are usually read by a chain of Sikhs and it takes about 48 hours. Invitations are sent out to people to attend an Akand Path on occasions such as weddings, special sports events and birthdays. The reading is an important occasion and means a great deal to Sikhs. Continuous reading allows the reader to travel through beautiful passages like Guru Nanak's Mul Mantra. It takes the reader and listeners through descriptions of God, spiritual teaching and discussions about such things as pretending to be loyal when you are not.

Nitnem and gutka: prayer and worship at home

> Whoever calls themselves a Sikh … should rise early in the morning and meditate on God's name.
>
> **Guru Ram Das**

Becoming less self-absorbed and more centred on God is the aim of a Sikh's private prayer and devotions. There are many instructions in the Guru Granth Sahib for private worship. Sikhs are expected to reach a high level of dedication and self-discipline in their lives if they want to experience fulfilment and happiness. Sikhs are encouraged to pray, but Guru Nanak warned that words by themselves are meaningless.

People use a prayer book called the **Nitnem**. It is a collection of poems but more prayers can be added to it. Ideally, Sikhs should pray at least three times a day, and certain poems are appropriate to different times of day.

Before worship a Sikh should bathe, emphasising the relationship between the worshipper and God, who is around and within. After bathing, he or she repeats the Japji of Guru Nanak, which starts with the Mul Mantra. Some Sikhs use a **mala** to help them focus on their meditation. The prayer rope has 108 knots and as a worshipper passes them through the fingers they repeat 'Waheguru', which means Wonderful Lord.

In the evening they repeat two more set hymns and may use the mala again. Some Sikhs have a complete copy of the Guru Granth Sahib in their homes, but because of its size and the fact that it needs its own room (gurdwara) in the house, most Sikhs use the Gutka for private worship instead. This a book containing a collection of fewer than 20 'shabads' - hymns from the Guru Granth Sahib. Sikhs often know all these shabads off by heart.

▲ A mala

What do you know? — AO1

1. What is Nam Japna and how do Sikhs perform it?
2. Describe how Sikhs discover the will of God (hukam).
3. What is an Akand Path?
4. On what occasions does an Akand Path happen?
5. Describe how Sikhs worship at home.

What do you understand? — AO2

6. Explain how performing Nam Japna might bring Sikhs closer to God.
7. Explain why hukam is so important to Sikhs.
8. Explain why Sikhs perform an Akand Path.
9. Explain the importance of prayer and meditation at home.

What do you think? — AO3

10. Is it possible to know the will of God?
11. Is it possible to meditate effectively without aids such as mala (prayer) beads?
12. Does reading through a complete sacred book at one sitting make you a better person?
13. Is public worship more important than private worship?

2.3 Festivals

Starter: How do festivals help to keep religious faith alive?

Festivals are an important part of the Sikh culture and are usually something to do with the lives of the gurus. They unite Sikhs in their faith and shared history and provide focal points in the year for celebrations.

There are two kinds of festival: **gurpurbs** and **melas**. Gurpurbs are holy days that honour the gurus and melas are celebrations that coincide with Indian festivals. Most of the festivals include a normal service in the gurdwara and an Akand Path.

The Guru Granth Sahib is usually processed with great ceremony and reverence. Songs are composed and sung about the gurus along with hymns from the Dasam Granth (a book of writings attributed to Guru Gobind Singh).

Vaisakhi

Originally Vaisakhi was an Indian festival to mark the spring harvest. Today it is kept on or around the 14th April and celebrates the birth of the Khalsa in 1699. This was when Guru Gobind Singh summoned all Sikhs to his HQ in Anandpur and formed the first Khalsa. (See page 144 for an account of what happened.) Vaisakhi today underlines the values of courage, strength and unity that Guru Gobind Singh so admired in his Panj Payares. It is also the time when Sikhs first started wearing the Five Ks. It is an important festival because it marks the birth of Sikhism as it is practised today.

▲ Celebrating Vaisakhi in the Punjab, India

How is Vaisakhi celebrated today?

The gurdwara is beautifully decorated. The Nishan Sahib (flagpole) is washed in diluted yoghurt outside the gurdwara and the old flag is replaced by a new one. This practice reflects Sikhism's Hindu origins because the cow is a sacred animal and, therefore, its milk is thought of as pure. The old flag is torn into pieces and anyone fortunate enough to acquire one of those pieces treasures it.

The Guru Granth Sahib is carried with great pomp and ceremony as a symbol of what unites and guides Sikh life. The procession starts at the gurdwara and is led by traditionally dressed 'Panj Payares'. In the procession, there are people performing martial arts and using swords as part of the performance. It may also feature energetic **bhangra** dancing. Everyone is in a good mood and joins in the singing of hymns and dancing, which is very popular. Double-sided drums, called dhol, accompany the dancing.

This noisy, colourful parade through the streets is called the Nagar Kirtan. People from other faiths and none are invited to join in. Other events include competitions like wrestling and table tennis, and sports such as football and hockey.

Diwali / Bandi Chhor Diwas

Diwali usually happens around October or November. It is called 'the Festival of Lights' and lights play a big part in the celebrations. It also marks the beginning of the Sikh and Hindu New Year. It is a huge occasion in both religions and the connection between the two faiths can be seen in this shared festival. However, for Sikhs the emphasis is on the actions of the gurus and so Diwali is sometimes called Bandi Chhor Diwas, which means 'prisoner release day'. This is because they remember the story of Guru Hargobind (see page 149).

Guru Hargobind had been imprisoned, as he was considered a threat to the state, but he was offered freedom at the festival of Diwali. Guru Hargobind refused to leave unless the 52 Hindu princes who shared his cell were also released. The emperor, thinking that he could be seen to be agreeing while making it impossible at the same time, ruled that anyone holding onto the guru's coat could also walk free. The guru ordered a long cloak with tassels down the sides to be brought into the prison. He put it on and all 52 men managed to hang onto the tassels as he walked out, so all were freed. He walked from Gwalior, where he had been imprisoned, to Amritsar, arriving at Diwali. Human rights and freedom are important to Sikhs so remembering this story at Diwali reminds them of their duty towards all people.

How is Diwali celebrated?

Sikhs clean their homes and workplaces. They decorate the outside of their buildings and put lighted candles in windows and doorways. Gurdwaras are filled with lights and, in India, the Golden Temple of Amritsar is covered in lights and its many treasures are put on display. Presents are exchanged and there are always sweets and a feast. Langar is served in every gurdwara after a special service remembering Guru Hargobind through prayer and meditation. Hymns are sung and there are readings from the Guru Granth Sahib. Karah parshad is shared. Firecrackers are set off and, in the evening, there are firework displays.

Manjeet Kaur, a Sikh from Stamford Hill, said:

'It's great to come together and celebrate. I love everything about this time of year, it's the fireworks, the food and visiting family and friends.'

Guru Nanak's birthday

The festival of Guru Nanak's birthday takes place on 4 November. It is celebrated because he is the founder of Sikhism and it is therefore one of the most sacred festivals. Guru Nanak's actual birthday is in April, on Vaisakhi Day, but as he was born during a full moon, controversies over the calendars led to it being celebrated for so long in November that it has become the official date.

How is Guru Nanak's birthday celebrated?

Two days before, the Guru Granth Sahib is read from cover to cover. This is called an Akand Path and takes 48 hours.

On the actual day, celebrations begin very early in the morning at the gurdwara with hymns and a sermon. There is then a procession called the Nagar Kirtan. It is led by the Panj Payares barefoot and in their traditional dress. They also carry the palki of the Guru Granth Sahib and are followed by a brass band and a crowd of people singing hymns. Sikhs stage mock battles and display their swordsmanship.

The Guru Granth Sahib is carried on a decorated float. There is music and fireworks and people throw confetti. Drink and food stalls line the route. People remember how Guru Nanak travelled thousands of miles, spreading his belief that there is only one God and that everyone is equal regardless of gender, caste, religion, race or wealth.

Often the procession will go from one gurdwara to another, culminating in a langar where lunch will have been prepared for the thousands of participants. There are always plenty of sweets, making it a popular festival for children.

Activity

Research one of the Sikh festivals. Send a friend a greeting card and invite them to join you in the festivities. Explain to them what it is about and what to expect.

What do you know? **AO1**

1 What do Sikhs remember at Vaisakhi?
2 Describe how Vaisakhi is celebrated.
3 How do Sikhs celebrate Diwali?
4 Describe what happens over Guru Nanak's birthday.
5 What features do all three festivals have in common?
6 What is the difference between gurpurbs and melas?

What do you understand? **AO2**

7 Explain why festivals are important in the Sikh tradition.
8 Explain why Sikhs celebrate Vaisakhi.
9 Explain why Diwali is about celebrating freedom and human rights.
10 Explain why Guru Nanak's birthday is important to Sikhs.

What do you think? **AO3**

11 Is one Sikh festival more important than the others?
12 Are festivals about God or about the community we live in?
13 Should all festivals be joyous occasions?

2.4 Rites of passage

Birth and naming ceremonies

Starter: Why are names so important?

The Sikh Rahit Maryada is the Sikh code of conduct and it contains instructions about what to do when important milestones in life are reached. When a baby is born, the words of the Mul Mantra are whispered into her ear and a drop of 'amrit' (a mixture of honey and water) is dropped into her mouth; its sweetness is a symbol of the sweetness of the gurbani. It is also a reminder to the parents of their duty to bring their child up in the faith. Sometimes this little ritual is done at the naming ceremony. This special ceremony is held in the gurdwara as soon as possible after the birth and usually within 40 days.

What happens at Naam Karan?

▲ A baby girl being brought for Naam Karan

This baby girl has been brought to the gurdwara for her naming ceremony. First of all she is presented to the Guru Granth Sahib. Her mother lays her on the carpet in front of the throne then both her parents touch their foreheads to the ground in respect to the Guru Granth Sahib. The holy book is opened in the middle, where the hymns are, and the pages are allowed to fall open at random. The granthi reads from that page. The first letter of the opening word on the top left-hand corner of the left-hand page provides the first letter of the baby's name. For this baby the letter was 'G' and her parents choose the name Ganeev, which means 'a priceless worth'. Kaur, which means princess, is added to her name in line with Sikh tradition. Boys have the name 'Singh' added, which means lion. Having the same name regardless of your status in life demonstrates equality within the Sikh community. Ganeev's name is announced to the whole congregation.

The granthi reads the first five verses of the prayer of joy, the Anand Sahib. Then the whole of the Ardas is read. When that is over, karah parshad is shared among the congregation. As is often the case, it had been prepared by Ganeev's parents.

Ganeev's parents made a presentation of a new romala (the decorated cloth covering for the Guru Granth Sahib) to the gurdwara. It is customary on these occasions to give a present to the gurdwara. This can be one of several things: food for the community to share, money or a new romala. Some parents pay for Akand Path, the whole of the Guru Granth Sahib to be read without a break. Ganeev's parents presented a new romala.

Activity
Research the first names in your family, including your name, and find out what they mean. What name might you choose for your own child? Give reasons for your choice.

The Five Ks

Starter: How can clothes, jewellery and things you use every day represent or remind you of something?

The Five Ks are five symbols to help Sikhs to remember the important things about their faith. Sikhs believe in integrity, equality and faithfulness. They believe in the importance of meditating on God and always being ready to defend other people from oppression and injustice. The Five Ks were first worn by the Panj Payares. They are what Guru Gobind Singh instructed all members of his new Khalsa to wear. Women and men wear all the Five Ks. As the Five Ks are ordinary items for Sikhs to wear (even the sword is part of everyday dress for men), they do not get forgotten but become a part of a Sikh's everyday life.

Kesh – This is the uncut hair and beard. Sikh men twist it up into a turban and women wear a long plait covered with a scarf although some wear a turban like the men. Sikhs believe that God is Nature and being in harmony with Nature is the way they are supposed to live. As hair grows naturally, they should not cut it. Long hair is a gift from God and keeping hair long is a sign of living a saintly life. It unites Sikhs and emphasises their identity as members of the Khalsa.

Kara – In Sikhism the circle is a symbol that God is eternal. He is without beginning or end, just like the bangle. Sikhs wear it round their right wrist as a symbol of their membership of the Khalsa and as a reminder that they should do good deeds. It is made of steel, which is a strong metal, reminding them of the strength they must show in protecting their freedom and that of others.

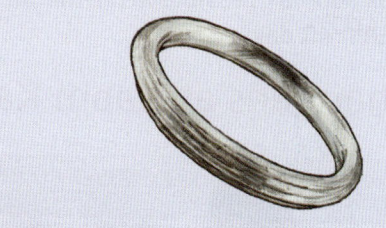

The Five Ks

Khanga – This is the comb used by men and women to keep the long hair tidy and to hold it up under the turban. Hair must be washed regularly and kept free of tangles.

Men don't shave and many of them wear a net over their beards.

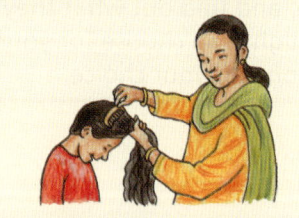

Kachha – Sikhs use clothing as a constant reminder of their duty to others. Kachha are shorts and they are worn by both men and women. They remind the wearer of the need for self-discipline. Kachha are easy to move about in so Sikhs can be ready for action wherever they are. Some women also carry kirpans for the same reasons.

Kirpan – A curved sword worn at the waist as a symbol of Sikhs' hard-won freedom. It is a reminder of their duty to defend the weak just as the gurus defended the Sikh and Hindu communities in the past.

What do you know?

AO1

1 What are the Five Ks?
2 What do they represent?
3 Describe what a Sikh boy or girl would wear on a typical day.
4 Imagine you are present at a Sikh baby naming ceremony. Describe your experience.
5 How is a baby's name chosen?
6 What do the names Singh and Kaur mean?
7 What is karah parshad?

What do you understand?

AO2

8 Explain why Sikh men and some women carry the kirpan.
9 Explain the importance of the kangha.
10 Explain the symbolism of the kara.
11 Why are babies brought to the gurdwara?
12 Explain the significance of the names Kaur and Singh.
13 Explain how the ceremony enables the parents to show their devotion to God.

What do you think?

AO3

14 How can what you wear influence who you are?
15 Should you be allowed to choose your own name?
16 Do our names influence the kind of people we become?

Amritsanskar and the importance of the Khalsa

Starter: Why is it so important to belong to something?

> Khalsa belongs to God, victory is God's.

The Ardas, Guru Gobind Singh

The Khalsa was started in 1699 by Guru Gobind Singh and is celebrated at the festival of Vaisakhi. The guru summoned all the Sikhs to the town of Anandpur and when they duly assembled before his tent, he emerged brandishing a sword and demanding the head of one loyal Sikh. One by one, five men went into the tent and the crowd heard the sound of heads being cut off. Then Guru Gobind Singh came back out with the five men, alive and all dressed the same. They were the 'Panj Payares', the first five members of the Khalsa (see page 144). The rite that followed was the initiation ceremony called Amritsanskar.

The importance of the Khalsa in the Sikh tradition cannot be overstated. It unites all Sikhs through a common name and common duty.

The Amritsanskar ceremony

▲ The amrit is stirred by the five amrit-dhari using a double-edged sword. The amrit-dhari are full members of the Khalsa and represent the Panj Payares

Amritsanskar is the most important ceremony for Sikhs because it is when they become full members of the Khalsa. They are ready to take on the responsibilities of the community and to be responsible for their own conduct. Boys and girls can join the Khalsa as long as they understand what it means and are committed to what it stands for.

The first ceremony was held in 1699 for the Panj Payares and what happens today is very similar to what happened then. Amritsanskar usually takes place in the gurdwara.

- The Khalsa community is represented by five amrit-dhari. They wear the ceremonial saffron dress of the Sikhs and the Five Ks.
- Hymns are recited from the Guru Granth Sahib and prayers are said.
- The candidates promise to follow the rules and lifestyle of the Sikhs, serving others and worshipping one God.
- The amrit-dhari prepare the amrit, which is a mixture of sugar and water, in a large metal bowl, stirring it with a double-edged sword. The sweet mixture is blessed and sprinkled on the candidates' hair and eyes. They then drink some from the same bowl.
- The candidates recite the Ardas each time they drink and they then recite the Mul Mantra.
- The ceremony ends with one more reading from the Guru Granth Sahib and with the eating of the karah parshad.

Activity

In groups, invent an initiation ceremony for entering Year 7 or 8. Think about the ideals of your school and what a person might hope to achieve in this year. Share your ideas with the rest of the class and explain the symbolism of what happens.

What do you know?   AO1

1 What is the Khalsa?
2 Describe how the first members of the Khalsa were chosen.
3 Who are the amrit-dhari?
4 What is amrit?
5 Describe a typical Sikh ceremony of Amritsanskar.

What do you understand?   AO2

6 Explain the importance of the Khalsa.
7 Explain the significance of Amritsanskar.

What do you think?   AO3

8 How might someone feel differently after they have been through Amritsanskar?

Marriage

Starter: Why are so many symbols used in a wedding ceremony?

Sikh marriages are more than the union of two people; they join two families. This is why Sikh parents usually choose their children's marriage partners. However, sons and daughters do have the right to refuse their parents' choice as it is very important that everyone is in agreement. Marriage is seen as a commitment before Waheguru. (Waheguru is the name in Punjabi given to God and means literally 'Wonderful God'.)

The purpose of marriage is described as the union between two souls and is primarily for companionship along life's spiritual path. On engagement there is usually a party in the gurdwara and the groom's mother visits the bride and gives her a gold ring.

Weddings generally happen in the morning, either at the bride's home or in the gurdwara, and can be performed by any Sikh. The important thing is that it is performed in the presence of the Guru Granth Sahib. The bride can choose to wear the traditional red of happiness, as is the custom in India, or white as is usual in the West. She must cover her head with a chunni (scarf). The groom wears a coloured turban and scarf and a kirpan hangs at his waist. Dowries are not allowed but, before the marriage, the two families meet up to exchange gifts and to eat a meal together. This ceremony is called 'Milni'.

Anand karaj or 'the ceremony of bliss'

▲ A Sikh marriage ceremony, Anand karaj

- The bride and groom sit facing the takht as the importance of marriage is explained to them and a blessing is said for them and their parents.

- The couple walk around the Guru Granth Sahib four times and bow to it. This shows that they accept its teachings and wish to support each other, physically and spiritually, for the rest of their lives. It shows that the Guru Granth Sahib will be central to their lives.

- Then the bride's father places a garland of flowers over the couple. He ties one end of the groom's scarf to the end of the bride's scarf. This is a symbol of the bride leaving her family and joining her husband's. He places the end of the scarf into the bride's hand and she keeps hold of it for the rest of the ceremony.

- The wedding hymn is sung at this point. It is called the Lavan and was written by Guru Ram Das. It explains the relationship between the individual and God. After each verse, the couple walk clockwise around the Guru Granth Sahib. The bride holds the end of the groom's scarf. Rose petals are thrown over them after the last circuit.

- The service ends with sharing karah parshad. Guests drop presents of money into the laps of the bride and groom.

- Everyone then enjoys a meal in the langar.

Activity
Imagine you are the brother or sister of the bride or groom. Write a letter to a friend describing the wedding.

What do you know? **AO1**
1 Describe what happens before the wedding ceremony.
2 Outline what takes place at a Sikh wedding ceremony.
3 Describe what the bride and groom wear at their wedding.

What do you understand? **AO2**
4 Explain the purpose of Sikh marriage.
5 Explain the symbolism of the scarves worn by the bride and groom.
6 Explain why the ceremony takes place in front of the Guru Granth Sahib.

What do you think? **AO3**
7 Why is it so important that the families of the couple get on well?
8 Should marriages be easy or difficult to end if they do not work out?

Essay practice
'Couples should only marry it they love each other.' Do you agree? Give reasons to support your answer. Show that you have considered more than one point of view.

Glossary

Buddhism

anatta Means 'no self' or 'no soul'. It is the second of the three marks of existence.

anicca Means 'impermanence'. It is the first of the three marks of existence.

ascetic Giving up all physical pleasures, eating almost nothing and practising some extreme spiritual exercises.

Asita A wise man who announced that Siddhartha would grow to be either a ruler or great religious teacher.

Avalokiteshvara A popular bodhisattva usually depicted with a thousand arms.

bhavana Means 'cultivating' or 'developing' a life of loving kindness.

Bodhi tree The fig tree under which Siddhartha achieved enlightenment. Bodhi means enlightenment.

bodhisattva An enlightened being who has vowed to practise Buddhism out of compassion for the world.

breath-control Used in samatha meditation to focus the mind.

Buddha Nature The belief that everyone has the capacity to become enlightened.

chanting Half way between singing a tune and singing a single note. This is done as a means of remembering the Buddha's teaching.

dana Means 'generosity'; lay people give gifts or dana to the ordained.

Dharma Means 'Truth' and is the teaching of the Buddha.

dukkha Means 'suffering'. It is the third of the three marks of existence.

dysentery Severe stomach upset.

Five Precepts The five basic Buddhist moral principles *(see pansils)*.

Four Noble Truths The four guiding principles the Buddha taught for living a happy life.

karma Means 'action with intention'; the law of nature that every action has a consequence.

karuna Means 'compassion'.

koans Are short perplexing stories designed to make one think.

lay people Members of the Buddhist community who are not ordained as monks or nuns.

Lumbini The place where Siddhartha was born.

magga Means 'the way' or 'path' and is the middle ground between a life of extremes *(see Noble Eightfold Path)*.

Mahayana Buddhism Mahayana means 'the great way' and refers to Buddhists who emphasise that compassion should be for all.

mantra A short phrase which is repeated over and over in meditation.

Mara The god of illusion who tried to tempt Siddhartha at his enlightenment.

metta Means 'loving kindness'.

mudra Hand gestures used in meditation.

nirodha Means 'cessation of suffering' and is the third of the Four Noble Truths.

nirvana Means 'extinguish' and describes the state when all desires are gone and a person is in bliss.

Noble Eightfold Path Is the eight means of everyday living the Buddhist life and for training the mind *(see magga)*.

pagoda A very elaborate monument or stupa in Japan with an inverted, umbrella-shaped spire on top *(see stupa)*.

pansils Are the Five Precepts *(see Five Precepts)*.

parinirvana The final state of nirvana after death. This term also describes the Buddha's death.

pilgrimage A spiritual journey often made to a special place.

prostrate Lying fully on the ground, face down, as a sign of humility and respect.

puja Worship at home or in a temple.

rupa A statue or picture of the Buddha or a bodhisattva used in puja and meditation.

samsara Reincarnation or the process of birth and rebirths over many lifetimes.

samudaya The cause of suffering, or dukkha. The second of the Four Noble Truths *(see the Second of The Four Noble Truths)*.

sangha The worldwide Buddhist community comprising of the ordained (monks and nuns) and lay people (non-ordained men and women).

satori A term used in Zen Buddhism to refer to the moment of spiritual awakening.

stupa A monument used to commemorate the Buddha or any great Buddhist teacher.

tanha Means 'craving' or 'desire' *(see three poisons)*.

Theravada Buddhism Is the oldest form of Buddhism and exists mainly in Sri Lanka, Burma and Thailand. It stresses the ordained path to enlightenment.

three great knowledges The knowledge gained by Buddha during his enlightenment in his previous lives, karma and the Four Noble Truths.

Three Refuges The three central beliefs of the Buddha, the Dharma and the Sangha.

three poisons The poisons or cravings of greed, hatred and ignorance *(see tanha)*.

vihara Buddhist monastery or temple.

Wheel of Life The wheel of samsara showing the six different realms of existence.

Christianity

altar The communion table where the Eucharist is offered. Usually at the east end of the church.

ascension The belief that Jesus went back into heaven.

atonement Being made right with God.

baptism Ceremony using water to welcome a person into the church family.

chapel A room attached to a building and used as a place of worship for some Christian groups, e.g.: Methodists and Baptists.

Chrismation In Orthodox baptisms the baby is anointed with oil on the forehead, chest, back, hands, feet, ears and mouth.

Christmas The day Christians celebrate the birth of Jesus.

church A gathering of believers; a building in which Christian worship takes place.

clergy The collective name for ordained men and women.

confirmation Ceremony marking a person's full membership of the church.

covenant The agreement between God and his people.

crucifixion Method of Roman execution used to kill Jesus.

doctrine Teaching about a belief.

Easter The day Christians celebrate the resurrection of Jesus.

Eucharist The service sharing bread and wine, celebrating the Last Supper.

font A pedestal with a holder for a basin of water, used for baptism.

Good Friday The day Christians remember the death of Jesus.

Holy Spirit The third person of the Trinity.

hymns Poems set to music and sung as part of worship.

incarnation God in human form.

intercessions Prayers for others and the world.

lectern The stand upon which the Bible rests in a church.

liturgy A formal type of service with set prayers and readings.

Maundy Thursday The Thursday of Holy Week when Christians remember the Last Supper that Jesus ate with his disciples before his death.

monogamous Being married to only one person at any one time.

new covenant The new agreement between God and his people made through Jesus.

omnibenevolent Means 'all good'.

omnipotent Means 'all powerful'.

omnipresent Means 'always present'.

omniscient Means 'all knowing'.

Palm Sunday The Sunday before Easter when Christians remember Jesus' triumphal entry into Jerusalem.

pilgrimage A special journey usually made for religious reasons.

prayer Communication with God.

pulpit A raised enclosed platform from which the sermon is given during a church service.

relics Remains, usually bones, of a saint or holy person.

Resurrection The belief that Jesus rose from the dead.

sacrament An outward sign of God's blessing/grace.

sacrifice Offering something of value to God.

sermon A short address given by the priest as part of a service.

shrine A place that is seen as holy because of something that happened there. There is usually a little niche in which a saint's statue or relics are kept.

sin Means 'wrongdoing'.

stewardship Taking care of the world for God.

testimony A person's story about what God means to them or how they came to faith.

Trinity The doctrine that God is three in one and one in three: Father, Son and Holy Spirit.

worship Offering praise to God.

Hinduism

Aum or Om A word which represents the deepest vibration or essence of the universe.

ashrama The four stages of life from student to wandering holy man.

atman Soul, spirit, true or unique self *(see jivatman)*.

arti Means 'complete love'. Arti is performed by waving a lighted candle in front of the deity.

avatars Means 'descent' and describes Vishnu's ten forms in which he appears on earth.

Badrinth A city in India whose temple is dedicated to Vishnu and is often visited by pilgrims.

bhajans Songs and dances used in worship.

bhakti yoga The path to enlightenment through love and devotion to God.

brahmin Teacher or priest.

Brahman The ultimate reality of the universe, invisible Spirit and source of all matter.

darshan Means 'viewing'; the blessing of God experienced through a murti or holy person.

Devi The Mother Goddess.

dharma Refers to the 'moral code' in Hinduism, constituting the fundamental laws of life and the universe.

divas Oil lamps lit at the festival of Divali.

Gayatri mantra An ancient and widely used mantra which meditates on the power of the sun.

guru A greatly respected wise person and teacher.

havan Means 'to offer'; a fire ceremony is used to make the offerings.

Holi A spring festival which celebrates the defeat of the wicked Princess Holika.

japa A mantra which is recited many times to a special rhythm.

jivatman The individual soul or spirit as distinct from the mind.

jnana yoga The path to enlightenment by knowing God through mind and meditation.

karma Law of cause and effect in nature.

kirtan A chant based on a mantra used in worship.

mandir A Hindu temple.

mandapa The main prayer hall in the mandir.

meditation A means of quietening the mind and body to become more aware of the self and of God.

moksha Means 'liberation' when all negative karma is overcome and the atman becomes one with Brahman.

murti An image or statue of a god or deity.

namakarana Naming ceremony of a child (fifth samskara).

prashad Blessed food prepared for the deity and distributed at puja to devotees.

puja Worship that takes place at home or in a temple.

raja yoga Or royal yoga; meditating on God by stilling the mind.

samsara Reincarnation or the process of birth and rebirths over many lifetimes.

samskara Sixteen stages of life each of which has a special ceremony.

sanatana dharma Eternal truth.

Shaivism Worship of and devotion to the Lord Shiva.

Shaktism Worship of and devotion to the Goddess.

shikhara External spire outside a mandir (temple).

shrine Most holy part of a temple or home where the deities are worshipped.

Tri-murti The three forms of God: Brahma, Vishnu and Shiva.

upananyana Sacred thread ceremony when a boy enters the student stage of his life.

Vaishnavism Worship of and devotion to the Lord Vishnu.

varna Caste or social groups in society.

Varanasi Holy city in the Himalayas visited by many pilgrims.

varnashrama dharma The moral duties performed according to a person's place in society and stage of life.

Islam

adhan The call to prayer.

akhirah The Last Day in the afterlife when God rewards the good and punishes the wicked.

Al Qadr The Divine Plan; God knows who will choose good and who will choose evil.

Allah Arabic word meaning God.

amal Means action and constitutes leading a moral Muslim life.

aqiqah Naming ceremony of a child.

ayah A verse from the Qur'an.

barzakh Means 'the barrier', where souls wait to be judged by God in the afterlife.

beneficence Means 'goodness' and refers to God's nature that He is all good and merciful.

bismillah The preface to all except the first chapters of the Qur'an, 'to God the Compassionate the Merciful'.

caliph A successor of Muhmmad who leads the Muslim community.

du'a Private prayer which is not one of the five compulsory daily prayers.

Hadith The sayings of Muhammad and stories about him.

hafiz Someone who can recite the whole of the Qur'an by heart.

hajji/hajjah Man/woman who has been on hajj.

halal Means 'permitted' or 'lawful'.

hijrah The migration of Muhammad's first followers from Makkah to Madinah

ibadah Worship of God.

id/eid Arabic word meaning festival.

Id-ul-Adha Or the festival of sacrifice, which remembers Ibrahim's (Abraham) near sacrifice of Ishmael.

Id-ul-Fitr Festival which marks the end of the Ramadan fast.

ihram State of religious purity required for pilgrims to carry out the hajj.

imam Muslim prayer leader.

iman Belief and trust in God.

immanent Means that God is very close to humanity and knows their thoughts.

iqama Means 'set up' the prayer and it is the call to prayer which summons worshippers to form up for prayer in the mosque.

Isa The Prophet Jesus.

Jummah Arabic word for Friday. Prayers at the mosque on Friday are called Jummah prayers.

ka'bah The sacred cube-shaped shrine in the centre of Makkah.

Khadija Muhammad's first wife.

khutba Formal sermon preached by the imam at Friday prayers.

madrassah Muslim school or place of study often attached to a mosque.

mahr Marriage dowry or gift given by the husband to his wife.

masjid Means 'place of prostration' or 'mosque' *(see mosque)*.

mihrab Alcove in the qiblah wall of a mosque indicating the specific direction of worship Makkah *(see qiblah)*.

mosque Muslim place of worship.

minaret Tower from which traditionally the muezzin makes the call to prayer *(see adhan)*.

muezzin The person who makes sure worship takes place properly in the mosque and who makes the call to prayer.

Night of Power Or Laylat ul Qadr, defining the night when God first revealed Himself to Muhammad.

nikah Arabic word for marriage.

niyah Means 'intention'.

omnipotent Means 'all powerful'; God the creator of the universe.

prophet A person chosen by God to deliver His message to the world.

qiblah Means 'direction' and is the wall in the mosque which indicates the direction of Makkah.

Qur'an The holy book of Islam; pure Word of God revealed to Muhammad.

rak'at Means 'bendings' and refers to the sequence of Muslim prayer postures.

Ramadan The month of fasting.

sawm Means 'fasting'; one of the five pillars of Islam.

sa'y The run the pilgrims make between two hills during hajj.

Shahadah Means 'witness' and expresses the promise to be obedient to God's will and the example of the Prophet Muhammad.

Shaitan Arabic for Satan.

shari'ah Islamic law.

Shi'ite Branch of Islam which believes Islam should be led by a member of Muhammad's family.

shirk Failing to respect the oneness of God by reducing Him to the human level.

sunnah The example of the Prophet Muhammad which Muslims should follow.

Sunni Branch of Islam which believes leadership should be given to the person best suited to govern.

surah Chapter of the Qur'an.

tahnik Ceremony that takes place at the birth of a child which involves rubbing honey on to its gums.

tawaf Circling of the Ka'bah during hajj.

tawhid The unity or oneness of God.

transcendent Means 'existing beyond' and refers to God who exists outside of time and space.

umma Muslim community.

wudu Ritual washing or cleansing in preparation for prayer.

wuquf Means 'standing'; the moment when pilgrims stand and confess their sins at Arafat on hajj.

zakah One of the five pillars of Islam; it is the obligation to give a percentage of money to charity.

Judaism

anti-Semitism Acts of violence and abusive language used against the Jews.

ark The box in which the Torah scrolls are kept.

atonement Making things right with God.

bar mitzvah Ceremony for a thirteen-year-old boy (son of the commandment).

bat mitzvah Ceremony for a twelve or thirteen-year-old girl (daughter of the commandment).

bimah Platform in the synagogue from which the Torah is read.

Brit Milah Ceremony of circumcision.

cantor The person who leads the singing in Jewish worship.

circumcision Cutting off the foreskin of the penis.

covenant The agreement between God and his people.

Gemara Commentary on the oral laws.

hallot Special loaves of bread used on Sabbaths and festivals.

Hasidic Jews A group of strict orthodox Jews.

huppah The canopy under which a couple are married.

kashrut Food laws.

ketubah The marriage contract.

Kiddush Blessing said over wine.

kiddushin The formal engagement to be married.

kippah Skullcap worn by Jewish men and boys.

kosher Lawful to eat.

mechitzah The screen dividing men and women in the synagogue.

menorah A candlestick with seven branches.

mezuzah Box containing parchment scroll fixed to the right-hand doorpost.

Mishnah The oral teaching of the rabbis.

mitzvot A commandment.

mohel The person who performs circumcision.

ner tamid The light that symbolises God's presence.

Olam Ha'Ba Describes heaven or the afterlife.

Pesach Passover.

rabbi Spiritual leader teaches the Torah.

Seder Passover ceremony.

Shabbat Sabbath - a day when no work is done.

Shekinah The presence of God.

Shema One of the most important prayers in Judaism.

shofar The ram's horn blown at Yom Kippur.

siddur The Jewish prayer book.

synagogue Jewish place of worship.

Tabernacle The tent containing the Ark of the Covenant before the Temple was built.

tallit Prayer shawl.

Talmud Basic code of living for Jews.

tashlikh The act of throwing leftover crumbs from the Rosh Hashanah meal into running water. It symbolises casting away their sins.

tefillin Leather boxes containing verses from the Hebrew scriptures, worn by Jewish men during services.

Tenakh Jewish scriptures (the Jewish bible).

Torah The Jewish books of the law.

trefa Unlawful to eat.

tzitzit Tassels on a prayer shawl (tallit).

worship Offering praise to God.

Sikhism

Adi Granth The first collection of the Gurus' teaching.

Akhand Pat The continuous non-stop recitation of the Guru Granth Sahib from beginning to end.

amrit Sugar and water mixture used at Sikh initiation.

amrit-dhar Sikhs who are full members of the Khalsa.

bhangra A kind of energetic dancing.

chauri Traditional, ceremonial fan waved over the Guru Granth Sahib.

daswandh A tenth of one's income which is given to God.

dhan Material service.

diwan The hall where worship takes place.

Five Ks The five items worn by members of the Khalsa.

gurbani The book containing the teaching of the Gurus.

gurdwara Sikh place of worship.

gurmukh Implies being God-centred.

gurpurb Festivals associated with the lives of the Gurus.

guru Spiritual teacher.

Guru Granth Sahib The Sikh's holy book.

haumai The idea of self-centredness, or a person's ego.

hukam Means 'divine order'.

Japji Morning prayer recited everyday by all people practising that faith.

kachha Shorts worn by all Sikhs; one of the Five Ks.

kara A steel bracelet worn by all Sikhs; one of the Five Ks.

Karah Parshad Sweet dish made from flour, semolina, butter and sugar.

Karma Means 'action with intention'; the law of nature that every action has a consequence.

Kaur The name 'princess' given to all Sikh girls.

kesh The uncut hair and beard worn by Sikhs; one of the Five Ks.

Khalsa The Sikh community.

khanda The curved sword carried by Sikhs.

khanga A small wooden comb; one of the Five Ks.

Kirat Karna To earn an honest living.

langar Community kitchen serving free food to visitors.

man Mental or intellectual service.

mala Prayer beads used during chants or repeating daily mantras.

manmukh Being self-centred.

martyred Being killed for your faith.

melas Traditional fairs or festivals.

mukti Freedom from the cycle of birth, life, death and rebirth.

Nishan Sahib The Sikh flag.

nitnem A Sikh book of prayers.

palki Canopy over the Guru Granth Sahib.

ragas The arrangement of the shabads into musical groupings.

raghi Music group.

sewa Service to others- both in the Sikh community and outside.

shabads Hymns.

Singh The name 'lion' given to all Sikh boys.

taan Physical service.

takht The throne that the Guru Granth Sahib rests on.

Waheguru Is the name in Punjabi given to God and has the literal meaning 'Wonderful God'.

Index

Acknowledgements

The Publishers would like to thank the following for permission to reproduce copyright material.

Photo credits

p.vi © Tarapong Pattamachaiyant/123RF; **p.1** © Stelian/stock.adobe.com; **p.3** b © Paul Almasy/Corbis/VCG/Getty Images; **p.4** © Living Room/Shutterstock.com; **p.5** © Godong/Robertharding/Alamy Stock Photo; **p.6** © Wirojsid/stock. adobe.com; **p.7** l © Glebchik/stock.adobe.com; **p.13** © Michalis Palis/stock.adobe.com; **p.14** © Pcalapre/stock.adobe. com; **p.17** © Wiktor Szymanowicz/Alamy Stock Photo; **p.19** © Aleksey/stock.adobe.com; **p.20** © Godong/Alamy Stock Photo; **p.21** © Leon Werdinger/Alamy Stock Photo; **p.22** © Rodney Forte/123RF; **p.24** b © Sarawutnam/stock.adobe.com; **p.25** bl © Serhii/stock.adobe.com; **p.28** © Beatrice Sirinuntananon/123RF; **p.30** © Foxaon1987/Shutterstock.com; **p.31** © kimberly kilborn/stock.adobe.com; **p.33** © Francis Dean/REX/Shutterstock; **p.34** © Alx/stock.adobe.com; **p.36** © SPUTNIK/ Alamy Stock Photo; **p.39** l © Lebrecht Authors/Lebrecht Music & Arts/Alamy Stock Photo; r © Fine Art Images/Heritage Image Partnership Ltd/Alamy Stock Photo; **p.40** © Jozef Sedmak/Alamy Stock Photo; **p.42** © Pmmart/stock.adobe.com; **p.45** © Francesca Moore/Alamy Stock Photo; **p.46** © Susan Grenfell; **p.49** © Ed Buziak/Alamy Stock Photo; **p.51** © Peter Grenfel; **p.55** © Jeff Gilbert/Alamy Stock Photo; **p.56** © Andreas Keuchel/Alamy Stock Photo; **p.57** © Seregayu/stock. adobe.com; **p.59** tr © Haydn Denman/Alamy Stock Photo; **p.61** l © Matt Hahnewald Photography/Alamy Stock Photo; r © https://en.wikipedia.org/wiki/The_Great_Banyan#/media/File:Great_banyan_tree_kol.jpg, https://en.wikipedia.org/ wiki/Creative_Commons; **p.64** tr © Raywoo/123RF; br © Dinodia Photos/Alamy Stock Photo; **p.67** © Godong/Alamy Stock Photo; **p.68** l © ArkReligion.com/Art Directors & TRIP/Alamy Stock Photo; r © Historic Images/Alamy Stock Photo; **p.69** t © The Picture Art Collection/Alamy Stock Photo; b © Philippe Lissac/Godong/Corbis Documentary/Getty Images; **p.70** t © Peter Horree/Alamy Stock Photo; b © Zoonar/Radek Kucharski/Alamy Stock Photo; **p.71** l © Shalini Saran/IndiaPicture/ Alamy Stock Photo; r © Ravi Varma/Wellcome collections; **p.72** © Helene Rogers/ArkReligion.com/Art Directors & TRIP/ Alamy Stock Photo; **p.73** t © Espies/stock.adobe.com; b © Martin Siepmann/imageBROKER/Alamy Stock Photo; **p.75** l © Ellen Clark/Danita Delimont/Alamy Stock Photo; **p.77** t © Dmitry Rukhlenko/stock.adobe.com; **p.78** © MarioPonta/Alamy Stock Photo; **p.79** r © Amlan Mathur/Alamy Stock Photo; **p.80** © Van der Meer Marica/Arterra Picture Library/Alamy Stock Photo; **p.81** © Galyna Andrushko/stock.adobe.com; **p.82** © Frank Bienewald/imageBROKER/Alamy Stock Photo; **p.83** t © Jakub Sliwa/Aurora Photos/Alamy Stock Photo; **p.84** © Dinodia Photos/Alamy Stock Photo; **p.89** l © Sonia Halliday Photo Library/Alamy Stock Photo; tr © CM Dixon/Print Collector/Hulton Archive/Getty Images; br © PRISMA ARCHIVO/Alamy Stock Photo; **p.90** © J.D. Dallet/Age fotostock/Alamy Stock Photo; **p.91** © Granger, NYC/TopFoto; **p.92** © Hasnuddin/ stock.adobe.com; **p.93** © ArkReligion.com/Art Directors & TRIP/Alamy Stock Photo; **p.94** l © Pambudi Yoga Perdana/ Shutterstock.com; r © Amalia Sari/Alamy Stock Photo; **p.96** © The Understand Quran Academy; **p.99** l © Rob Stothard/ Stringer/Getty Images News/Getty Images; **p.101** l © Om Yos/stock.adobe.com; r © Oleksandr Rupeta/Alamy Stock Photo; **p.102** l © Saiyood/stock.adobe.com; **p.104** t © ArkReligion.com/Art Directors & TRIP/Alamy Stock Photo; **p.105** © Images & Stories/Alamy Stock Photo; **p.109** © Nic I'Anson/Eye Ubiquitous/Alamy Stock Photo; **p.110** l © Antony SOUTER/Alamy Stock Photo; r © Aleksandar Todorovic/stock.adobe.com; **p.111** l © Georg Berg/Alamy Stock Photo; r © Distinctive Images/ stock.adobe.com; **p.112** © Kevin Carden/stock.adobe.com; **p.116** l © Ira Berger/Alamy Stock Photo; r © Vitaly tiagunov/ stock.adobe.com; **p.119** © Ira Berger/Alamy Stock Photo; **p.122** © Maria Grin/stock.adobe.com; **p.125** © DBtale/stock. adobe.com; **p.126** © a|s|a|p Creative Production/ASAP/Alamy Stock Photo; **p.127** © Andrzej Golik/Shutterstock.com; **p.128** © Howard Sandler/Fotolia; **p.131** © PhotoStock-Israel/Alamy Stock Photo; **p.133** © Donna Ellen Coleman/Shutterstock.com; **p.134** © Rafael Ben-Ari/stock.adobe.com; **p.137** © Howard Sandler/Shutterstock.com; **p.138** © BJ Warnick/Ron Sachs/CNP/ Newscom/Alamy Stock Photo; **p.139** © BirchTree/Alamy Stock Photo; **p.142** © Buddy Mays/Alamy Stock Photo; **p.146** © Dharam Kaur Khalsa; **p.149** © Boris Stroujko/stock.adobe.com; **p.150** © Dinodia Photos/Alamy Stock Photo; **p.151** © Ruby/ Alamy Stock Photo; **p.152** © Sameer Sehgal/Hindustan Times/Getty Images; **p.153** b © Christine Osborne/World Religions Photo Library/Alamy Stock Photo; t © Roberto Lacaze/Alamy Stock Photo; **p.154** © Khalsa Aid International; **p.157** t © Parmorama/Alamy Stock Photo; **p.159** b © Dinodia Photos/Alamy Stock Photo; **p.160** © David Cumming/Eye Ubiquitous/ Alamy Stock Photo; **p.162** © Stefano Montesi/Corbis News/Getty Images; **p.164** © Vectomart/stock.adobe.com; **p.165** © Truetube/CTVC Ltd; **p.168** © Paul Gapper/Alamy Stock Photo; **p.170** © Ira Berger/Alamy Stock Photo.

Text permissions

The Holy Bible, New International Version®, NIV®. Copyright© 1973, 1978, 1984, 2011 by Biblica, Inc.®
Used by permission. All rights reserved worldwide.